British English

Personal Best

Student's Book

B1
Pre-intermediate

Series Editor
Jim Scrivener

Authors
Bess Bradfield with
Graham Fruen

Richmond

CONTENTS

Personal Best Language App, unit-by-unit grammar and vocabulary games

CONTENTS

Language App, unit-by-unit grammar and vocabulary games

UNIT 1

All about me

LANGUAGE present simple and adverbs and expressions of frequency ■ personality adjectives

1A The only friends you need

1 Here are some words to describe a good friend. Order the words from 1 (very important) to 6 (less important).

honest funny patient kind polite generous

Personal Best

Go to Vocabulary practice: personality adjectives, page 136

2 Read the introduction to the text. Are the sentences true (T) or false (F)?

1 You need lots of friends to be happy. ____
2 There are four different types of friends. ____
3 It is important to have different types of friends in your life. ____

3 **A** 1.3 Match the types of friend in the box with descriptions 1–4. Listen and check.

the super planner the party animal the good listener the straight talker

B Do you have any friends like these? What type of friend are you?

THE FOUR FRIENDS YOU NEED

We all know that friends are important … but do we have the 'right' friends? Dr Adam Greenberg, a psychologist, doesn't think we need lots of friends to be happy. Instead, he says the types of friends we have is more important. He believes that there are four types of friends and they all help us in different ways. So, what are these four friends like?

1 ________
You share everything with these friends and you often tell them all your secrets. They're patient when you ring them late at night with a problem and they don't complain when you tell them the same stories again … and again!

2 ________
These friends know you very well and they're honest … *really* honest. They always tell you the truth, even when you don't want to hear it, but this is because they care about you and they don't want you to make a mistake and get hurt.

3 ________
These friends are very sociable and you usually have a good time when you are with them. They're very funny and they make you laugh when you're sad. All your friends and family love them, too. With friends like these, life is never boring!

4 ________
These friends are very organized, but they're sometimes a bit serious. They hardly ever forget important dates … like your birthday! They're very busy and have lots of things to do every day, but they always find time to have a coffee with you.

4 Choose the correct words to complete the sentences. Check your answers in the text.

1 *Do* / *Does* we have the 'right' friends?
2 Dr Greenberg *don't* / *doesn't* think we need lots of friends to be happy.
3 He *say* / *says* the types of friends we have is more important.
4 They *don't* / *doesn't* want you to make a mistake and get hurt.
5 You usually have a good time when you *is* / *are* with them.
6 They hardly ever *forget* / *forgets* important dates.

5 A Complete the diagram with the adverbs of frequency in the box.

hardly ever never often usually

100% — 0%

always ¹ ________ ² ________ sometimes ³ ________ ⁴ ________

B Underline the adverbs of frequency in the text and complete the rule. Then read the Grammar box.

Adverbs of frequency go *before / after* most verbs, but they go *before / after* the verb *be*.

Grammar present simple and adverbs and expressions of frequency

Things that are always true:
Does Ahmet live in Ankara? No, he lives in Istanbul.
Do you speak Spanish? Yes, I speak a little.

Routines and habits:
How often do you see him? I usually see him at the weekend.
How often are you late? I'm never late!

Look! We also use expressions of frequency for regular routines e.g. *once a week*, *every month*

Personal Best

Go to Grammar practice: present simple and adverbs and expressions of frequency, page 112

6 A 1.5 **Pronunciation:** final *-s/-es* sound Listen and repeat the sentences. Then match the verb endings in **bold** with the sounds: /s/, /z/ or /ɪz/.

1 She like**s** Italian food. ____ 2 He teach**es** at the university. ____ 3 My brother know**s** him. ____

B 1.6 How do you say the verbs? Listen, check and repeat.

believe**s** say**s** change**s** think**s** use**s** want**s** goe**s** watch**es** hope**s**

7 A Add adverbs and expressions of frequency to make sentences about your partner.

She usually catches the bus to work. He catches the bus to university every day.

1 He/She catches the bus to work/university.
2 He/She goes to bed at 11.00 at night.
3 He/She is patient.
4 He/She drinks coffee in the morning.
5 He/She watches films in English.
6 He/She is late for class.

B Read your sentences to your partner. He/She will tell you if you are correct.

Go to Communication practice: Student A page 158, Student B page 166

8 Read the text about two friends. Complete the text with the correct form of the verbs in the box.

get have not have invite like think

MY BEST FRIEND IS THE EXACT OPPOSITE OF ME

Lots of people ¹ ________ I'm really serious and I never go out, but that's not true! I'm very hard-working and my job in the bank is difficult, so I ² ________ much free time. I play the guitar in a jazz group and we usually practise two or three times a week. I ³ ________ cooking, so I often ⁴ ________ people to my house for dinner.
My best friend is Luca. He's the singer in the group and he's completely different from me. He's a student at university and, to be honest, he's a bit lazy and he hardly ever ⁵ ________ to lessons on time. But he's funny and generous and we always ⁶ ________ a great time when we go out.

9 A Choose a friend and tell your partner his/her name.

B In pairs, use the prompts to ask and answer questions about your friends.

1 What / be / he/she / like?
2 Where / he/she / live?
3 What / he/she / do?
4 Where / he/she / work/study?
5 How often / you / talk to / him/her?
6 What / you / usually / talk about?
7 How often / you / see / him/her?
8 Where / you / meet / him/her?

Personal Best Write a description of yourself and of someone you know who is the opposite of you.

Learning Curve

1B 21st century hobbies

1 Match the activities in the box with pictures a–h.

meet up with friends · go to concerts · bake cakes · play chess · go on social media · collect records · do exercise · shop online

a
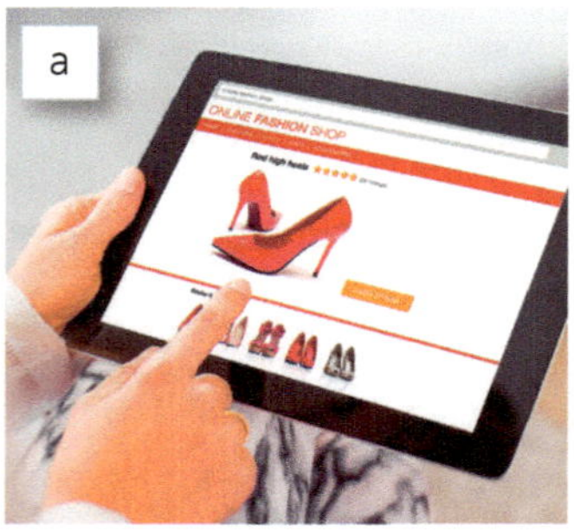
b

c

d

e

f

g

h

2 In pairs, ask and answer the questions *Do you ...?* and *How often do you ...?* for the activities in exercise 1.

A *Do you collect records?* **B** *No, I don't.*
A *How often do you do exercise?* **B** *I go to the gym once or twice a week.*

Personal Best

Go to Vocabulary practice: hobbies and socializing, page 137

Skill listening for the main idea

It is important to understand the main idea when someone is speaking.

- Think about who is speaking and what they are talking about.
- Don't worry if you don't understand all the words.
- Remember that speakers often talk about the main ideas more than once.

3 ▶ 1.8 Read the Skill box. Watch or listen to the first part of a webshow called *Learning Curve* and tick (✓) the main idea.

1 People have less time for socializing today. ☐
2 Many popular hobbies are now online. ☐
3 Old hobbies are becoming popular again. ☐

4 **A** ▶ 1.8 Watch or listen again. Complete the table with the online activities Kate mentions.

Traditional activity	Online activity
play team sports	
take cooking classes	
go to a shopping centre	
go out to meet new people	

B In pairs, think of more traditional activities that you can now do online.

5 1.9 Watch or listen to the second part of the show. Choose the correct options to complete the sentences about the main ideas.

Viktor

David

Suzie

Rebecca

1 Viktor ...
 a plays chess a lot. b does lots of activities online. c meets up with friends every day.
2 David ...
 a likes computers. b exercises at home. c prefers exercising at the gym.
3 Suzie ...
 a downloads lots of music. b prefers to relax at home. c does her hobby with other people.
4 Rebecca ...
 a does lots of activities online. b doesn't like meeting new people. c spends lots of time with her family.

6 1.9 Watch or listen again. Are the sentences true (T) or false (F)?

1 Viktor plays chess with friends every day. ____
2 David goes to the gym five times a week or more. ____
3 Suzie loves music from the 1980s. ____
4 Rebecca makes videos of her cat. ____
5 Kate only likes traditional hobbies like rock climbing. ____

7 **A** Ask your classmates the questions in the boxes and write down their answers.

What do you do in your free time? | Do you have any online hobbies?

B Do you think online hobbies are more popular than traditional hobbies?

8 1.10 In pairs, complete the sentences from the show with the contractions in the box. Listen and check.

don't I'm he's that's what's can't

1 ________ your name?
2 ________ really enjoying the game.
3 Computers ________ interest me.
4 You ________ do that online!
5 I use it when ________ not at the gym.
6 Wow, Suzie, ________ amazing!

Listening builder contractions

When people speak, they usually make contractions:
We do not meet up with friends. → *We do**n't** meet up with friends.*
She is not very sporty. → *She**'s not** very sporty / She **isn't** very sporty.*
I am ready to go rock climbing. → *I**'m** ready to go rock climbing.*

9 1.11 Read the Listening builder. Listen and circle the contraction that you hear.

1 *We're / We aren't / We can't*
2 *He's / He isn't / He doesn't*
3 *My teacher's / My teacher's not / My teacher isn't*
4 *It's / It isn't / It doesn't*
5 *They don't / They can't / They aren't*
6 *I'm / I'm not / I don't*

10 Discuss the questions in pairs.

1 Is it important to have a hobby? Why/Why not?
2 Which hobbies are most popular in your country?
3 Do men and women usually like different hobbies?
4 Are your hobbies different now from when you were a child? If so, how?
5 Can you think of any dangerous hobbies? Would you like to try them? Why/Why not?

Personal Best Write a paragraph about one of your partner's answers in exercise 10.

1C Famous families

1 Who are musicians a–c? In pairs, match them with their relatives: Anaïs, Skip and Eve. Read the text and check.

THE NEXT GENERATION OF STARS

a

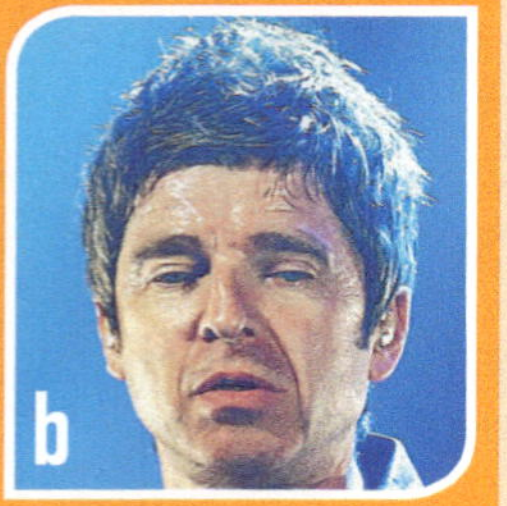
b

c

Their faces may look familiar, but if you're wondering who these cool young people are, the clue is in their names. Meet the children – and grandchildren – of some of music's biggest stars.

Anaïs Gallagher is the daughter of Noel Gallagher, former guitarist and songwriter with Oasis. In our photo, she's wearing a gold hat and already looks like a star! Anaïs, 16, goes to school in London, and is currently presenting a music and fashion show on children's TV. She lives in London with her mum and, in the future, she wants to be a film director.

Skip Marley wears his hair in dreadlocks and looks just like his famous grandfather, Bob. He's just 20, but he's also a musician who sings and plays the guitar, the piano and the drums. He lives in Miami, where he's studying Business at university. Right now, he's recording some new songs and planning to go on tour.

Eve Hewson is the daughter of Paul Hewson, better known as Bono, from the rock band U2. Eve, 25, is an actress and is living in New York at the moment, where she's playing the part of a nurse in a TV series. Does she miss her hometown of Dublin? Yes, but her sister and a lot of her friends from home live nearby, and her parents often visit.

With so much talent – never mind those famous connections – we can expect to see a lot more of Anaïs, Skip and Eve in the future.

Anaïs

Skip

Eve

2 Read the text again. Complete the sentences with the correct name: *Anaïs, Skip or Eve*.

1 ________ lives in Miami.
2 ________ is wearing a white hat in the photo.
3 ________ goes to school in London.
4 ________ is living in New York at the moment.
5 ________'s parents often visit.
6 ________ is recording some new songs right now.

3 **A** Underline the verbs in exercise 2. Which verbs are present simple and which are present continuous? What is the difference between them?

B Choose the correct tenses to complete the rules. Then read the Grammar box.

1 We use the *present simple / present continuous* to talk about actions that are happening now or actions that are temporary.
2 We use the *present simple / present continuous* to talk about things that happen regularly or things that are always true.

Grammar present continuous and present simple

Things that are happening now or are temporary:	Things that happen regularly or are always true:
*She's **living** in Lima for three months.*	*He **lives** in Istanbul.*
*I'**m not wearing** my glasses.*	*They **don't wear** coats in the summer.*
***Is** she **working** in Paris at the moment?*	***Do** you **work** as a teacher?*

Personal Best

Go to Grammar practice: present continuous and present simple, page 113

4 A 1.13 **Pronunciation:** *-ng* sound Listen and repeat the words. Pay attention to the /ŋ/ sound.

bring**ing** meet**ing** runn**ing** si**ng**ing study**ing** so**ng** tak**ing** you**ng**

B 1.14 Practise saying the sentences. Listen, check and repeat.

1 She's wear**ing** a lo**ng** coat.
2 She's carry**ing** a lo**ng** coat.
3 He's bri**ng**ing me a stro**ng** coffee.
4 He's tak**ing** a stro**ng** coffee to the meet**ing**.

5 Match the sentences in exercise 4B with pictures a–d.

a

b

c

MEETING ROOM
d

Personal Best

Go to Vocabulary practice: useful verbs, page 138

6 A Choose the correct form of the verb to complete the questions.

1 What clothes *do you wear / are you wearing* today?
2 *Do you have / Are you having* a dictionary with you at the moment?
3 What *do you look forward to / are you looking forward to* this year?
4 *Do you think / Are you thinking* it will rain today?
5 What clothes *do you usually wear / are you usually wearing* if you go to a party?
6 What *do you do / are you doing* right now?

B In pairs, ask and answer the questions.

Go to Communication practice: Student A page 158, Student B page 166

7 1.16 Complete the conversation with the present simple or present continuous forms of the verbs in the box. Listen and check.

meet work (x2) be do (x2) write not know want

Ruben Karen!
Karen Hi, Ruben. How [1] ________ you?
Ruben I'm fine, thanks. What [2] ________ you ________ here?
Karen I [3] ________ my sister for lunch.
Ruben Oh, great. Your sister ... what [4] ________ she ________ ?
Karen She [5] ________ for a bank.
Ruben Here in the city centre?
Karen Not normally, but she [6] ________ in the main office this week. Hey, [7] ________ you ________ to have lunch with us?
Ruben OK, but I [8] ________ your sister.
Karen Don't worry. It'll be fine. So, how's university?
Ruben Good, but I'm really busy. I [9] ________ my final-year project at the moment, so ...

8 Imagine you meet your partner in the street. Ask and answer the questions in pairs.

1 How are you?
2 What are you doing here?
3 Where are you working/living at the moment?
4 How's it going?
5 How's your ...?
6 What does he/she do?
7 What's he/she like?
8 What's he/she doing now?

Personal Best Write about someone in your family with the present simple and present continuous.

1D Me in three objects

1 Read the blog and look at the pictures. Discuss the questions in pairs.

1 What can you find out about Sasha, Brady and Julio?
2 Who do you think is the most interesting?
3 Who do you think is most similar to you?
4 Is it possible to know what someone is like by looking at the things they own?

MSD COLLEGE REPLIES: You in three objects . . . . *Learning for life*

You in three objects . . . .

POSTED:
5 November, 16:00

You can discover a lot about people by looking at the objects that are important to them. Post photos of three things that represent you, tell us why they are important and introduce yourself to the rest of the class!

my laptop
coffee
my running shoes
my paints
music
my backpack
my cat
Mexican food
cinema tickets

Sasha — POSTED: 5 November, 18:26 — SEE MORE ...

Brady — POSTED: 5 November, 18:44 — SEE MORE ...

Julio — POSTED: 6 November, 09:15 — SEE MORE ...

2 Look at the mind map. Who drew it: Sasha, Brady or Julio? Complete the diagram with the correct objects. Then read the Skill box.

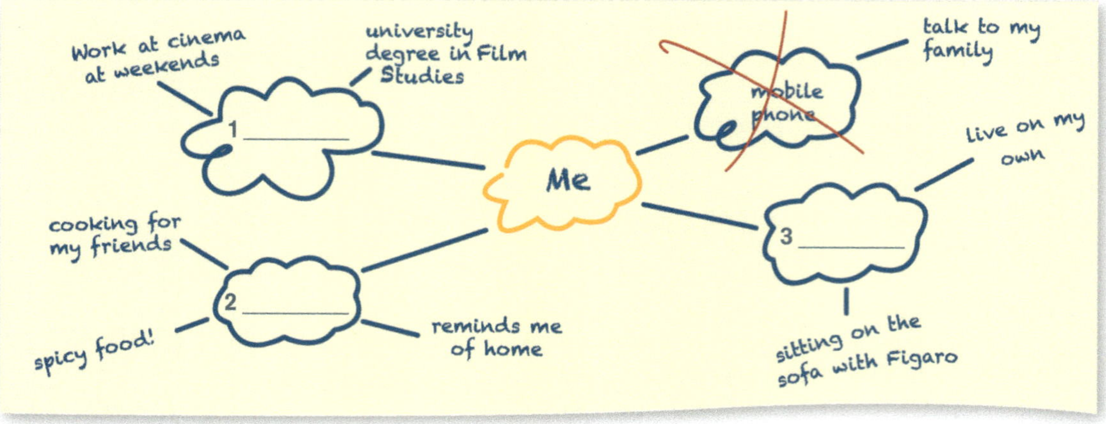

Work at cinema at weekends
university degree in Film Studies
1 ___________
Me
mobile phone
talk to my family
live on my own
3 ___________
sitting on the sofa with Figaro
cooking for my friends
2 ___________
spicy food!
reminds me of home

Skill making notes

Making notes before you write is a good way to plan your work.
- Write as many ideas as you can about the main topics.
- Use diagrams like mind maps to see the ideas more clearly.
- Choose the best ideas and organize them into paragraphs.

3 **A** Look at the mind map again. Which idea doesn't Julio use? How many paragraphs do you think he will write?

B Read Julio's blog post in exercise 4 and check your answers to the questions above.

4 1.17 Complete Julio's blog post with the present simple or present continuous form of the verbs in the box. Listen and check.

not agree love cook do live sit watch study

Julio's blog

First, I chose a photo of Figaro, my cat, because he's very important to me. I [1] ________ on my own at the moment, so it is good to see a friendly face when I come home. I [2] ________ animals, especially cats. In the photo, he [3] ________ on the sofa with me. He often sits with me and we watch films together.

I [4] ________ at university in the USA now, but I come from Mexico. That's why I also chose Mexican food. I love spicy food and I often [5] ________ a big meal and invite all my friends to dinner. It's great to meet up with friends and when I taste the food, I remember my friends and family back home.

I chose some cinema tickets, because I work at a local cinema at the weekends. I [6] ________ a degree in Film Studies at the moment, so movies are a really important part of my life. Some people say I [7] ________ too many films, but I [8] ________ . I want to be a film director and I learn something new from every film I watch.

5 Look at the phrases with the highlighted words in the text. Answer the questions.

1 What type of information comes after *because*? *a reason for something / a result*
2 What type of information comes after *That's why* and *so*? *a reason for something / a result*

Text builder expressing reasons and results

Reasons: *I chose a photo of my cat,* ***because*** *he's very important to me.*
Results: *My cat is very important to me,* ***so*** *I chose a photo of him.*
My cat is very important to me. ***That's why*** *I chose a photo of him.*

6 **A** Read the Text builder above. Complete the sentences with *because*, *so* or *That's why*.

1 I think it's really important to keep fit, ________ I chose my running shoes.
2 I didn't choose my mobile phone, ________ everybody has one and it's not very special.
3 I design websites and I'm always connected to the internet. ________ I chose my laptop.
4 My backpack is important to me, ________ it reminds me of travelling to lots of countries.
5 I love art, but I'm too shy to take a photo of one of my paintings. ________ I chose my paints.

B Who wrote the sentences: Sasha, Brady or Julio?

7 **A** Complete the sentences with your own ideas. Write three true sentences and three false sentences.

1 My favourite ________ is ________ , because ...
2 I think ________ is very ________ , so I ...
3 I'm a very ________ person. That's why I never ...
4 It's really important to ________ , so I always ...
5 I am ________ at the moment, because ...
6 I'm frightened of ________ . That's why ...

B Listen to your partner's sentences. Which sentences do you think are true?

8 **A** PREPARE Draw a mind map of some objects that represent you. Then add reasons why the things are special. Look at your diagram and choose three objects you want to include in your blog post.

B PRACTISE Write a blog post with the heading *Me in three objects*. Use your notes from Stage A to help you organize the paragraphs.

C PERSONAL BEST Swap your blog post with your partner. Read his/her work and correct any mistakes. How could you improve it?

Personal Best Write six sentences with *because*, *so* and *That's why* about your friends, family and hobbies.

UNIT 2

Stories and pictures

LANGUAGE past simple and time expressions ■ *-ed/-ing* adjectives

2A That's me in the photo!

1 A Look at the photos in the text below and say what is happening. What do you call these types of photos?

B Read the text quickly. Match descriptions 1–3 with photos a–c.

the STORY OF SELFIES

The 'age of selfies' began in the early 21st century when people started using smartphones with digital cameras. We now take over a million selfies every day! Here are three interesting selfies with their stories:

1 Robert Cornelius made the world's first 'selfie' when he experimented with a camera in 1839. He tried to take a photo of himself, but early cameras worked very slowly so Robert didn't move for one minute and he couldn't smile. That's why the final photo wasn't very exciting!

2 This frightening selfie is of Alexander Remnev, from Russia. In May 2014, Alexander travelled to Dubai with a friend. They weren't interested in taking normal photos, so they decided to climb the Princess Tower, which is over 400 m tall. They opened a door at the top of the building and climbed out … and they didn't use any safety equipment. Why did they do it? They said they were bored!

3 Teenager Jack Surgenor was very excited when he saw Queen Elizabeth II in Northern Ireland on 24 June 2014. He quickly took a selfie and sent it to all his friends. He was very pleased, but how did the Queen feel about being in someone else's photo? We don't know, but she looked a bit annoyed!

a

b

c

2 Read the text again. Complete the sentences with the names in the box.

Alexander Remnev	Jack Surgenor	Queen Elizabeth II	Robert Cornelius

1 ________ took a very dangerous photo.
2 ________ wasn't happy to be in a photo.
3 ________ waited a long time to take the photo.
4 ________ took a photo of a famous person.

3 A Write the past simple form of the verbs. Check your answers in the text.

1 begin ________
2 make ________
3 try ________
4 work ________
5 travel ________
6 decide ________
7 be ___ / ___
8 send ________

B Which verbs are regular and which are irregular?

4 Underline all the past simple negative sentences and questions in the text. Complete the rules, then read the Grammar box.

1 To make a negative in the past simple, we normally use ________ + infinitive.
2 To make a question in the past simple, we normally use ________ + subject + infinitive.
3 The negative of *was*/*were* is ________ /________ and the negative of *could* is ________ .

Grammar **past simple and time expressions**

	Regular verbs	Irregular verbs
Positive:	*Alexander* ***travelled*** *to Dubai.*	*He* ***took*** *a photo.*
Negative:	*Alexander* ***didn't travel*** *to Dubai.*	*He* ***didn't take*** *a photo.*
Questions:	*Why* ***did*** *he* ***travel*** *to Dubai?*	*Why* ***did*** *he* ***take*** *a photo?*

Look! Time expressions go at the end or at the beginning of sentences:
Alexander travelled to Dubai ***in May 2014****.* ***In May 2014****, Alexander travelled to Dubai.*

Personal Best

Go to Grammar practice: past simple and time expressions, page 114

5 **A** 2.3 **Pronunciation:** *-ed* **endings** Listen to three phrases from the text. Say how the *-ed* endings are pronounced: /t/, /ɪd/ or /d/.

1 People start**ed** using smartphones. 2 They open**ed** a door. 3 Early cameras work**ed** very slowly.

B 2.4 Say how the *-ed* endings are pronounced for the verbs: /t/, /d/ or /ɪd/. Listen, check and repeat.

climb**ed** decid**ed** experiment**ed** look**ed** travell**ed** watch**ed**

Go to Communication practice: Student A page 158, Student B page 166

6 **A** Choose the correct adjectives to complete the sentences. Check your answers in the text.

1 That's why the final photo wasn't very *excited* / *exciting*!
2 This *frightened* / *frightening* selfie is of Alexander Remnev, from Russia.
3 They said they were *bored* / *boring*!
4 Teenager Jack Surgenor was very *excited* / *exciting* when he saw Queen Elizabeth II.

B Look at sentences 1–4 again and answer the questions.

1 Which adjectives describe people's feelings? ________ , ________
2 Which adjectives describe someone/something that causes a feeling? ________ , ________
3 How many more *-ed* and *-ing* adjectives can you find in the text? ________

Personal Best

Go to Vocabulary practice: *-ed*/*-ing* adjectives, page 139

7 **A** Complete the questions with the past simple form of the verbs in brackets.

When was the last time you ...

1 ________ embarrassed? (feel)
2 ________ frightened? (be)
3 ________ something tiring? (do)
4 ________ something interesting? (eat)
5 ________ some surprising news? (receive)
6 ________ annoyed with your best friend? (get)

B In pairs, ask and answer the questions and explain what happened.

8 Think about a selfie or photo you took. Ask and answer the questions in pairs.

1 When did you take the photo?
2 Where were you?
3 What did you do?
4 Why did you take the photo?
5 How did you feel?
6 Did you send the photo to anyone?

Personal Best Write down three important dates. Then write sentences explaining what happened and why they are important.

2B Party like it's 1829

trpid

1 Describe the picture of a party. Discuss the questions in pairs.

1 Why do people have parties?
2 What do you usually do when you go to a party?
3 Do you prefer to organize parties or to be a guest?
4 What's the worst thing about parties?

Skill approaching a text

Before you read a text, predict as much information as you can.

- Read the title of the text. Can you guess what it means?
- Look at the pictures. What people, places and things do they show?
- Read the headings of the different sections. What do you think they are about?

2 **A** Read the Skill box. Try to predict the answers to the questions about the text on page 15.

1 Who was Andrew Jackson?
2 Where did he live?
3 What did the guests do at the 1829 party?
4 What did the guests do at the 1837 party?

B Read the whole text quickly and check your answers to the questions.

3 Read the text in more detail. Look at the sentences and write: *1829 party*, *1837 party* or *both*.

1 There was food at the party. ________
2 Some guests caused damage. ________
3 All the guests had a good time. ________
4 Jackson didn't stay until the end. ________
5 Jackson received a strange present. ________
6 The guests ate in the gardens. ________

4 Discuss the questions in pairs.

1 Were you surprised by the text? Why/Why not?
2 How would a party at the White House be different today?
3 What kind of person was Andrew Jackson?
4 Would you like to go to a party like one of Andrew Jackson's? Why/Why not?

5 Complete the sentences with the words in the box. Check your answers in the text.

after after that later then

1 ... they soon pushed their way inside. ________ , the party got out of control.
2 Eight years ________ , an American farmer gave the president an enormous cheese.
3 Jackson didn't know what to do with it; he couldn't eat it himself, but ________ he had an idea.
4 ________ just two hours, it was gone.

Text builder sequencers

To say one action happened after another:
*I went to the gym and **then** I went home.* *I went to the gym. **After that**, I went home.*
To say one action happened after a period of time:
*Two hours **later**, I made dinner.* ***After** two hours, I made dinner.*

6 Read the Text builder. In pairs, talk about an important party or celebration you went to. Use sequencers to explain what happened.

- What was the party or celebration?
- How many guests were there?
- What did you eat and drink?
- What did you do?
- Did you have a good time?
- Were there any problems?

ANDREW
JACKSON

PARTY LIKE A PRESIDENT

Andrew Jackson was president of the United States between 1829 and 1837. He was the first president from the Democratic party and a very popular politician, but he's also famous for some surprising events which took place at the White House. The pictures below show two memorable parties held there when Jackson was president.

THE 1829 CELEBRATIONS

On 4 March 1829, when Jackson became president, he invited his supporters to visit the White House and thousands of people followed him to his new home. At first, the crowd waited in the gardens, but they were very excited and they soon pushed their way inside. After that, the party got out of control. People stood on tables and chairs, broke glasses and some even fell and hurt themselves. Jackson escaped out of a window and went to a nearby hotel, but his staff stayed because they were worried about the building. In the end, they put lots of food onto tables in the gardens and the hungry guests followed them outside to eat the food. The White House was safe ... for the moment!

THE LAST PARTY, 1837

Eight years later, an American farmer gave the president an enormous cheese, which weighed over 600 kg. Jackson didn't know what to do with it; he couldn't eat it himself, but then he had an idea. He decided to have another party to celebrate the end of his presidency. In February 1837, thousands of guests arrived and started to eat the only thing on the menu – the cheese. After just two hours, it was gone and everyone was very happy, but the expensive carpets in the White House were covered in smelly cheese. This time, Jackson wasn't worried about the mess. He left the White House two weeks later and the next president, Martin van Buren, was very annoyed because the building still smelled of cheese!

Personal Best Choose one of the parties from the text. Write a summary of what happened.

2C Behind the camera

1 In pairs, order the phases from 1 (birth) to 8 (death).

start a career get engaged die go to university
be born have children leave school get married

Go to Vocabulary practice: life stages, page 140

2 Read the radio guide about Mario Testino. What is his job? Why is he famous?

YESTERDAY	TODAY	TOMORROW	THURSDAY	FRIDAY	SATURDAY	SUNDAY	MONDAY
8.00PM	9.00PM	10.00PM	10.30PM	11.00PM	12.00PM	12.10AM	4.00AM

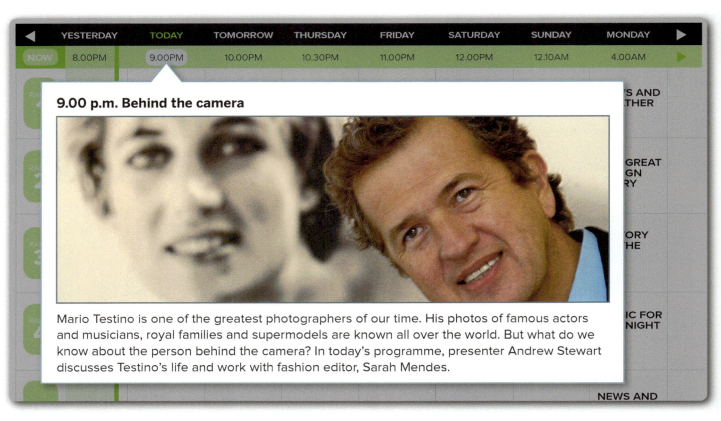

9.00 p.m. Behind the camera

Mario Testino is one of the greatest photographers of our time. His photos of famous actors and musicians, royal families and supermodels are known all over the world. But what do we know about the person behind the camera? In today's programme, presenter Andrew Stewart discusses Testino's life and work with fashion editor, Sarah Mendes.

3 2.7 Listen to the radio programme. Choose the correct options to complete the sentences.

1 Mario was born in *Italy / Peru*.
2 He grew up in *Lima / New York*.
3 After school, he *went to university / travelled round the world*.
4 In London, he got a job in a *restaurant / hospital*.
5 He started his career by photographing *models and actresses / people he worked with*.
6 He became famous when he photographed *Madonna / Gianni Versace*.
7 He photographed Princess Diana in *1995 / 1997*.
8 In 2012, he opened a gallery in *London / Lima*.

4 2.8 Complete the presenter's questions with the words in the box. Listen again and check.

does did from is what who

1 Where is he ________ ?
2 ________ did he do after he left school?
3 How ________ his career start?
4 ________ did he work with?
5 What ________ he doing at the moment?
6 ________ he still live in London?

5 Look at exercise 4 again and answer the questions. Then read the Grammar box.

1 Which question doesn't have a question word? ______
2 In questions 1–6, which auxiliary verbs are used for:
  a the present simple? ______
  b the past simple? ______
  c the present continuous? ______
3 Which question doesn't have an auxiliary verb? ______

Grammar question forms

Most verbs:	**(question word) + auxiliary verb + subject + main verb**		
	Where do you live?	*Does your brother live near here?*	*What do we know about Mario Testino?*
	When did you arrive?	*Did you see him?*	*How did his career start?*
	What are you doing?	*Is Mario working today?*	*What am I doing?*
The verb *be*:	**(question word) + *be* + subject**		
	Where is he from?	*Was he late for work?*	

Look! Prepositions don't usually come before the question word: *Who did he work* ***with****?* NOT *~~With who did he work?~~*

Personal Best

Go to Grammar practice: question forms, page 115

6 2.11 **Pronunciation:** question intonation Listen to two of the questions from the radio programme. Does the intonation go up ⤴ or down ⤵ at the end of the questions?

1 How did his career start? *up* ⤴ / *down* ⤵
2 Does he still live in London? *up* ⤴ / *down* ⤵

7 **A** Put the words in brackets in the correct place in the questions.

1 Was Mario's father Peru? (from)
2 Why he take Mario to New York? (did)
3 When did move to London? (Mario)
4 Did Princess Diana in 1997? (die)
5 Does live in New York now? (he)
6 Which does the radio presenter play? (song)

B 2.12 Say the questions with the correct intonation. Listen, check and repeat. Then ask and answer the questions in pairs.

Go to Communication practice: Student A page 159, Student B page 167

8 In pairs, ask and answer questions with the words.

1 you / busy / at the moment?

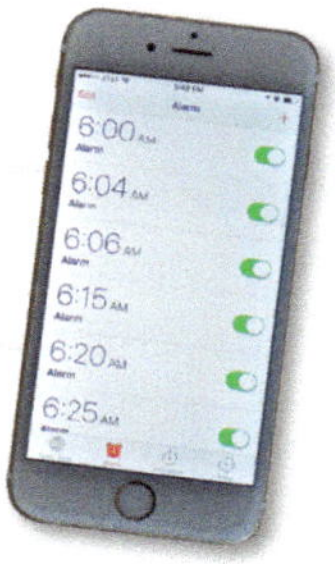
6:00
6:04
6:06
6:15
6:20
6:25

2 what time / you / wake up / this morning?

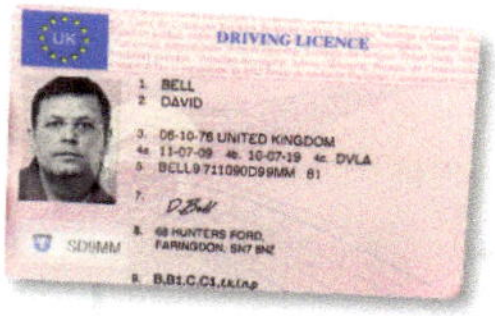
DRIVING LICENCE

3 you / have / a driving licence?

4 where / you / go on holiday / last year?

5 how often / you / take / photographs?

6 which TV series / you / watch / at the moment?

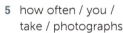

9 Write four sentences about you and your family. Read the sentences to your partner. He/She must ask questions to find out more information.

A *I went to university in São Paulo.* **B** *What did you study there?*
A *My father retired last year.* **B** *What was his job?*

Personal Best Write five quiz questions about a famous person.

Learning Curve

2D That reminds me of ...

1 2.13 Look at the pictures. In pairs, predict what happened on Taylor's first day at work. Watch or listen to the first part of *Learning Curve* and check.

2 2.13 Are the sentences true (T) or false (F)? Watch or listen again and check.

1 Taylor's new job is in a fitness centre. ____
2 She was worried about being late. ____
3 She arrived at work fifteen minutes early. ____
4 A big car hit her car. ____
5 The man in the car shouted at her. ____
6 She was embarrassed. ____

Conversation builder telling a personal story

Starting the story:
Something similar happened to me.
That reminds me of ...
Let me tell you about ...

Involving the listener:
You'll never guess ... (who it was / what happened next / what she said)
Can you imagine?
But that's not all.

Saying how you felt:
It was so ...
I felt really ...
At first, I felt ...

3 2.14 Read the Conversation builder. Match the sentence halves from the conversation. Listen, check and repeat.

1 Let me tell you about
2 At first, I felt
3 I felt
4 But that's
5 You'll never guess
6 It was so

a embarrassing.
b not all.
c my first day.
d great.
e really angry.
f who took my parking spot.

4 In pairs, write three phrases that Taylor's new boss could use to tell the story of what happened.

5 A 2.15 In pairs, order phrases a–h from Penny's story. Watch or listen to the second part of the show, and check.

a ☐ I sent the message to him by mistake!
b ☐ My boss had the same name as my friend – Steve Jones.
c ☐ He thought it was funny, but can you imagine how I felt?
d ☐ Everyone in the office could hear him! It was quite embarrassing.
e ☐ Something similar happened to me at my last job.
f ☐ You'll never guess what he said. 'I'm glad you think I'm handsome and amazing, but it isn't my birthday!'
g ☐ I worked at a radio station in London before I moved to New York.
h ☐ I sent my good friend Steve an email message for his birthday. It said, 'Happy birthday to my handsome, amazing friend!'

B 2.15 Watch or listen again. How are Taylor and Penny's stories similar?

6 2.16 Listen and repeat the phrases when you hear the beeps. How do Taylor and Penny show they are interested in each other's stories?

Skill showing interest

Good listeners show that they are interested in what someone else is saying.
- Use short response expressions such as *Oh, no! Really?* etc.
- Ask questions about what happened.
- Use the correct intonation to show you are interested.

7 Read the Skill box. Put the phrases in the correct columns.

What happened? That's amazing! Really? What did he do then?
Oh no! You're kidding! That's awful! Lucky you! Poor you! Great!

Responding to something positive	Responding to something negative	Showing interest or asking for more information

8 A 2.17 Listen to phrases 1–6. Which speaker sounds more interested: A or B?

1 What happened? _____ 3 Really? _____ 5 You're kidding! _____
2 That's amazing! _____ 4 Oh no, that's awful! _____ 6 Lucky you! _____

B 2.18 In pairs, say phrases 1–6 to show you are interested. Listen, check and repeat.

Go to Communication practice: Student A page 158, Student B page 166

9 A PREPARE Choose one of the ideas. Make notes on what happened and how you felt.

your first day at work/ school/university

a birthday or celebration

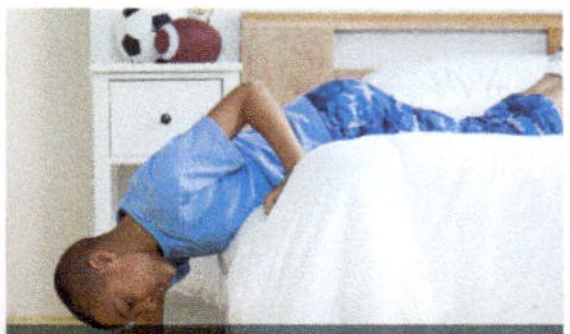
a time when you lost something important

a difficult day

B PRACTISE In pairs, take turns to tell your stories. Listen to your partner and show you are interested by responding to what he/she says or by asking questions.

C PERSONAL BEST Find another partner and tell your story again. How is your storytelling better this time?

Personal Best How well did you listen to your partner's story? Write about what happened and how he/she felt.

Grammar

1 Choose the correct options to complete the sentences.

1. ________ married?
   - a You are
   - b Are you
   - c Is you
2. She ________ Japanese food.
   - a 's liking
   - b like
   - c likes
3. ________ take a message?
   - a I can
   - b Can I
   - c Do I can
4. In the summer I ________ .
   - a every day go running
   - b go running every day
   - c go every day running
5. When ________ here?
   - a do you got
   - b did you get
   - c are you get
6. We went to Brazil ________ year.
   - a last
   - b past
   - c ago
7. The train ________ in the morning.
   - a late is always
   - b always is late
   - c is always late
8. ________ time did you wake up yesterday?
   - a Which
   - b When
   - c What

2 Rewrite the sentences using the tenses in brackets.

1. I work in a restaurant.
   I *worked* in a restaurant. (past simple)
2. I don't wear dark clothes.
   I ________ dark clothes. (present continuous)
3. Where do you go to school?
   Where ________ to school? (past simple)
4. What do you do?
   What ________? (present continuous)
5. Did you take a lot of photos on holiday?
   ________ a lot of photos on holiday? (present simple)
6. I buy bread in the supermarket.
   I ________ bread in the supermarket. (past simple)

3 Complete the text with the correct forms of the verbs in brackets.

Ishita Malaviya

Where [1]________ (be) Ishita from?

She [2]________ (grow up) in Mumbai, India and now she [3]________ (live) in Manipal, in the state of Karnataka, 875 km away.

What [4]________ she ________ (do)?

A few years ago, she [5]________ (become) India's first professional female surfer and now she [6]________ (have) a surf school, where she [7]________ (teach) tourists and local people to surf.

How [8]________ she ________ (start) surfing?

When she [9]________ (go) to university in 2007, she met a German student with a surfboard. At first, she [10]________ (not can) believe that people surfed in India, so she asked him about it and started to learn.

What [11]________ she ________ (do) at the moment?

She [12]________ (make) a film about her story. She hopes it makes more people come to surf in India.

Vocabulary

1 Match the adjectives with the definitions.

shy embarrassed patient annoying confused disappointed lazy generous

Someone who ...

1. feels bad because he/she made a mistake. ________
2. doesn't want to work or try hard. ________
3. is happy to give money, help or his/her time. ________
4. doesn't mind waiting a long time for something. ________
5. doesn't understand something. ________
6. feels sad because something bad happened. ________
7. doesn't like meeting lots of new people. ________
8. makes other people feel a bit angry. ________

2 Circle the word that is different. Explain your answer.

1	wear	carry	bring	funny
2	rude	tired	honest	sociable
3	boring	excited	interesting	disappointing
4	retire	keep fit	grow up	leave school
5	tell	expect	remind	unkind
6	yoga	Pilates	swimming	exercise
7	get up	get married	get engaged	get divorced
8	hope	relax	expect	look forward to

3 Choose the correct options to complete the sentences.

1 Thank you for eating at our restaurant. Please ________ soon!
 a go back **b** grow up **c** come back
2 She really ________ her mother. They have the same eyes.
 a looks **b** looks like **c** reminds
3 Hayley is really ________. She spends ten hours a day in the office.
 a hard-working **b** serious **c** patient
4 I ________ the meeting to finish at about 3.00.
 a wait **b** expect **c** look forward to
5 Can you ________ me your name please?
 a tell **b** say **c** remember
6 Ravi ________ most weekends with his family.
 a joins **b** spends **c** keeps
7 When I was a child, I ________ swimming every Sunday.
 a went **b** did **c** played
8 My football team lost the game. I feel so ________!
 a excited **b** relaxed **c** disappointed

4 Complete the sentences with the verbs in the box.

go on lose retire wait remember
learn have leave miss meet

1 In Britain, you can ________ school when you are 16 years old.
2 Sonia didn't ________ the train, but she arrived late.
3 All my friends ________ social media every day.
4 Did Alex ________ to buy some eggs?
5 My father is 62 and he wants to ________ next year.
6 When you go to university, you ________ lots of interesting people.
7 How often do you ________ your glasses?
8 I'm married, but I don't want to ________ any children.
9 This year, I want to ________ to play a musical instrument.
10 Can you ________ for me after the lesson?

Personal Best

Lesson 1A
Describe two friends using personality adjectives.

Lesson 2A
Write two things you did last weekend.

Lesson 1A
Describe one thing you do every month and one thing you do every year.

Lesson 2B
Write a sentence about what you did yesterday using *after*.

Lesson 1B
Name five hobbies or activities you like doing.

Lesson 2C
Write two questions for an interview with a musician you like.

Lesson 1C
Write a sentence using the present simple and present continuous.

Lesson 2C
Think of a relative and describe two of his/her life stages.

Lesson 1D
Write a sentence about yourself using *because*.

Lesson 2D
Give an expression to start telling a story.

Lesson 1D
Write a sentence about someone you know using *so*.

Lesson 2D
Give an expression to show you are interested in a story.

UNIT 3

Keep on travelling

LANGUAGE comparatives, superlatives, *(not) as ... as* ■ useful adjectives

3A Tourist or traveller?

1 **A** Look at the title of the quiz. What is the difference between a 'tourist' and a 'traveller'?

B Match the speech bubbles with the people in the pictures.

1 I want to go to different countries, try unusual food and have an adventure.

2 I prefer to stay in nice hotels, visit famous sights and have a good time.

2 Underline all the adjectives in the speech bubbles.

Personal Best

Go to Vocabulary practice: useful adjectives, page 141

3 **A** Do the quiz in pairs. Write down your partner's answers.

B Look at the results on page 174. Are you and your partner similar?

ARE YOU A TOURIST OR A TRAVELLER?

1 What do you usually do on holiday?
- **a** I try to see the most famous sights in a city or visit the big museums.
- **b** I like to go somewhere unusual and discover new things.

2 Do you prefer to stay in the city centre or out of town?
- **a** The city centre can be more expensive, but it's the best place to be.
- **b** I prefer to be further away from the centre. It's cheaper to stay out of town.

3 Do you use a guidebook?
- **a** Yes, I do. I like to plan my trip carefully before I go.
- **b** Never! Reading guidebooks isn't as good as speaking to local people.

4 Do you ever explore new places alone?
- **a** No, I don't. Holidays are about spending time with friends and family.
- **b** Yes, I do. You discover more about yourself when you're on your own.

5 What time of year do you prefer to travel?
- **a** In the summer, when the weather is hot and everyone is happier.
- **b** The summer is the worst time! Places aren't as crowded at other times of the year.

a

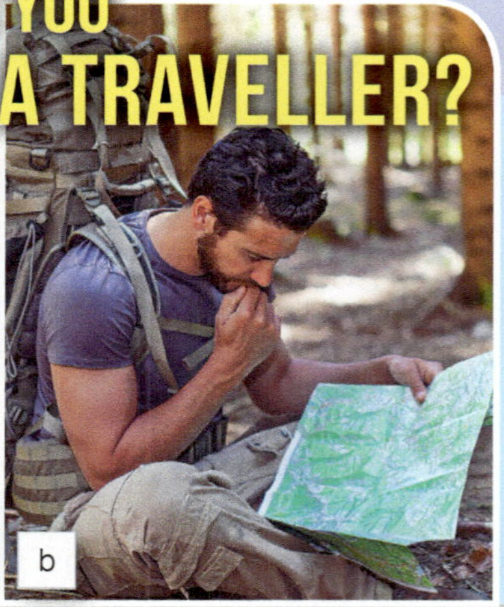
b

4 Complete the table with comparative and superlative adjectives from the quiz. Can you complete the other forms?

	famous	cheap	happy	far	good	bad
comparative						
superlative	*the most famous*					

5 Match sentences 1–2 with the correct meanings a–b. Then read the Grammar box.

1 Reading guidebooks isn't as good as speaking to local people. ____
2 Reading guidebooks is as good as speaking to local people. ____

a Reading guidebooks and speaking to local people are equally good.
b Reading guidebooks is less good than speaking to local people.

Grammar comparatives, superlatives, *(not) as … as*

Comparatives:
*Your hotel is **cheaper** than my hotel.*
*The festival is **more exciting** than the castle.*

Superlatives:
*This is **the biggest** museum in the country.*
*The castle is **the most famous** building in the city.*

(not) as … as:
*The beaches **aren't as crowded as** they are in the summer.*

Personal Best

Go to Grammar practice: comparatives, superlatives, *(not) as … as*, page 116

6 3.3 Listen to Michelle ask three friends for advice. Tick (✓) the advice they recommend.

PARIS TRIP

Transport:
roller skates ☐ bus ☐ metro ☐

Attractions:
the Eiffel Tower ☐ the Louvre ☐ Buttes-Chaumont Park ☐

Food:
a restaurant ☐ a picnic ☐ fast food ☐

7 **A** 3.4 **Pronunciation:** sentence stress Listen to four sentences from the conversations in exercise 6. Underline the stressed words.

1 The metro is the quickest way.
2 The restaurants are much more expensive than I thought.
3 The ones in the city centre are the worst.
4 It's as cheap as fast food, but it's a lot better.

B 3.4 Listen again and repeat.

Go to Communication practice: Student A page 159, Student B page 167

8 **A** Complete the sentences to make recommendations for your town or city.

1 ________ is the most popular tourist attraction.
2 ________ isn't as famous as ________ , but I prefer it because ________________________________ .
3 ________ is the best way to travel, because ________________________________ .
4 ________ is a great place to buy ________ , and it isn't as expensive as ________________________________ .
5 ________ is the most traditional food, and the best restaurant for it is ________________________________ .
6 ________ is the most interesting place for lunch, because ________________________________ .

B Compare your recommendations in pairs. Say if you agree or disagree.

9 **A** Complete the questions with the correct form of the adjectives in brackets.

1 In your opinion, is a city break as ________ as a beach holiday? (relaxing)
2 Do you think holidays in your country are ________ than going abroad? (good)
3 Where is ________ place in your country? (hot)
4 Do you think travelling by car is as ________ as travelling by train? (expensive)
5 Do you think holidays with friends are ________ than family holidays? (enjoyable)
6 In your opinion, what is ________ thing about a holiday? (bad)

B Ask and answer the questions in pairs. Try and give more information.

Personal Best Choose three places and make sentences about them with comparatives, superlatives and *(not) as … as*.

Learning Curve

3B Staycation or vacation?

1 Match the activities in the box with the pictures. Which activities do you usually do on holiday?

sunbathe visit a museum go sightseeing buy souvenirs
hire a car eat out go abroad stay in a hotel

a
b
c
d
e
f
g
h
H
I NY

Personal Best

Go to Vocabulary practice: holiday activities, page 138

2 Discuss the questions in pairs.

1 How often do you have a holiday?
2 Do you ever go abroad? Why/Why not?
3 Where do you usually stay?
4 Who do you usually go with?
5 What do you enjoy doing most on holiday?
6 What is the worst thing about a holiday?

3 ▶3.7 Guess the correct definition of a 'staycation'. Watch or listen to the first part of *Learning Curve* and check.

A 'staycation' is a holiday where you stay ...

a in your country. **b** at your own home. **c** at a friend's house.

Skill Identifying key points

When people speak, listen for the important things they say.

- People usually emphasize the most important ideas.
- After an important idea, they sometimes give an example or more information.
- Find the key words in the questions and listen very carefully when the speaker talks about this point.

4 ▶3.7 Read the Skill box. Watch or listen again and tick (✓) the key points Penny mentions.

1 Holidays need a lot of planning. ☐
2 They can be expensive. ☐
3 Hotels are great for relaxing. ☐
4 Travel can be tiring. ☐
5 You don't need to travel on a staycation. ☐
6 You can go to your favourite places. ☐
7 You can relax at home. ☐
8 You can continue your daily routine. ☐

Penny
Learning Cu

5 ▶3.8 Watch or listen to the second part of the show. Tick (✓) the type of holiday the people are having.

1 Terry and Carol staycation ☐ vacation ☐
2 Ayoku staycation ☐ vacation ☐
3 Lisa staycation ☐ vacation ☐

6 3.8 Watch or listen again. Are the sentences true (T) or false (F)?

1 Terry and Carol are having a bad time on holiday. ____
2 They're in Ireland. ____
3 They think staycations can be boring. ____
4 Ayoku has two weeks off work. ____
5 He wants to spend the time relaxing in his apartment. ____
6 Last year he went on holiday but didn't relax much. ____
7 Lisa's cousins have come to visit her in New York. ____
8 She prefers to show them popular tourist attractions. ____

Terry and Carol

Ayoku

Lisa

7 Discuss the questions about your last holiday in pairs.

Where did you go? / Where did you stay? / What did you eat? / What did you do? / What was the weather like? / Did you have a good time? / Who did you go with?

Listening builder sentence stress

English speakers usually stress the most important words in a sentence. You can usually understand the general idea if you only hear these words.

*A **staycation** is a **holiday** where you **stay** at your **own home**.*
*You can **make time** to **eat out** at your **favourite restaurant**, or **drive** to the **beach**.*

8 **A** Read the Listening builder. Look at the words in the sentences 1–5 from the show. Can you understand the general ideas?

1 ________ hired ________ car ________ came ________ ________ lovely national park!
2 ________ usually stay ________ home ________ ________ often boring.
3 ________ doing all ________ things ________ don't usually ________ time ________ do.
4 ________ ________ actually ________ stressful ________ everything ________ planned.
5 ________ ________ family visits, ________ take ________ ________ places ________ many tourists never see.

B 3.9 In pairs, try to complete the sentences with the unstressed words. Listen and check.

9 Discuss the questions in pairs. Give reasons for your answers.

Which is better...

1 sunbathing or going sightseeing?

3 flying or travelling by train?

HOTEL

2 staying in a hotel or going camping?

4 packing a big suitcase or taking a small rucksack?

Personal Best Write a paragraph explaining to tourists what there is to do in your town or city.

3C A traveller's tale

1 A Read the introduction of the text and look at the pictures. Answer the questions in pairs.

1 How long do you think Alastair's trip took?
2 How many countries do you think he visited?
3 What type of problems do you think he had on the journey?
4 What kind of person do you think Alastair is?
5 Would you like to go on an adventure like this? Why/Why not?

B Read the rest of the text and check your answers.

Round the world by bike

In 2001, Alastair Humphreys was doing a course to become a teacher, but he really wanted to do something different. A few months later, he surprised his friends and family by beginning an amazing journey that took him around the world ... on his bike!

In all, Alastair visited 60 countries, and throughout the trip he kept a blog to record all of his experiences. Although there were some special moments on the road, there was also disappointment and disaster.

One disappointment came early. Alastair's dream was to cycle all the way except for taking boats to cross the oceans. Unfortunately, this was impossible. The police stopped him while he was travelling across Egypt and he had to ride on a truck. He was angry, but there was no other way to continue.

The rest of the time, he rode, rode, rode. On one occasion, he was crossing the Arizona desert when his bike broke. Help came from a surprising place. To his amazement, complete strangers bought him a new bike so that he could continue his incredible journey.

The trip was tough and Alastair didn't have enough money to stay in nice hotels. While he was cycling through Patagonia, he didn't have a shower for 24 days!

However, one of the hardest parts of his trip came when he travelled across Russia in winter. Luckily, a friend joined him so he wasn't travelling alone, but it was so cold that while they were cycling through Siberia, Alastair's beard froze.

But none of these problems could stop him from completing the journey. Four years and 75,000 km later, Alastair finally arrived back at his home in Yorkshire with lots of stories to tell.

2 In pairs, answer the questions. Read the text again and check your answers.

1 Why didn't he cycle all the time?
2 How did he get a new bike?
3 What was his accommodation like?
4 Where did he experience the worst weather?

3 A Complete the sentences with the correct verbs. Check your answers in the text.

1 He _________ the Arizona desert when his bike _________ .
2 While they _________ through Siberia, Alastair's beard _________ .

B Look at the sentences again and answer the questions. Then read the Grammar box.

1 Which verbs describe completed actions in the past? _________ , _________
2 Which verbs describe actions happening at the time of the completed action? _________ , _________

Grammar past continuous and past simple

Actions in progress at a time in the past:
*In 2001, Alastair Humphreys **was doing** a course to become a teacher.*

Actions in progress when a completed action happened:
*The police **stopped** him **while** he **was travelling** across Egypt.*
*He **was travelling** across Egypt **when** the police **stopped** him.*

Personal Best

Go to Grammar practice: past continuous and past simple, page 117

4 A 3.11 **Pronunciation:** *was/were* Listen to the sentences and underline the stressed words. How do you pronounce *was* and *were*?

1 I was driving home at 6.00 yesterday evening.
2 They were working hard when I got to the office.
3 It didn't rain while Anita was staying in Scotland.
4 What were you doing at 8.00 this morning?

B Practise saying the sentences in pairs.

5 In pairs, ask and answer the question *What were you doing ...?* with the times in the boxes. Pay attention to how you say *was* and *were*.

in 2014 | at 7.30 this morning | this time last week | one hour ago | yesterday evening at 6.00 | last year

6 A Look at the pictures. Complete the sentences with your own ideas.

1 I was sleeping in bed when ...

3 While Barbara was cooking dinner, ...

2 They were running in the park when ...

4 My boss phoned me while ...

B Compare your answers in pairs.

Go to Communication practice: Student A page 160, Student B 168

7 3.12 Choose the correct form of the verbs to complete the conversation. Listen and check.

David Did I ever tell you about how I [1]*met / was meeting* a museum guide in Hamburg?
Emma No, I don't think so.
David It was in 2012, while I [2]*travelled / was travelling* around Germany. I [3]*waited / was waiting* for a train to Berlin, but I was hungry, so I [4]*went / was going* to a café to buy a sandwich. While I [5]*sat / was sitting* there, a man at another table [6]*got up / was getting up* and [7]*left / was leaving* his wallet.
Emma Oh no! What did you do?
David I [8]*ran / was running* after him and [9]*gave / was giving* him the wallet back. But the funny thing is, when I [10]*got / was getting* to the platform later, the same man [11]*waited / was waiting* for the train.
Emma Really?
David Yes, and he [12]*was / was being* a museum guide at the Pergamon Museum in Berlin! He [13]*offered / was offering* to show me around to thank me for finding his wallet. The museum was amazing!

8 Think about a holiday or travel experience you had. Discuss the questions in pairs.

1 Where and when did you go?
2 What were the best/worst moments?
3 What were you doing when the best/worst moments happened?

Personal Best Describe an important event in your life. Use the past simple and past continuous to explain what happened.

3D Travel problems

1 Discuss the questions in pairs.

1 When was the last time you were at an airport?
2 Why were you there?
3 How do you normally feel when you are at an airport?
4 What problems can happen at an airport?

2 3.13 Look at pictures a–f and order them from 1–6. Listen and check.

a
Wedding Invitation
b
c
d
CHIUSA
e
f
Flight Booking
London → Naples
Naples → London

3 3.13 Complete the text with the correct form of the verbs in the box. Listen again and check.

arrive book buy have open carry receive run see wait

In 2013, Martin Hendon was living in London. One morning, he [1] ________ a quick breakfast, when he [2] ________ a letter from his best friend, Tony. It was an invitation to Tony's wedding … in Naples, Italy, in two weeks! So Martin quickly [3] ________ a flight and [4] ________ a new suit.

The day before the wedding didn't start well. Martin [5] ________ patiently at the airport when he [6] ________ that his flight was cancelled. He caught a later flight and arrived in Naples the next morning, but he was very tired and accidentally took the wrong suitcase. When he [7] ________ it in his hotel room, he found someone else's clothes!

He [8] ________ down the street desperately looking for a new suit, but it was Sunday and the shops were closed. Just then, he recognized a passenger from his plane walking slowly down the street. She [9] ________ a suitcase the same colour as Martin's. He asked her politely to open it, and there was Martin's new suit inside!

He changed his clothes and jumped in a taxi to the wedding. When Martin [10] ________ , he opened the door nervously. Inside, everyone was waiting for the wedding to begin. Tony looked at him and smiled. He was only a few minutes late.

4 Match the paragraphs from exercise 3 with descriptions a–d. Then read the Skill box.

Paragraph 1 a the problem (what happened)
Paragraph 2 b the resolution (how he solved the problem)
Paragraph 3 c the background (who, when, where)
Paragraph 4 d the ending (what happened in the end, how he felt)

Skill writing a narrative

When you write a story, make it easy to follow and interesting.

- Tell the story in chronological order.
- Organize your ideas into four paragraphs (the background, the problem, the resolution, the ending).
- Use adjectives and adverbs to make the text more interesting.

5 **A** Complete the sentences from Martin's story. Check your answers in the text.

1 One morning, he was having a ________ breakfast. 2 Martin ________ booked a flight.

B Answer the questions about sentences 1 and 2.

1 Which word is an adjective and describes a noun? ________
2 Which word is an adverb and describes a verb? ________
3 What letters do we add to most adjectives to make an adverb? ________

6 Underline seven more adverbs that describe verbs in Martin's story.

Text builder adverbs of manner

We use adverbs of manner to say how someone does an action:
*Martin was waiting **patiently** at the airport.*

Most adjectives:	*quiet → quietly, slow → slowly*
Adjectives ending in -y:	*happy → happily, angry → angrily*
Irregular adverbs:	*good → well, fast → fast, hard → hard*

Look! Adverbs of manner come at the end of the phrase:
He speaks Spanish ***well.*** NOT ~~*He speaks well Spanish.*~~

7 Read the Text builder. Choose the correct words to complete the first paragraph of another story.

Ana Carvalho is from Goiânia, Brazil, but in 2015 she was studying [1]*hard / hardly* at university in São Paulo. After her exams, she was waiting [2]*nervous / nervously* for the results, but she was also very [3]*happy / happily* because it was her birthday soon. She planned to go home and celebrate with her friends and family in Goiânia. Ana was very [4]*practical / practically*, and the night before the flight she packed her suitcase [5]*careful / carefully*, checked she had her passport and tickets and slept [6]*good / well*.

8 **A** PREPARE Match phrases 1–6 with pictures a–f. In pairs, discuss what happened to Ana Carvalho. Put your ideas into three groups for the next three paragraphs of the narrative.

1 apologize and give her a ticket to Goiânia ____
2 began to worry on the plane ____
3 realize that the plane is flying to Guyana ____
4 receive the exam results at her party ____
5 not hear her correctly ____
6 ask which gate is for Goiânia ____

Goiânia?
INFORMATION
a
b
Hello...
c
GUYANA
GOIÂNIA
SÃO PAULO
d
e
f

B PRACTISE Use your notes to help you write the rest of Ana's story. Remember to use adverbs.

C PERSONAL BEST Swap stories with another pair. Tick (✓) three sentences you think are well written.

Personal Best Write five sentences about a holiday experience you had. Use a different adverb in each sentence.

UNIT 4

The working world

LANGUAGE *will*, *may* and *might* for predictions ■ jobs

4A The future of work

1 **A** Look at the title of the text and the picture. What do you think it is about?

B In pairs, decide which jobs machines will do in the future and which jobs will always need people.

accountant fashion designer farmer journalist model police officer
receptionist salesperson surgeon tour guide waiter/waitress

Personal Best

Go to Vocabulary practice: jobs, page 142

2 Read the text. Which jobs do experts think that machines will do?

WILL A ROBOT TAKE MY JOB?

I'm at the Henn-na Hotel in Japan. A smartly-dressed Japanese woman welcomes me and asks if I have a reservation. But this is no ordinary receptionist. She is in fact a robot, one of several at the hotel that can carry your bags to your room, and even give you travel suggestions.

Robots and computers are taking our jobs. According to experts, ninety years from now, machines will replace 70% of today's occupations. Accountants and telephone salespeople may be the first to lose their jobs. In restaurants, robots might replace waiters and waitresses. Models might also disappear – the fashion designer Ralph Lauren is already experimenting with holographic models for his clothes. And in the future, when you go to hospital for an operation, even the surgeon probably won't be real.

So, should we be worried? The answer is no. History shows us that as old jobs die, new jobs replace them. So, what jobs will exist for us in the future? Here are our top three predictions:

1 Drone controller
Drones will deliver our shopping, remove our rubbish and may even act as police officers, but people will still need to control these flying devices from the ground.

2 Vertical farmer
Transporting food will probably become more expensive, and with crowded cities, there will only be one way to grow food and vegetables – upwards! Supermarkets will grow all their food above them in special glass buildings.

3 Space tour guide
In the future, people won't want to travel round the world on holiday. Space tourism will create thousands of jobs for space pilots and tour guides to take tourists out of this world!

3 Match the halves to make complete sentences. Check your answers in the text.

1 Ninety years from now, machines will
2 Accountants and telephone salespeople may
3 Models might
4 The surgeon probably won't
5 Transporting food will probably
6 People won't

a become more expensive.
b also disappear.
c want to travel round the world on holiday.
d replace 70% of today's occupations.
e be the first to lose their jobs.
f be real.

4 **A** Answer the questions about the predictions in exercise 3.

1 Which two sentences are about things that are likely? _______ , _______
2 Which two sentences are about things that are possible? _______ , _______
3 Which two sentences are about things that are unlikely? _______ , _______

B Choose the correct words to complete the rule. Then read the Grammar box.

When we use *probably*, it comes *before / after will* and *before / after won't*.

Grammar *will*, *may* and *might* for predictions

Predictions which are sure/very likely:	Predictions which are less sure/possible:	Predictions which are very unlikely:
*The traffic **will** be very bad tonight.*	*It **might** rain tomorrow.* *The train **may** be late.*	*Chelsea **won't** win the FA cup next year.*

Look! We can use *probably* with *will* and *won't*: *I'**ll probably** fail the exam / I **probably won't** pass the exam.*

Personal Best

Go to Grammar practice: *will*, *may* and *might* for predictions, page 118

5 A 4.4 **Pronunciation:** *want/won't* Listen and repeat the sentence from the text. Match the words in **bold** with the sounds /ɒ/ and /əʊ/.

In the future, people **won't want** to travel round the world on holiday.

B 4.5 How do you say the sentences? Pay attention to *want* and *won't*. Listen, check and repeat.

1 He might **want** to look for a new job.
2 Robots **won't** replace politicians.
3 My boss will probably **want** to travel by boat.
4 In the future, you **won't** have to go to school.

Go to Communication practice: Student A page 160, Student B page 168

6 A Work in pairs and look at the topics below. What do you think will happen in the future? Make nine predictions.

Students won't go to school. Computers will probably replace teachers.

IN 50 YEARS FROM NOW…

HOW WILL EDUCATION CHANGE?

1 Students / go to school/university.
2 Computers / replace / teachers.
3 Students / study / different subjects.

HOW WILL TRANSPORT BE DIFFERENT?

4 Cars / need / drivers.
5 There / be / more traffic.
6 We / use / electricity as fuel.

MEDICAL CARE
HEALTH

WHAT WILL THE HEALTH SYSTEM BE LIKE?

7 There / be / more healthcare jobs.
8 Robots / replace / doctors.
9 We / go to the doctor's / when we are ill.

B 4.6 Listen to an expert talking about the topics. What predictions does she make? How sure is she?

7 Did you agree with the expert? Can you think of any other predictions about these topics?

8 In pairs, make predictions about the topics. Say if you agree or disagree with your partner.

- the weather tomorrow
- your country winning the World Cup
- your next English exam
- the town or city where you live
- your journey home tonight
- tomorrow at work/school/university

Personal Best Write predictions about how five different jobs will change in the future.

4B I'm so bored

1 Look at the title and the pictures on page 33. Which jobs can you see? Discuss the questions in pairs.

1 How often do you feel bored?
2 What jobs do you think are boring?
3 Do you think boredom is a bad thing? Why/Why not?
4 What can you do to stop feeling bored at work?

Skill skimming a text

When we skim a text, we read it quickly to understand the main ideas.

- Look at the title, pictures and any headings, and predict what the text is about.
- Read the first sentence in each paragraph carefully. These are 'topic sentences' and are usually a summary of what the paragraph is about.
- Think about the ideas from all the topic sentences to understand the general meaning of the whole text.

2 Read the Skill box. Then read the highlighted topic sentences in the text and tick (✓) the best description of the text.

1 Modern technology makes us feel bored more quickly. ☐
2 People can have better ideas after they do boring activities. ☐
3 Boredom in offices is a serious problem for companies. ☐

3 Answer the questions in pairs. Read the text again and check your answers.

1 What do most people do when they are bored?
2 How did the scientists use the plastic cups to test people's creativity?
3 What activity did some people do first to make them bored?
4 Who was more creative in the experiment? What ideas did they have?
5 What does Jack White do to give him ideas for new songs?
6 What kind of activities make us feel more/less creative?

4 Has the text changed your opinion about being bored? Why/Why not?

5 **A** Look at the extract from the text. Who or what does *They* refer to?

*Some scientists think we're making a mistake. **They** believe that boring activities can be good for us.*

B Read the Text builder. Find pronouns 1–8 in the text and say what they refer to.

Text builder pronoun referencing

We use pronouns and possessive adjectives to avoid repeating nouns:
*Sharon had **a fantastic idea** yesterday. **It** was really creative.*
***Carlos** always works late. I saw **him** in the office at 8.00 last night.*
***My parents** earn a lot of money, but I think **their** jobs are very boring.*

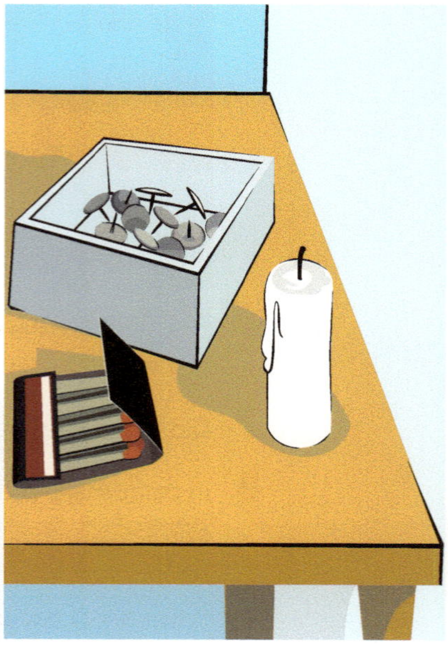

6 **A** Complete the text with the pronouns in the box. What do the pronouns refer to?

his it he them

Karl Duncker was a German psychologist. [1] _________ is most famous for thinking of a problem to test creativity. In [2] _________ experiment, he gave students a candle, a book of matches and a box of pins. He asked [3] _________ to fix the candle to a wall and light [4] _________ without dripping any wax on the table.

B In pairs, try to solve Duncker's problem. Explain your solution to the class.

THE TRUTH ABOUT BOREDOM

PASSHOLDERS
ONLY

We all hate being bored, particularly at work. In fact, most of us try hard to avoid [1] **it** and, thanks to modern technology, there are now hundreds of ways to keep us entertained. People watch videos or play games on the way to work, check their phones when they're in boring meetings, and chat to friends or listen to music while they do dull administrative tasks. But some scientists think we're making a mistake. They believe that boring activities can be good for us and a recent psychology experiment tests this idea.

In 2013, Dr Sandi Mann and Rebekah Cadman did an experiment to test people's creativity, i.e. how well we can think of ideas. [2] **Their** idea was to see if boredom had an effect on how creative we are. They gave 140 people some plastic cups and asked [3] **them** to think of different ways to use them. However, half of the people spent 15 minutes doing some very boring activities first. They had to read telephone numbers from a long list and copy [4] **them** onto paper.

The results of the experiment were very interesting. The people who did the boring activities first were much more creative and thought of lots of ideas. Some people suggested wearing the cups as party hats or filling [5] **them** with fruit juice and freezing them to make ice-lollies. Whereas, the people who didn't do any boring tasks found it hard to think of many ways to use the cups.

Dr Mann says a little boredom can be positive for us. [6] **She** thinks that we shouldn't be afraid of 'doing nothing'. Many very successful people do 'boring' activities in their free time. For example, the US rock musician Jack White repairs furniture. [7] **His** hobby helps him to relax and think of ideas for new songs. At work, some successful people do similar things to be creative, like tidying their desk or deleting old emails.

However, there are good and bad ways to be bored. You should only do boring activities for a short time and you should avoid physical activities which make you feel tired, as this can make you less creative. So, if you usually listen to music, read the news and send messages to friends when you're bored at work, why not try doing less? Make a cup of coffee, organize your paperwork or look out of the window – maybe [8] **it** will change your life … and you can always tell your boss that you're being creative.

Personal Best Write about a time you thought of a creative solution to a problem.

4C The secret boss

1 Look at the two people in the pictures. What is the relationship between them? Read the text and check.

Carla Pine is the managing director of Cibus, a chain of Italian restaurants. She works in London and is responsible for twenty restaurants in the UK. Next week, she's visiting two of her restaurants to find out what it's like to be a worker in the company, but she's going to do it in secret! She's going to dress as a member of staff, but because people might recognize her, she's going to change the colour of her hair and the style of her clothes, and become … Katie Rose.

She's going to Manchester and she has a busy few days ahead of her. On Monday and Tuesday, she's working as a kitchen assistant with George Nowak. On Wednesday and Thursday, she's working as a waitress in another restaurant in the city with Lucy Mendez … and on Friday, she's going to tell George and Lucy who she really is!

Carla Pine

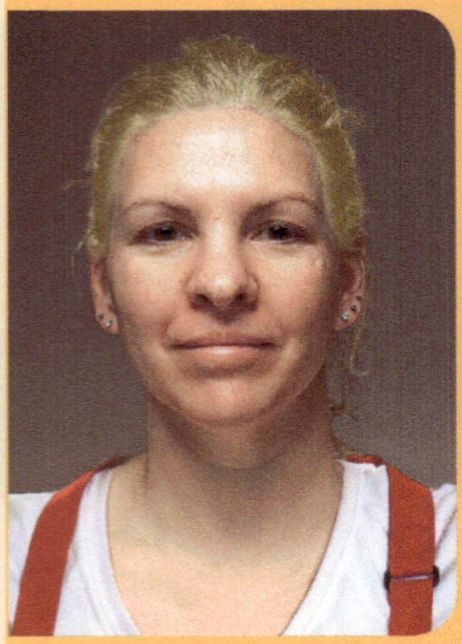

Katie Rose

2 Choose the correct options to complete the sentences. Read the text again and check.

1 Carla is visiting *one* / *two* / *three* of her restaurants next week.
2 She is going to change her *appearance* / *opinion* / *voice* so people don't recognize her.
3 She's going to see what it's like to work as *a hair stylist* / *a boss* / *an employee*.
4 On Monday and Tuesday, she's working as a *managing director* / *waitress* / *kitchen assistant*.
5 On Wednesday and Thursday, she's working with *Lucy Mendez* / *George Nowak* / *Katie Rose*.

3 Answer the questions about the sentences in exercise 2. Then read the Grammar box.

1 Do the sentences refer to the past, the present or the future? _________
2 Which sentences say *when* and/or *where* she will do things? _________
3 Which use the present continuous? _________ Which use *be going to*? _________

Grammar *be going to* and present continuous

Future plans:
*I'**m going to do** a training course.*
*The company **isn't going to open** a new office.*

Future arrangements (with a fixed time and place):
*He'**s travelling** to Manchester on Monday.*
*What **are you doing** this evening?*

Look! We can also use *be going to* with arrangements:
*He'**s going to** travel to Manchester on Monday.* *What **are** you **going to** do this evening?*

Personal Best

Go to Grammar practice: *be going to* and present continuous, page 119

4 **A** 4.9 **Pronunciation:** *going to* and *want to* Listen to Carla speaking quickly. How are *going to* and *want to* pronounced?

I **want to** find out what it's like to work for my company, so I'm **going to** visit two of my restaurants … in secret.

B 4.10 In pairs, say the conversation quickly. Listen, check and repeat.

A What are you **going to** do tonight?
B I'm **going to** try that new Chinese restaurant. Do you **want to** come?
A I can't. I'm **going to** work late tonight. I'm free tomorrow, if you **want to** meet up.
B Yes, that's great. I **want to** hear all your news!

5 Tick (✓) the things you have done from the box below. Tell your partner when and why.

apply for a job ☐ go on a training course ☐ get a promotion ☐ leave a job ☐ write a CV ☐

When I was a student, I applied for a job as a radio DJ. I didn't get it.

Personal Best

Go to Vocabulary practice: phrases about work, page 143

6 **A** 4.13 Listen to the conversation between Carla, Lucy and George. Complete the table.

Name	Problems	Solutions
 George Nowak, Head chef	*George's kitchen wasn't clean.*	
 Lucy Mendez, Head waitress		

B Check your answers in pairs.

George's kitchen wasn't clean, so Carla is going to ...

7 **A** In pairs, look at the problems and think of the best way to solve them.

1

Your colleague is going on holiday, so you'll have to use a complicated new computer program at work.

2

Your boss does no work, but she wants you to work at the weekends to finish a project.

3

You want to buy a house, but your salary is the same as when you started work ten years ago!

B Tell the rest of the class your plans.

We're going to go on a training course to learn about the new program.

Go to Communication practice: Student A page 160, Student B page 168

8 In pairs, ask and answer the question *What are you doing ...?* with the future times in the boxes below.

A *What are you doing tonight?*
B *I'm meeting some friends in the city centre. We're going to have dinner together.*

tonight | tomorrow | next weekend | next summer | in two weeks' time | the day after tomorrow | next year

Personal Best Write about your work plans for the future.

4D Can I leave a message?

1 Look at the reasons for making telephone calls. Can you think of any more?

book a taxi   speak to a colleague   call in sick to work   ask for technical help
book a table at a restaurant   make an appointment   call a shop for information

2 Discuss the questions in pairs.

1 How often do you phone people?
2 Who do you usually speak to on the phone?
3 How do you feel when you speak to someone you don't know on the phone?
4 What problems can you have when you speak in English on the phone?

3 ▶ 4.14 Watch or listen to the first part of *Learning Curve*. Who called these people, and why did they call?

Ethan

Receptionist

Penny

Mo

4 ▶ 4.14 Watch or listen again. Are the sentences true (T) or false (F)?

1 Penny thinks that communication is easier with modern technology. ____
2 Penny and Ethan have a video conference call with Simon and Kate at 10.00. ____
3 Ethan makes an appointment with the dentist for 9.50. ____
4 Mo says it will take ten minutes to fix the internet connection. ____
5 Mo says he will bring Penny a telephone to call Simon and Kate. ____

Conversation builder telephone language

Caller:
Hello, this is ...
Could I speak to ...?
Can you tell him/her that ...?
Could you ask him/her to call me back, please?
Thank you, goodbye.

Person being called:
Good morning, ... How can I help you?
Hello, ... speaking/calling.
I'm afraid he/she's not available at the moment.
Can I take a message?
I think you have the wrong number.
Thanks/Thank you for calling.

5 **A** ▶ 4.15 Read the Conversation builder. In pairs, order the conversation from 1–9. Listen and check.

a ☐ Thanks for calling.
b ☐ Yes, can you ask her to call Fiona when she can?
c ☐ Hello, Mo Bensallem speaking.
d ☐ Yes, of course.
e ☐ Oh hello, could I speak to Julia, please?
f ☐ I'm afraid she's not at her desk at the moment.
g ☐ Sorry, I don't know. Can I take a message?
h ☐ Do you know when she will be back?
i ☐ Thank you, goodbye.

Fiona
Mo

B In pairs, practise saying the conversation. You can change the names and any details.

6 4.16 Watch or listen to the second part of the show. Does Penny speak to Kate and Simon?

7 4.16 Tick (✓) the problems Penny has. Watch or listen again and check.

1 She dials the wrong number. ☐
2 Simon forgot about the conference call. ☐
3 Kate doesn't answer the phone in time. ☐
4 Charlotte can't hear Penny very well. ☐
5 Charlotte doesn't understand English well. ☐
6 Penny forgot to leave her number. ☐

Charlotte

8 4.17 Listen and repeat the phrases when you hear the beeps. How do the speakers deal with difficulties?

Skill dealing with difficulties

It is sometimes difficult to understand people when they speak, especially on the telephone.

- Ask the speaker politely to speak louder or repeat what he/she said.
- Ask the speaker to spell any difficult words.
- Repeat what the speaker says to make sure it is correct.
- Stress the word or phrase you want to check if you have a doubt.

9 Read the Skill box. Put the phrases in the correct column.

I'm afraid I didn't catch that. Sorry, did you say ...? And was that ... or ...? Sorry, could you speak up? Can you spell that, please? Could you speak more slowly, please? Could you repeat that, please?

You don't hear something	You need to check or confirm specific information

10 **A** 4.18 Listen to five conversations and underline the information the speaker wants to check.

1 Sorry, did you say you needed three blue shirts?
2 And you bought the product on 5 June 2015?
3 So your flight is at 5.00 p.m. on Wednesday next week?
4 Sorry, did you say you wanted to book a double room next week?
5 Was that vegetable soup for table 12?

B In pairs, repeat questions 1–5. Pay attention to the words you stress.

Go to Communication practice: Student A page 159, Student B page 167

11 **A** **PREPARE** In pairs, look at the situations below. Decide which role you will have and think about what you will say.

	Situation 1	Situation 2
Student A	You have arranged to meet a colleague. Call to cancel the meeting.	You are going on holiday to London. Book a hotel room for your trip.
Student B	Answer the phone. The person the speaker wants to talk to is not in the office. Take a message.	You are a receptionist in a hotel. Take details of the booking. It is very noisy and you can't hear the speaker well.

B **PRACTISE** Sit back to back with your partner so you can't see him/her. Practise the telephone conversation.

C **PERSONAL BEST** Are you more confident at speaking on the telephone in English? How could you improve? Swap partners and practise the conversations again.

Personal Best Write down one of the conversations from exercise 11.

Grammar

1 Cross (**X**) the sentence which is NOT correct.

1 a This hotel is more expensive than Hotel Atlanta. ☐
b This hotel is the most expensive as Hotel Atlanta. ☐
c Hotel Atlanta isn't as expensive as this one. ☐

2 a Simon was cutting his finger while he was cooking. ☐
b Simon cut his finger while he was cooking. ☐
c Simon was cooking when he cut his finger. ☐

3 a I don't think he'll win the race. ☐
b He might not win the race. ☐
c He might won't win the race. ☐

4 a This phone is the smallest in the shop. ☐
b This phone is smaller than the others. ☐
c This phone as small as in the shop. ☐

5 a It may be hot tomorrow. ☐
b It will be probably hot tomorrow. ☐
c It might be hot tomorrow. ☐

6 a What do you do next week? ☐
b What are you doing next week? ☐
c What are you going to do next week? ☐

7 a I met Jamal while I was studying at university in 2010. ☐
b In 2010, while I was studying at university, I met Jamal. ☐
c I was meeting Jamal in 2010, while I studied at university. ☐

8 a She isn't meeting up with her friend tonight. ☐
b She isn't going to meet up with her friend tonight. ☐
c She doesn't meet up with her friend tonight. ☐

2 Use the words in brackets to complete the sentences so they mean the same as the first sentence.

1 London isn't as hot as Madrid.
Madrid ________ London. (hotter)

2 I don't think I will pass the exam.
I ________ the exam. (probably / pass)

3 Kelly is shorter than Nicki.
Kelly ________ Nicki. (as / tall)

4 My phone rang while I was cooking dinner.
________ my phone rang. (when)

5 He's arriving at 6.00 p.m.
He's ________ at 6.00 p.m. (going)

6 The shop may be closed.
The shop ________ open. (might)

7 I was speaking on the phone when I missed my train.
I missed my train ________. (while)

8 What are you going to do on Saturday?
What ________ on Saturday? (doing)

3 Choose the correct options to complete the text.

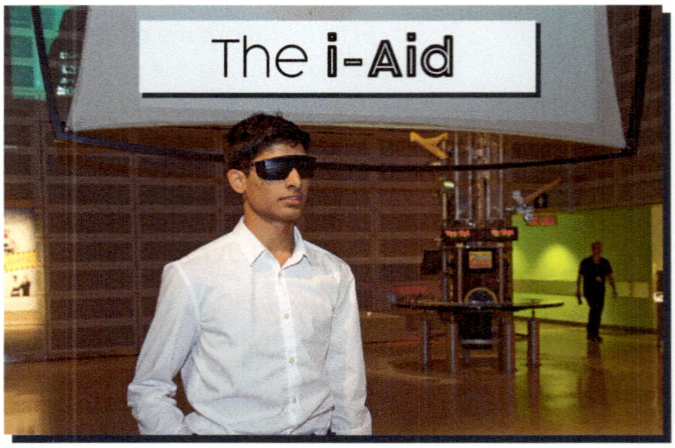
The i-Aid

In 2009, Canadian Alex Deans [1]*watched* / *was watching* a blind person cross the road when he [2] *had* / *was having* a great idea. He realized that he could use sound to help blind people know where things are, like some animals do.

Even though he [3]*still studied* / *was still studying* at high school, he [4]*found* / *was finding* time to develop his idea, and four years later, he finished work on the i-Aid – a device that makes it [5]*easier* / *easiest* for blind people to move around objects.

In 2013, he won an award for the [6]*better* / *best* invention in Canada and gained a great deal of interest from tech companies. In fact, the Canadian Institute for the Blind were so impressed, that the blind people at the institute started testing the device and the results were very positive.

Deans will [7]*might* / *probably* have to wait a couple of years to see the i-Aid on sale, but he is just as [8]*busy* / *busier* as before. At the moment, he [9]*is studying* / *going to study* Engineering at university, and whichever project he's working on, it [10]*will* / *may* definitely be just as exciting as the i-Aid.

Vocabulary

1 Match the words in the box with the definitions.

souvenir	modern	sunbathe	resort
famous	tidy	crowded	pack

1 to put things in a bag for a holiday ________
2 something that reminds you of a holiday ________
3 known and recognized by many people ________
4 to relax in the sun ________
5 full of people ________
6 up to date ________
7 everything organized in the right place ________
8 an area where tourists stay and do activities ________

2 Circle the word that is different. Explain your answer.

1	lively	busy	quiet	quickly
2	a hotel	a flight	a museum	a double room
3	surgeon	model	firefighter	police officer
4	CV	promotion	salary	attend
5	scientist	salesperson	travel agent	shop assistant
6	advert	apply	career	degree
7	lively	polluted	crowded	ugly
8	hire	abroad	eat out	pack

3 Complete the sentences with the words in the box.

tour guide   film director   fashion designer
flight attendant   football coach   news reporter

1 He's my favourite ________ , but his clothes are really uncomfortable. You can't wear them for long.
2 The ________ was happy when the team won. It was a difficult game, though. They only won 1-0.
3 The ________ will meet you in the main square. It's very busy, so look for this sign.
4 My sister is a ________ . She flew to 50 different foreign countries last year.
5 My cousin is a ________ . He knows lots of famous actors.
6 I work as a ________ for my city's radio station. I talk about interesting events in the area.

4 Complete the conversation with the verbs in the box.

write   get   go (x2)   start   see   book
visit   leave   apply

Omar Did you [1]________ the job advert in yesterday's newspaper?
Nuria No, I didn't.
Omar Royal Airlines are looking for new flight attendants. You said you wanted to [2]________ your job.
Nuria Do you think I should [3]________ for the job?
Omar Yes – it's perfect for you! Didn't you want to [4]________ abroad more often?
Nuria Yes, but on holiday. I don't think you have much time to [5]________ sightseeing or [6]________ local attractions.
Omar Not when you're working, but you'll probably get a discount when you [7]________ flights ... so you can travel more on holiday!
Nuria Hmm, maybe. What's the salary?
Omar It's quite low when you [8]________ work, but you might [9]________ a pay rise after a year or two. I'll help you [10]________ a CV, if you want.
Nuria OK, I'll do it!

Personal Best

Lesson 3A Write two sentences about your friends using *(not) as ... as.*

Lesson 4A Write two predictions about next year.

Lesson 3A Write two sentences about where you live using comparatives and superlatives.

Lesson 4B Name three pronouns and three possessive adjectives.

Lesson 3B Name five things you usually do on holiday.

Lesson 4C Name three things an employee usually does.

Lesson 3C Write what you were doing at this time yesterday.

Lesson 4C Think of three plans or arrangements you have for tomorrow.

Lesson 3C Write a sentence using the past simple and the past continuous.

Lesson 4D Give three expressions you can use if someone calls you on the telephone.

Lesson 3D Describe three things you did yesterday using adverbs of manner.

Lesson 4D Give three expressions you can use when you have problems understanding something.

UNIT 5

Mind and body

LANGUAGE *should/shouldn't* ■ health and medicine

5A Should I see a doctor?

1 Match the speech bubbles with the pictures.

a
b
c
d
e

1 I have a headache.

2 I cut my finger.

3 I'm feeling stressed.

4 I have the flu.

5 I have a cough.

Go to Vocabulary practice: health and medicine, page 144

2 Look at the title and the pictures in the text. In pairs, try to match the strange health tips with the problems in exercise 1. Read the text quickly and check.

Five strange health tips that you should know about

The internet is full of websites that offer health tips – some serious and some strange. Here are our top five tips from the web ... do they work? You can decide on that!

Do you have a temperature or the flu? Then you should put some onion in your socks and wear them at night. You'll feel much better the next morning. Remember though, you shouldn't eat the onion afterwards!

You're chopping vegetables in the kitchen and you cut your thumb. What should you do? Put a little black pepper on the cut, of course! It stops the bleeding and helps the cut get better. But you should only do this for small cuts. For anything serious, you should see a doctor.

Do you have regular headaches? Then you should always have an apple nearby. Some studies have found that the smell of green apples can help with headaches and can also make you feel less anxious.

Are you feeling stressed? You should call your mum. A study at the University of Wisconsin showed that people who had more contact with their mothers had lower levels of stress. So you shouldn't delay – call her today!

If you have a cough that won't go away, then you should eat some chocolate. Scientists say that chocolate contains a chemical that is better at stopping coughs than many cough medicines. So you shouldn't go to a chemist's – go to a sweet shop instead!

3 Discuss the questions in pairs.

1 Would you try any of the tips? Why/Why not?
2 Do you know any other strange health tips?
3 Do you ever use the internet to look for health advice?
4 What are the advantages and disadvantages of using the internet for this?

4 **A** Look at the question and sentence from the text. Tick (✓) the correct meaning.

Are you feeling stressed? You should call your mum.

1 It's necessary to call your mum if you feel stressed. ☐
2 It's a good idea to call your mum if you feel stressed. ☐
3 It's a bad idea to call your mum if you feel stressed. ☐

B Complete the sentences with the words in the box. Check your answers in the text. Then read the Grammar box.

do go put should (x2) shouldn't

1 What ________ you ________?
2 You ________ ________ some onion in your socks.
3 You ________ ________ to a chemist's.

Grammar ***should/shouldn't***

Ask for advice: *What **should** I do?*
Say something is a good idea: *You **should** see a doctor.* *I think you **should** get help.*
Say something is a bad idea: *You **shouldn't** trust tips on the internet.* *I don't think you **should** go to work.*

Personal Best

Go to Grammar practice: *should/shouldn't*, page 120

5 **A** 5.3 **Pronunciation:** *should/shouldn't* How do you say *should* and *shouldn't?* Listen to the sentences and check.

1 What should we do?
2 Why shouldn't I speak to him?
3 I think you should talk to an expert.
4 You shouldn't believe him.

B 5.3 Underline the stressed words in each sentence. Listen, check and repeat.

6 **A** Complete the conversation with *should* and *shouldn't* to give health advice.

Paul I'm feeling really stressed. I can't sleep. What [1]________ I do?
Doctor Well, I don't think you [2]________ work so many hours, and you [3]________ go to bed so late. You [4]________ try and do more exercise. That will help you to sleep better.
Paul [5]________ I drink less coffee?
Doctor Yes, you [6]________! And you [7]________ drink more water, too.
Paul OK, thank you.
Doctor If that doesn't help, you [8]________ come and see me again.

B 5.4 Listen and check. Repeat the conversation in pairs.

Go to Communication practice: Student A page 161, Student B page 169

11-21
WALL ST

7 **A** Discuss these situations in pairs. What advice would you give?

I forgot my friend's birthday and now she's really angry with me. What do you think I should do?
Sara

My flatmate is really messy. The kitchen is always dirty after he cooks and he takes my food from the fridge without asking. I don't know what to do!
Enrico

My boss wants me to go to a work conference in New York. The only problem is that it's the same date as my wedding anniversary. What should I tell my wife?
Julio

B Tell the rest of the class your advice. Who had the best ideas?

Personal Best Think of a common health problem and write down five pieces of advice.

5B Modern life is stressful

1 Look at the pictures. In pairs, order them from 1 (most stressful) to 5 (least stressful).

a interviews

b presentations

c exams

d traffic

e moving house

2 Read the text. Complete the tips with *do*, *make*, *have* or *take*.

The best ways to beat stress

Over 60% of adults say their lives are too stressful. So if you're feeling stressed right now, you should stop for a minute and read our tips – they might be very helpful!

1 First, ________ **a deep breath** and give yourself time to think.
2 Then, ________ **a list** of everything you have to do.
3 Next, ________ **a decision** about what you can realistically do today.
4 Remember to ________ **a break** every two or three hours.
5 When you finish your tasks for today, ________ **a rest**.
6 You should ________ **something** that makes you feel happy.
7 Try and ________ **a chat** with friends and family about the situation.
8 And finally, ________ **your best** to eat well and sleep for at least eight hours.

Personal Best

Go to Vocabulary practice: collocations with *do*, *make*, *have* and *take*, page 145

3 Ask and answer the questions in pairs.

1 Do you think your life is stressful? Why/Why not?
2 What things make you feel stressed?
3 Do you think the tips are useful? Why/Why not?
4 Can you think of any other ways to beat stress?

Skill listening in detail

It is often important to understand what someone says in detail.

- Read the questions carefully and think about the possible answers.
- Listen carefully to everything the speaker says before you answer the question.
- Pay attention to how the things the speaker says relate to each other.
- Be careful in case the speaker changes his/her mind or corrects himself/herself.

4 **A** 5.6 Read the Skill box. Watch or listen to the first part of *Learning Curve*. Choose the correct options to answer the questions.

1 How does Simon beat stress?
  a He makes a list of jobs. **b** He walks around. **c** He speaks to his brother.
2 How many people in the USA suffer from stress every day?
  a 77% of citizens **b** 400,000 people **c** only a small number of people
3 What do some scientists say about a small amount of stress?
  a It can make us ill. **b** It makes us bored. **c** It can help us to work better.

B 5.6 Compare your answers in pairs. Watch or listen again and check.

5 A 5.7 Watch or listen to the second part of the show. Match the names of the speakers with the tips for beating stress.

1 running ________ 2 speaking to family ________ 3 doing yoga ________

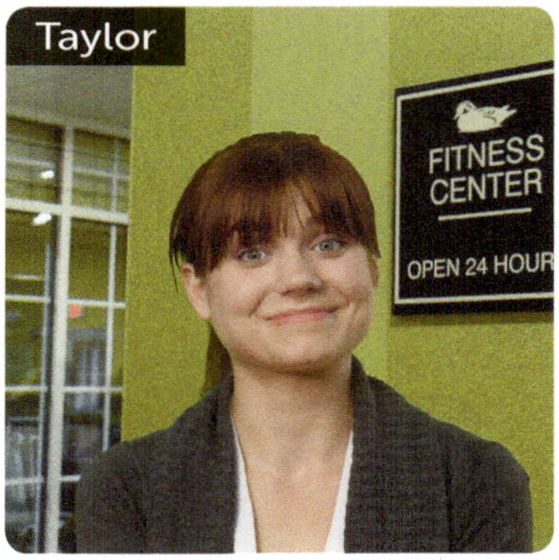
Taylor
FITNESS
CENTER

Edward

Maurice

B 5.7 Watch or listen again. Are the sentences true (T) or false (F)?

1 Taylor helps people who suffer from stress. ____
2 She thinks complaining about stress can help. ____
3 Edward's boss makes him feel stressed at work. ____
4 He listens to music while he's running. ____
5 Maurice had a stressful job. ____
6 He uses his phone to beat stress. ____

6 Discuss the questions in pairs.

1 Do you think life today is more stressful than 50 years ago? Why/Why not?
2 Do you think a little stress can be good for us? Why/Why not?

Listening builder **linking consonants and vowels**

When a word ends in a consonant sound and the next word begins with a vowel sound, we usually link the words together:
Kate likes to take‿a break once‿an‿hour‿and walk‿around.

7 5.8 Read the Listening builder. Look at the sentences from the programme and mark where you think the words link. Listen, check and repeat.

1 After a long day I take a hot shower.
2 Kate is on the street with an interview.
3 After work, I run about five miles a day.
4 And we have a chat on my phone every day.

8 5.9 Listen and complete the conversation.

Edward I don't think I can ____________ more.
Lara What's wrong, Edward? Tell ____________.
Edward I ____________ work to do ... and no time!
Lara I can help. Let's ____________ your jobs for today.

9 Discuss the questions in pairs.

1 What do you think the biggest cause of stress is for most people?
2 What do you think the most stressful stage of our lives is?
3 Think of three stressful jobs. Are there any advantages to these jobs?
4 Think of three low-stress jobs. What kind of job would you prefer? Why?

5C How to be happy

1 A How do you think the woman is feeling? Match the adjectives in the box with the pictures.

calm delighted upset cheerful nervous

a b c d e

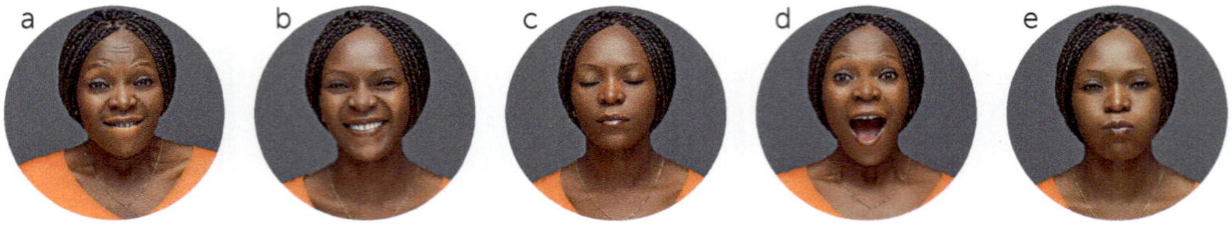

B In pairs, think of situations that make people feel these emotions.

An exam can make you feel nervous.

Personal Best

Go to Vocabulary practice: emotions and feelings, page 146

2 A Do you think money makes people happy? Why/Why not?

B Read the text. Tick (✓) the sentence that best summarizes the main idea.

1 People with lots of money often feel miserable. ☐
2 If people have less money, they often feel envious of others. ☐
3 Spending money on other people can make you feel good. ☐

CAN MONEY BUY YOU HAPPINESS?

The Beatles may have been right when they sang 'money can't buy me love', but according to a new study, it can buy you happiness – if you spend it in the right way. Many people think that they'll be happier if they earn more money. But Dr Michael Norton from Harvard Business School believes that it's not about how much money you make, but about how you spend it.

Dr Norton tried an experiment with people in different countries. At the start of the experiment, he asked people how happy they were. Then he gave them an envelope with some money and instructions on how to spend it. Some people had to spend the money on themselves and others were told to spend it on someone else. At the end of the experiment, they measured how happy the people felt again.

The results show that if you spend money on other people, you'll feel happier. And if you only spend money on yourself, you won't feel any different. So the next time you want to buy a new TV or some new clothes, ask yourself, 'If I buy this, will it make me happier?'. According to Dr Norton, we should think less about ourselves and more about others because if we do that, we'll feel much better!

3 A Complete the sentence. Check your answers in the text.

If you ________ money on other people, you ________ feel happier.
(A: If you ________ money on other people,) (B: you ________ feel happier.)

B Answer the questions about the two parts of the sentence: A and B. Then read the Grammar box.

1 Which part of the sentence is a possible future action? ____ What tense is the verb? ________
2 Which part of the sentence is the result of that action? ____ What tense is the verb? ________
3 Can we rewrite the sentence so that part B comes first and part A comes second? ________

Grammar first conditional

Possible future action:	Result of action:
*If it **rains** tomorrow,*	*Laura **won't go** to the beach.*
*If the train **doesn't arrive**,*	*I**'ll be** late for the meeting.*
*If she **fails** the exam,*	***will** she **have** to do it again?*

Look! We can swap the order of the clauses: *Laura won't go to the beach if it rains tomorrow.*

Personal Best

Go to Grammar practice: first conditional, page 121

4 A 5.12 Listen to the conversation. Why doesn't Sam accept the cinema ticket? Do you think this is a good reason?

B Complete Sam's reason. Listen again and check.

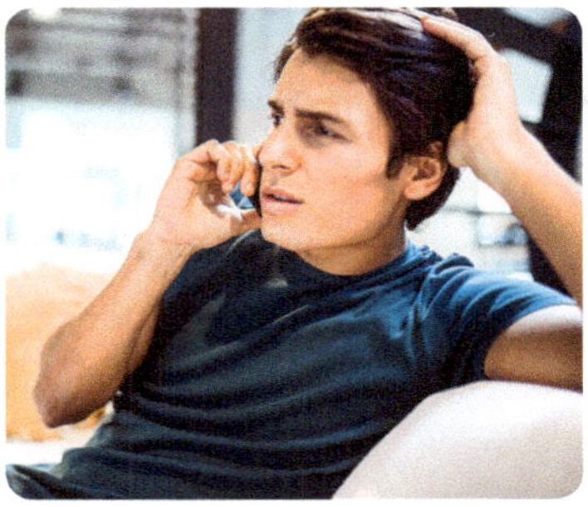

If I [1]________ to the cinema, we [2]________ a scary film. And if I [3]________ a scary film, I [4]________ nervous. And if I [5]________ nervous, I [6]________ well tonight. And if I [7]________ well, I [8]________ late for work. And if I [9]________ late for work, my boss [10]________ angry. And if my boss [11]________ angry, I [12]________ a pay rise. And if I [13]________ a pay rise, I [14]________ on holiday. And if I [15]________ on holiday, I [16]________ miserable. So, no thank you!

5 A 5.13 **Pronunciation:** *'ll* contraction How do you say *'ll*? Listen, check and repeat.

I'll you'll he'll she'll it'll we'll they'll

B 5.14 Match the halves to make sentences. In pairs, say the sentences. Pay attention to the *'ll* sound. Listen, check and repeat.

1 I'll be really envious
2 You'll miss your flight
3 If you give her your phone number,
4 If you can fix the computer now,
5 If she fails her exam,
6 They'll get a taxi

a she'll call you later.
b if you go to Jamaica for work.
c she'll be really upset.
d if you can't take them to the station.
e if you don't leave now.
f it'll be very helpful.

Go to Communication practice: Student A page 161, Student B page 169

6 A Do the quiz in pairs. Write down your partner's answers.

B Go to page 174 and look at the results. Do you agree with them? Why/Why not?

How happy are you?

1 If I wake up very early tomorrow morning, ...
a I'll feel miserable all day.
b I'll try to go back to sleep.
c I'll get up and make a big breakfast.
d I might go running or do some exercise.

2 If my best friend buys a new laptop, ...
a I might feel a bit envious.
b I'll buy an even better one.
c I might look for a new one, too.
d I'll be delighted for him/her.

3 If I find some money in the street next week, ...
a I'll put it in my bank account.
b I'll buy myself some new clothes.
c I'll give it to the police.
d I'll donate it to charity.

4 If my boss asks to speak to me, ...
a I'll think he/she wants to fire me.
b I'll probably feel quite nervous.
c I'll be calm and find out what he/she wants.
d I'll think I'm going to get a promotion.

5 If my parents give me a present that I don't really want, ...
a I'll ask for the receipt and change it for something I like.
b I'll thank them, but say I don't want the present.
c I'll say thanks, but use it as a present for someone else.
d I'll tell them I love it and try to use it in some way.

7 A In pairs, complete the sentences.

1 If I make a lot of money, ...
2 If I get a headache later, ...
3 I won't believe it if ...
4 I'll be delighted if ...
5 If I don't come to class next week, ...
6 I'll have a big party if ...

B Tell the class what your partner said.

Personal Best Write twelve first conditional sentences with all the emotions and feelings words from the Vocabulary practice on p. 146.

5D I need your advice

1 In pairs, order the work problems from 1 (most serious) to 6 (least serious).

lazy colleagues unkind boss
boring work too many working hours
low salary long journey to work

2 Look at the picture of Tom, who works at a busy health club. Guess the answers to the questions in pairs.

1 How is he feeling?
2 What problems does he have at work?

3 Read the email and check your answers to exercise 2.

1 ________ Catch up

2 ________ Hi Duncan,

3 ________ How's it going? Hope you're well. I'm still working at the health club, but I'm not very happy. That's why I'm writing. I wanted to ask you for some advice.

4 ________ One of my colleagues, Sebastian, is really lazy and he isn't very nice to me either. Whenever there's a problem, our manager always blames me! I also think his friends use the gym without paying. What do you think I should do? If I tell the manager, it might cause even more problems with Sebastian!

5 ________ Anyway, I saw an advert for a job at a new gym the other day. If I start work there, the salary will be lower, but it's a large chain, so there might be more opportunities in the future. Do you think I should apply? Do you fancy meeting up for a coffee some time this week so we can chat about it? Let me know when you're free.

6 ________ See you later,
Tom

4 Label the sections of the email with the words in the box.

details ending subject reason for writing greeting request for response

Skill writing an informal email

We write informal emails to people we know well, such as friends, family and colleagues.

- Structure the email with a subject, greeting, reason for writing, details, request for response and an ending.
- Use contractions like *I'm, he's* and *don't*.
- Use informal words and phrases like *Hi, How's it going?* and *anyway*.

5 Read the Skill box. Find the informal words and phrases in the email for phrases 1–6.

1 Hello ________
2 How are you? ________
3 On another subject ... ________
4 Would you like to ... ________
5 Please tell me ________
6 Goodbye ________

6 Discuss the questions in pairs.

1 Do you ever have problems similar to Tom's?
2 Who do you talk to about problems at work?
3 What should Tom do about Sebastian?
4 What should Tom do about the job advert?

7 Read Duncan's reply. Do you agree with him? Why/Why not?

RE: Catch up

Hi Tom,
Good to hear from you! I'm OK, thanks, but I was **very** sorry to hear your news about work. Everyone has colleagues who are **a bit** lazy like Sebastian, but the problem with his friends using the gym is serious. I think you should speak to him first. Explain that it's like stealing money from the company and if he doesn't stop, you'll have to tell the manager. I know she's **not very** nice, but it's **really** important she knows.
You also mentioned applying for another job. I think it's an **extremely** good idea. If you get the job, you can ask for the same money as you earn now, and you might get a promotion **quite** quickly in the future. I'd love to meet up. I'll be in town next Thursday evening. Let me know where and when you want to meet.

All the best,
Duncan

8 **A** Look at the modifiers in **bold** in Duncan's email and complete the rules.

1 Modifiers make adjectives and adverbs *stronger / weaker / both stronger and weaker.*
2 Modifiers come *before / after* adjectives and adverbs.

B Put the words in **bold** in the correct places in the diagram.

1 *extremely*   2 ________   rather   a little   6 ________
3 ________   4 ________   5 ________

Text builder **modifiers**

We use modifiers to make adjectives and adverbs stronger or weaker:
*Be careful, the soup is **extremely** hot.*
*She was driving **quite** fast when the accident happened.*
*I'm **a bit** nervous about the exam next week.*

Look! We usually use *a bit* and *a little* with negative adjectives:
*She's **a bit** upset today* NOT ~~*She's a bit cheerful today.*~~
Also remember that *a little* is formal, *a bit* is informal.

9 Read the Text builder. Complete the sentences with a modifier and an adjective. Compare your answers in pairs.

1 Most of my friends are ...
2 Learning English is ...
3 Today, I'm feeling ...
4 My job is ...
5 The weather is ...
6 Eating out is ...

10 **A** **PREPARE** Choose one of the problems.

- Your parents want you to study medicine, but you don't want to. You would prefer to study music.
- You want to get fit, but you only have a few hours a week free and you don't have very much money.
- Your boss gives you too much work. You are worried that if you refuse to do it, you might lose your job.

B **PRACTISE** Write an email to a friend asking for advice about the problem.

C **PERSONAL BEST** Swap emails with a partner. Underline five things that you think are very good.

Personal Best Write a reply to your partner's email. Try and use different modifiers.

UNIT 6

Risks and experiences

LANGUAGE present perfect with *ever* and *never* ■ phrasal verbs

6A Try something new

1 Look at the pictures. Ask and answer the questions in pairs.

1 Which activities are the most difficult, in your opinion?
2 Which activities would you like to try? Why/Why not?
3 What stopped you from doing these activities in the past?

learn an instrument

climb a mountain

cycle to work

VICTOR HUGO
Les Misérables
read a book in a foreign language

do an extreme sport

2 Read the text. Which activities from exercise 1 has Matt Cutts done?

June
SUN MON TUE WED THU FRI SAT

The 30-day Challenge

Have you ever wanted to try something new? Perhaps you've wanted to take up a new hobby or learn a new skill. What stopped you? Not enough time? The fear of failure? Was it difficult to change your routine?

Matt Cutts is an American software engineer. A few years ago, he felt bored with his life. That's when he decided to try the 30-day challenge. The idea is simple. You think of something you haven't done before, but you've always wanted to do, and you try it for 30 days. He started with small challenges, such as walking more, cycling to work, and giving up sugar for a month. Gradually, his challenges became bigger and more difficult. Now, Matt has written a novel, he's taught himself to play the ukulele, and he's even climbed Mount Kilimanjaro!

Trying something new can be a bit frightening, but doing it for just 30 days doesn't seem so hard. At the end of the month, you can stop … or who knows? You might decide to carry on with your new activity. For example, Matt gave up TV and did other things like reading books, instead. After 30 days, the first thing he did was turn on the TV. However, he found that he watched less TV than before because he enjoyed doing the other things, too.

Matt says that the challenges have made his life much more interesting. He's also become more confident. So, what about you? Is there something you've always wanted to do? What are you waiting for? **Try it for 30 days!**

3 Answer the questions in pairs.

1 Why did Matt start doing 30-day challenges?
2 Why is it easier trying something for 30 days?
3 How have the challenges helped Matt?
4 What challenge would you do for 30 days?

4 Choose the correct words to complete the sentences. Check your answers in the text.

1 Perhaps you've wanted to **take** *up* / *over* / *in* a new hobby or learn a new skill.
2 You might decide to **carry** *over* / *in* / *on* with your new activity.
3 Matt **gave** *under* / *up* / *above* TV and did other things like reading books, instead.
4 After 30 days, the first thing he did was **turn** *on* / *in* / *around* the TV.

Go to Vocabulary practice: phrasal verbs, page 145

Personal Best

5 **A** Complete the sentences about Matt from the text. Check your answers in the text.

1 A few years ago, he ________ bored with his life.
2 Matt has ________ a novel.

B Answer the questions about sentences 1 and 2 in exercise 5A.

1 Which sentence is about an event at a particular time in the past? ____
What is the tense? *past simple / present perfect*
2 Which sentence is about a general experience in Matt's life? ____
What is the tense? *past simple / present perfect*
3 How do we form the present perfect tense? the verb ________ + past participle

6 Underline a present perfect question and an example of the present perfect negative in the text. Then read the Grammar box.

Grammar **present perfect with *ever* and *never***

Experiences in your life:
__Have__ you __ever eaten__ Japanese food? *I__'ve been__ to Australia, but I__'ve never seen__ a kangaroo.*
She __hasn't seen__ the new Star Wars film.

Look! We use the past simple to talk about **when** an event happened and to give more details:
I've been to the USA. I __went__ to California in 2015. It __was__ great!

Personal Best

Go to Grammar practice: present perfect with *ever* and *never*, page 122

7 6.4 **Pronunciation:** irregular past participles Listen and repeat the words. Pay attention to the /ən/ sound in the *-en* endings.

brok**en** chos**en** driv**en** eat**en** fall**en** forgott**en** giv**en** spok**en** tak**en** writt**en**

8 **A** 6.5 Practise saying the questions. Listen, check and repeat.

1 Have you ever writt**en** a poem?
2 Have you ever eat**en** Indian food?
3 Have you ever driv**en** a fast car?
4 Have you ever brok**en** your arm or leg?
5 Have you ever forgott**en** an important birthday?
6 Have you ever fall**en** asleep in class or at work?

B Ask and answer the questions in pairs. If you answer *Yes, I have*, give more information in the past simple.

A *Have you ever written a poem?* B *Yes, I have. I had to write a poem when I was at school.*

Go to Communication practice: Student A page 161, Student B page 169

9 **A** 6.6 Complete the text with the present perfect form of the verbs in the box. Listen and check.

study give up write win work be

DID YOU KNOW ...?

Natalie Portman is a world-famous actress. You probably know that she [1] ________ an Oscar, but here are some facts you might not know.

- She [2] ________ with Britney Spears.
- She [3] ________ two scientific papers, which [4] ________ published.
- She [5] ________ Japanese, German and Arabic.
- She [6] ________ watching TV.

B 6.6 Listen again. Are the sentences true (T) or false (F)?

1 Natalie was the main character in a musical when she was 10 years old. ____
2 She studied Psychology at Harvard University. ____
3 She started learning languages when she was a child. ____
4 She never watches any TV programmes. ____

10 **A** Write down some of your experiences that not many people know about.

B In pairs, talk about your experiences and give more information.

Personal Best Write ten sentences about yourself using the phrasal verbs in the Vocabulary practice.

6B An amazing story

1 Look at the pictures on page 51. Discuss the questions in pairs.

1 Have you seen the film *127 Hours?*
2 If you have seen it, what is it about? If you haven't, can you guess what happens in it?
3 Have you ever tried rock climbing?
4 What problems could you have doing this activity?

2 Read the safety advice and guess which three mistakes Aron made. Read the text quickly and check your answers.

BLUE JOHN CANYON: SAFETY ADVICE

1 Always tell someone where you are going to climb.
2 Only climb here if you are an experienced climber.
3 Pack at least three litres of water and lots of food.
4 Take a knife and a first-aid kit for emergencies.
5 Always take a mobile phone to call for help.

3 Read the text again. Order the events from 1–8.

a ☐ He wrote a book.
b ☐ A helicopter rescued him.
c ☐ He cut off his hand.
d ☐ He ran out of food and water.
e ☐ A rock fell and trapped his hand.
f ☐ He started climbing in the canyon.
g ☐ In a dream, he saw a little boy.
h ☐ He had a son called Leo.

Skill guessing the meaning of words from context

You can sometimes guess the meaning of a word you don't know without using a dictionary.
- Look at the words before and after it to identify what type of word it is (noun, adjective, verb, adverb, etc.).
- Read the whole sentence carefully and guess what the word means.

4 **A** Read the Skill box. Look at words 1–8 in the text and identify what type of words they are: *noun*, *adjective*, *verb* or *adverb*. Can you guess what they mean?

1 remote ________
2 stuck ________
3 loudly ________
4 realized ________
5 dawn ________
6 wound ________
7 eventually ________
8 hurried ________

B Match definitions a–h with words 1–8 to check if you guessed correctly.

a a large cut or injury ☐
b far away ☐
c the first light of the day ☐
d moved quickly ☐
e with lots of sound ☐
f after some time ☐
g understood a fact ☐
h unable to move ☐

Text builder linkers to add extra information

We use the linkers ***and***, ***also***, ***as well*** and ***too*** to add extra information:
- *and* comes between two phrases: *It's a very beautiful place* ***and*** *it's very remote.*
- *also* comes before the main verb: *He* ***also*** *gives talks about his adventure.*
- *as well* and *too* come at the end of a phrase: *... he was alone* ***as well****. ... he pushed with his feet,* ***too****.*

5 Read the Text builder. Discuss the questions in pairs and add extra information with the linkers.

A *I think Aron was stupid because he didn't take a phone.*
B *Yes, but he was brave as well.*

1 How would you describe Aron?
2 What would you do in Aron's situation?
3 What advice do you think he gives in his talks?
4 What would you pack on a trip to the desert?

ARON RALSTON'S AMAZING STORY

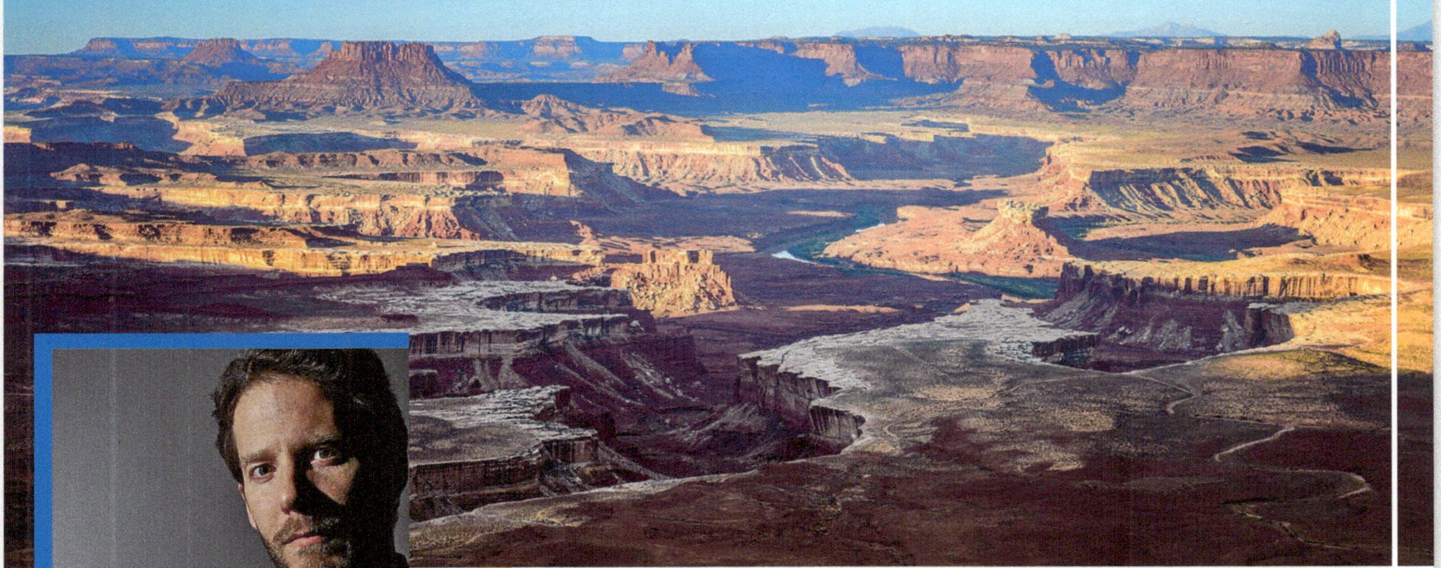

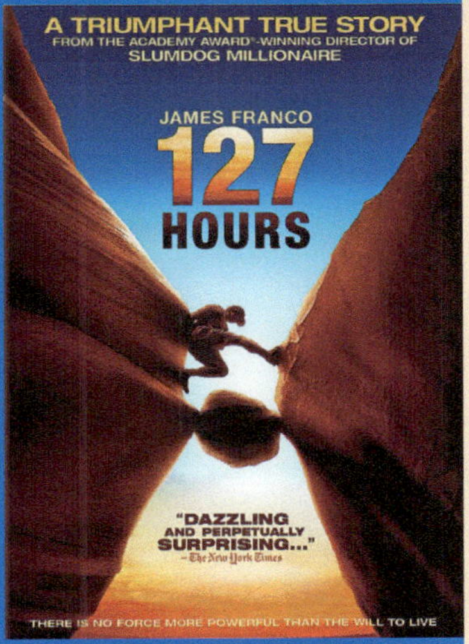
A TRIUMPHANT TRUE STORY
FROM THE ACADEMY AWARD®-WINNING DIRECTOR OF SLUMDOG MILLIONAIRE
JAMES FRANCO
127 HOURS
"DAZZLING AND PERPETUALLY SURPRISING..."
–The New York Times
THERE IS NO FORCE MORE POWERFUL THAN THE WILL TO LIVE

Aron Ralston is an experienced climber, but one day in 2003 he forgot a few basic rules and a day in the desert turned into a nightmare which lasted nearly a week. That particular day, he went rock climbing in Blue John Canyon in Utah, USA. It's a very beautiful place and it's very [1]**remote** – a long drive from the nearest town. The problems began when he didn't tell anyone where he was going, so nobody knew he was there.

A few hours later, he was climbing in the canyon when suddenly a big rock fell and trapped his right hand against the canyon wall. Trying not to panic, he pulled with his left arm and pushed with his feet, too, but he couldn't move the rock one centimetre – he was [2]**stuck** and alone as well.

He looked for his phone, but it was in his car, so he couldn't call for help. He tried shouting [3]**loudly**, but there was nobody to hear him. In his bag, there was a small bottle of water, two burritos and some chocolate – enough food for a short walk. Waiting for help day after day, he ate his food and drank the water slowly, but no help came. He [4]**realized** he was probably going to die and recorded video messages for his family on a camera.

After five days, all of his food and water was finished. That night, he had a strange dream and saw a small boy who was his future son. He woke up at [5]**dawn** the following morning and he knew what he had to do. The only way to escape was to cut off his hand!

First, he broke his arm and then he used a small knife to remove his hand. It took an hour and was extremely painful. He used a small first-aid kit on the [6]**wound**, but he was losing a lot of blood. He managed to climb down the canyon and walked slowly towards his car. [7]**Eventually**, he met a Dutch family who gave him food and [8]**hurried** to find help. Soon after, a helicopter arrived to rescue him.

Aron wrote a book about his experience and the director Danny Boyle made the story into a film. Seven years after the accident, Aron had a son called Leo, and today he still goes climbing. He also gives talks about his adventure to help other people. ■

Personal Best Find more words in the text that you don't know and guess their meaning. Check your answers in a dictionary.

6C Into the wild

1 Read the text and answer the questions in pairs.

1 Would you like to have Gemma's job?
2 What are the best and worst things about it?
3 Do you think you could survive in the wild?
4 Which photo do you prefer? Why?

Gemma Tang is a professional photographer and survival specialist. She grew up in Guangzhou, China, but has spent years travelling around the world, taking amazing photos of wildlife and spectacular landscapes. She is currently living in Cuzco, Peru, where she runs survival courses in the Amazon Rainforest. A new exhibition of her photos has just opened in London. Here are two of the best.

1
2
3

4
5
6

2 Match the words in the box with parts of the landscapes.

cliff waves peak sunset waterfall rocks

1 ________ 2 ________ 3 ________ 4 ________ 5 ________ 6 ________

Personal Best

Go to Vocabulary practice: the natural world, page 147

3 **A** 6.8 In pairs, do the survival quiz. Listen to Gemma and check your answers.

B Look at page 174 and read the results. Do you agree? Why/Why not?

SURVIVAL QUIZ

1 If I were in the mountains and I saw a bear outside its cave, …
a I'd run away as fast as possible.
b I'd climb the nearest tree.
c I'd take a photo. What an opportunity!

2 If I were on a trek in the rainforest and I ran out of food, …
a I'd eat a small animal, like a tarantula.
b I'd find some plants and eat them.
c I wouldn't eat anything.

3 If I were swimming in the ocean and I saw a shark in the water, …
a I'd scream and swim in the opposite direction.
b I'd move towards the shark and kick it on the nose.
c I'd try to swim quickly and quietly away.

4 If I were hiking and I needed to drink some water, …
a I'd drink the water from a river or lake.
b I'd find a stream to get water.
c I wouldn't drink any water.

4 6.8 Listen again and answer the questions.

1 Why should you climb up high in a tree? ________
2 What do tarantulas taste like? ________
3 What percentage of sharks don't attack humans? ________
4 What can river water contain? ________

5 A 6.9 Match the halves to make sentences from the audio. Listen and check.

1 If you ran,
2 If I were in this situation,
3 If you needed water,

a I wouldn't take a photo.
b would you look for a stream?
c the bear would follow you.

B Answer the questions. Then read the Grammar box.

1 Which tense do we use after *if*? ________
2 Which auxiliary verb do we use with the infinitive in the second part of the sentence? ________
3 Are these situations impossible or unlikely? ________
4 What do you notice about the past tense of *be* in sentence 2? ________

Grammar second conditional

Impossible or very unlikely situations:
***If** I **saw** a bear in the mountains, I'**d run**.*
***If** he **ran out** of food in the rainforest, he **wouldn't eat** anything.*
*What **would** you **do if** you **saw** a shark in the ocean?*

Look! We can use ***were*** instead of ***was*** in the second conditional:
*I wouldn't drink the river water if I **were** you.*

Personal Best

Go to Grammar practice: second conditional, page 123

6 A 6.11 **Pronunciation:** sentence stress Listen to the sentences from the conversation in exercise 3. Underline the stressed words.

1 If I saw a bear, I'd run.
2 If you ate a poisonous one, it would make you sick.
3 I wouldn't eat a spider if it were the last food on earth.
4 I wouldn't survive five minutes in the wild!

B Practise saying the sentences in pairs.

7 In pairs, look at the situations and make sentences about what you would and wouldn't do. Pay attention to the sentence stress.

If I found a wallet in the street, I wouldn't spend the money. I'd try and find the owner.

1 If I found a wallet in the street, ...

a give it to the police
b spend the money
c try and find the owner

2 If I accidentally hit a parked car with my car, ...

Mégane

a leave my phone number
b drive away
c wait for the owner to return

3 If I was invited to a fancy-dress party, ...

a make an excuse and not go
b make an amazing costume
c wear a silly hat

Go to Communication practice: Student A page 161, Student B page 169

8 Discuss the questions in pairs.

What would you do if ...
1 you didn't have to work?
2 a shop assistant gave you too much change?
3 you saw a colleague stealing from work?
4 you found a spider in the bath?
5 your boss offered you a job in New York?
6 your parents forgot your birthday?
7 you couldn't use the internet for a week?
8 you met a famous person in the supermarket?

Personal Best Write a paragraph about what you would do if you won a competition to go anywhere in the world.

Learning Curve

6D Would you take the risk?

1 A Are you a risk-taker? In pairs, ask and answer the questions to find out.

B Look at the results on page 174. Do you agree? Why/Why not?

Would you ...

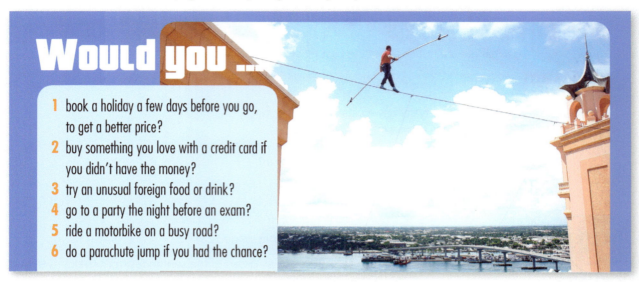

1 book a holiday a few days before you go, to get a better price?
2 buy something you love with a credit card if you didn't have the money?
3 try an unusual foreign food or drink?
4 go to a party the night before an exam?
5 ride a motorbike on a busy road?
6 do a parachute jump if you had the chance?

2 6.12 Watch or listen to the first part of *Learning Curve*. Match the phrases in the box with the people.

has tried parachuting   works as a chef   went to university with Jack   left a job to travel and work

Simon

Jack

Alyssa

Kate

3 6.12 Read the statements below. Who says each one: Simon or Kate? Watch or listen again and check.

1 We should see the world when we're young. ____
2 You should never leave a job without having another one. ____
3 There aren't that many jobs for vets at the zoo. ____
4 I can go for days without my cell phone. ____

Conversation builder agreeing and disagreeing

Agreeing:
Exactly! *You're right.*
I suppose so. *True*
Absolutely!

Disagreeing:
I don't think so. *Oh, come on!*
I don't know. *I'm not sure about that.*

4 A Read the Conversation builder. Which expressions did Simon and Kate use to agree/disagree?

B 6.13 Put the phrases in the correct columns from the Conversation builder. Listen, check and repeat.

agree/disagree strongly	agree/disagree	agree/disagree with doubts

5 A Look at sentences 1–6. Tick (✓) the box to show how much you agree or disagree.

	agree strongly	agree	not sure	disagree	disagree strongly
1 English is a difficult language to learn.	☐	☐	☐	☐	☐
2 We should all give up watching TV.	☐	☐	☐	☐	☐
3 People use mobile phones too much.	☐	☐	☐	☐	☐
4 True love only exists in fairy tales.	☐	☐	☐	☐	☐
5 Music was better 20 years ago.	☐	☐	☐	☐	☐
6 Money doesn't make you happy.	☐	☐	☐	☐	☐

B In pairs, read the sentences to each other and agree or disagree using the phrases from the Conversation builder. Explain your reasons.

6 6.14 Watch or listen to the second part of the show. What is Jack's news?

7 6.14 Choose the correct options to answer the questions. Watch or listen again to check.

1 What does Jack think about Alyssa's plan to travel to Africa?
a It's a good idea. **b** It could be dangerous. **c** It will be difficult without Wi-Fi.

2 What does Jack say about being on social media?
a It's not expensive. **b** It's risky. **c** It will be good for his business.

3 What does Simon say about cooking?
a He's bad at it. **b** He's good at it. **c** He can only cook eggs.

4 What do Kate and Simon offer to do?
a help Jack to cook **b** pay for the dessert **c** help Jack to make a video

Skill taking turns

When people talk in groups, they take turns.
- Wait until someone has finished their point before you start speaking.
- If you start speaking at the same time, stop and apologize.
- If someone isn't speaking much, encourage them to join in.

8 A 6.15 Read the Skill box. Listen and repeat the phrases when you hear the beep.

1 Sorry, go on.
2 Don't you think, Jack?
3 Sorry, you were saying?
4 What about you Simon?

B Why do the speakers use phrases 1–4?

9 6.16 Listen and tick (✓) the conversation in which the speaker waits the right amount of time before speaking.

Conversation 1 ☐ Conversation 2 ☐ Conversation 3 ☐

Go to Communication practice: All students page 174

10 A PREPARE Choose one of the statements and decide if you agree or disagree. Think of arguments and examples to support your opinion.

1 If you want a good job, you need to speak English.
2 Friends are more important than families.
3 There is a perfect partner for everyone.
4 Sugar is dangerous for our health.

B PRACTISE In groups of three, take it in turns to talk about the statements you chose. Encourage other students to give their opinions. Take turns politely.

C PERSONAL BEST Whose arguments did you agree with the most? Why?

Personal Best Write a conversation where two people disagree about something strongly.

Grammar

1 Choose the correct options to complete the sentences.

1 I'd meet up with her if I ________ more time.
- **a** had
- **b** 'll have
- **c** have

2 Be careful! You ________ risks.
- **a** won't take
- **b** shouldn't take
- **c** wouldn't take

3 If it's cold tomorrow, I ________ a jacket.
- **a** 'd take
- **b** 'll take
- **c** take

4 If the bus ________ , I'll walk to work.
- **a** doesn't arrive
- **b** didn't arrive
- **c** won't arrive

5 **A:** I have the interview today. Do I look OK?
B: I ________ wear those shoes.
- **a** don't think you should
- **b** think you should to
- **c** shouldn't think you

6 Have you ________ to Mexico?
- **a** ever been
- **b** ever go
- **c** went ever

7 What ________ if you saw an accident?
- **a** did you do
- **b** will you do
- **c** would you do

8 I ________ Turkish food.
- **a** never have eaten
- **b** have never eaten
- **c** have eaten never

2 Use the words in brackets to write sentences that mean the same as the first sentence.

1 I haven't eaten sushi in my life.
I ________ sushi. (never)

2 I haven't got my phone, so I can't call him.
If ________ my phone, I ________ him. (had / call)

3 It's a bad idea to go to the party.
I ________ you ________ to the party. (think / should)

4 I think you should look for a new job.
If ________ you, I ________ for a new job. (were / look)

5 They might lose the game. Mo will be upset if that happens.
If ________ the game, Mo ________ happy. (lose / be)

6 Where's Julio? Is he in Paris for the meeting?
Where's Julio? ________ to Paris for the meeting? (has / go)

3 Complete the text with the correct forms of the verbs in brackets.

The truth about Murphy's Law

Have you ever [1] ________ (drop) a piece of toast and wondered why it always seems to land with the buttered side on the floor? Or, when you leave the house in the morning, have you ever [2] ________ (think), 'If I [3] ________ (take) an umbrella, it [4] ________ (not rain), but if I [5] ________ (not take) one, it [6] ________ (rain)?' These are examples of Murphy's Law – the law that says if something can go wrong, it will go wrong. We've all [7] ________ (have) experiences like this, but what [8] ________ we ________ (should / do) about it?

Well, maybe we [9] ________ (not should / worry) too much. Professor Richard Dawkins, at the University of Oxford, doesn't think Murphy's Law is really true. He says that certain things happen all the time, but we only notice them when they cause us problems. Imagine if you [10] ________ (be) outside making a film and a noisy plane [11] ________ (fly) by, you [12] ________ (think) it was Murphy's Law. However, planes fly by all the time. It's only when they cause us a problem that we notice them!

So next time something goes wrong, don't blame Murphy, think positively and try to remember the other times that things went well.

Vocabulary

1 Match the words in the box with the definitions.

ache give up take a break make an excuse lonely miserable run out of roots valley have a chat

1 low land between mountains ________
2 to finish, use or sell all of something ________
3 to talk in a friendly way ________
4 to rest for a moment before starting again ________
5 very unhappy ________
6 to stop ________
7 a pain somewhere in your body ________
8 sad because you are alone ________
9 the parts of a tree that are underground ________
10 to explain why something bad happened ________

2 Choose the correct words to complete the sentences.

1 When will you find ________ your results?
 a out b about c of
2 I ________ my best, and that's all I can do.
 a did b made c was
3 He's very ________ today. He isn't worried at all.
 a calm b guilty c upset
4 I'll ________ the train times on the internet.
 a fill in b look after c look up
5 She broke my laptop. She feels really ________ .
 a guilty b envious c jealous
6 I ________ a big argument with my parents.
 a had b did c made

3 Circle the word which is different. Explain your answer.

1	backache	earache	sore throat	nosebleed
2	cliff	sunset	lightning	thunderstorm
3	flu	cold	cough	stressed
4	calm	upset	confident	cheerful
5	a rest	a chat	a coffee	a mistake
6	lake	cave	river	stream
7	lonely	guilty	miserable	delighted
8	a break	an effort	a chance	your time

4 Complete the conversation with the words in the box.

waves wildlife hurt made cut take down have rainforest rocks

Matt Hi, Kerry. Did you [1]________ a good time on holiday?
Kerry Not really. In fact, it was a disaster.
Matt Oh no! What happened?
Kerry Well, I tried surfing for the first time, but the [2]________ were so big!
Matt Did you have an accident?
Kerry Yes, I hit some [3]________ that were under the water and I [4]________ my leg.
Matt Oh dear! Does it still [5]________ now?
Kerry Yes, it does. And another day, I went on a boat trip through the [6]________ to see the animals that live there, but the boat broke [7]________ and we had to wait for hours for another one to rescue us.
Matt Did you see any [8]________ ?
Kerry Just mosquitoes!
Matt Oh no. What a pity.
Kerry I think I [9]________ a mistake. Next year, I'm going to stay at home and [10]________ no chances.

Personal Best

Lesson 5A
Write three pieces of advice to stay healthy.

Lesson 6A
Write a question with *ever*, and a sentence with *never*.

Lesson 5A
Name five reasons to see a doctor.

Lesson 6A
Name five phrasal verbs.

Lesson 5B
Name four verb collocations with *make*.

Lesson 6B
Write a sentence using *also*, and another using *as well*.

Lesson 5C
Name five feelings or emotions.

Lesson 6C
Name five natural features you could see in a rainforest.

Lesson 5C
Write a sentence using the first conditional.

Lesson 6C
Write a sentence beginning *If I were …*

Lesson 5D
Describe three things using adjectives and modifiers.

Lesson 6D
Give two expressions to agree with someone, and two to disagree.

UNIT 7

City living

LANGUAGE present perfect with *just, yet* and *already* ■ city features

7A Life in the city

1 Discuss the questions in pairs.

1 Do you live in a city, a town or a village?
2 Do you like where you live?
3 What are the good and bad things about it?

1
2
3
4
5
6

2 A Look at the picture. Which city is it?

B Match the words in the box with the parts of the city.

pavement	traffic lights	bridge
bike lane	pedestrian crossing	bench

1 ________ 2 ________ 3 ________ 4 ________ 5 ________ 6 ________

Personal Best

Go to Vocabulary practice: city features, page 148

3 A Read the text. Who is more positive about the city: Alex or Megan? ________

B Read the text again and match the headings in the box with the paragraphs.

Cost of living	Job opportunities	The weather	The people	Transport	Entertainment

Big City

San Francisco is one of the fastest growing cities in the USA. Today, we speak to two people who recently moved here and find out their first impressions of living in the city.

Alex, 25, is an IT professional and has just moved to San Francisco from London.

1 ________
There are so many tech companies here; it's really exciting. I've joined a networking group to meet people from the industry and I've already been to a couple of events. Have I found a job yet? No … but I'm sure I will soon! At least I have my visa!

2 ________
In my apartment block, there are people of all nationalities, as well as from other places in the USA. I haven't met all my neighbours yet, but I love living in a city where everyone is different.

3 ________
Whatever you're interested in, there's always something going on. I've already been to the theatre twice and seen a baseball game, and I only arrived two weeks ago!

Megan, 27, has moved to San Francisco from her hometown in Idaho to study Engineering.

4 ________
San Francisco is expensive and you need a good salary to live here. I've rented a room in a shared house, but after I've paid the rent, it doesn't leave me with much money for other things.

5 ________
All my friends told me that the summers wouldn't be as good as back home. It hasn't been too cold yet, but it can get really foggy, especially when you're near the ocean.

6 ________
The traffic here is terrible, so forget driving! Public transport can get really crowded, too, so I've just bought myself a bike. It's one of the best ways to get around the city, and the bike lanes are great.

4 **A** Who said sentences 1–4: Alex or Megan?

1 I've ________ bought myself a bike.
2 Have I found a job ________?
3 It hasn't been too cold ________.
4 I've ________ been to the theatre twice.

B Complete the sentences with the words in the box. Check your answers in the text.

already just yet (x2)

5 Answer the questions about the sentences in exercise 4. Then read the Grammar box.

1 Which tense is used in the sentences? ________
2 Which word do we add in questions and negative sentences to talk about something we expected to happen before now? ________
3 Which word do we add to sentences to talk about something that happened earlier than we expected? ________
4 Which word do we add to sentences to talk about something that happened very recently? ________

Grammar **present perfect with *just*, *yet* and *already***

Something that happened very recently: *I've **just seen** Peter in the street.*
Something that happened earlier than we expected: *He's **already** finished his homework.*
Something we expected to happen before now: ***Have** you **had** lunch **yet**? I **haven't seen** the film **yet**.*

Personal Best

Go to Grammar practice: present perfect with *just*, *yet* and *already*, page 124

6 **A** 7.3 **Pronunciation:** *just* and *yet* Listen and repeat the words. Pay attention to the /j/ sound *(yet)* and the /dʒ/ sound *(just)*.

1 /j/ **y**et **y**oung **y**ou **u**sually
2 /dʒ/ **j**ust **j**ob **g**ym bri**dge**

B 7.4 How do you say the sentences? Listen, check and repeat.

1 Have **y**ou **j**oined a club **y**et?
2 She's **j**ust **u**sed the machine.
3 I already have a **j**ob.
4 An**g**ela hasn't arrived **y**et.

Go to Communication practice: Student A page 162, Student B page 170

7 7.5 Complete the phone conversation between Alex and his friend Josh. Use the present perfect form of the verbs in the box and *just*, *yet* and *already*. Listen and check.

find have (x2) make meet not see

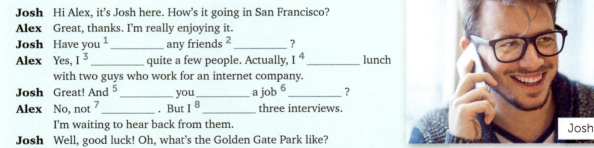

Josh Hi Alex, it's Josh here. How's it going in San Francisco?
Alex Great, thanks. I'm really enjoying it.
Josh Have you [1] ________ any friends [2] ________ ?
Alex Yes, I [3] ________ quite a few people. Actually, I [4] ________ lunch with two guys who work for an internet company.
Josh Great! And [5] ________ you ________ a job [6] ________ ?
Alex No, not [7] ________ . But I [8] ________ three interviews. I'm waiting to hear back from them.
Josh Well, good luck! Oh, what's the Golden Gate Park like?
Alex I [9] ________ it [10] ________ ! I'm too busy ... but I might go this weekend.

Josh

8 **A** Make a list of things you have already done and things you still have to do this week.

B In pairs, ask and answer the question *Have you ... yet?* about your partner's list. Give more information in your answers.

A *Have you been to the supermarket yet?*
B *Not yet. I'm going shopping tonight, though.*
A *Have you called your parents yet?*
B *Yes, I've already called them twice this week.*

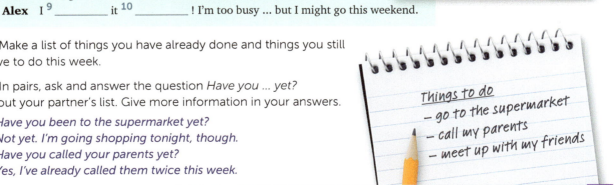

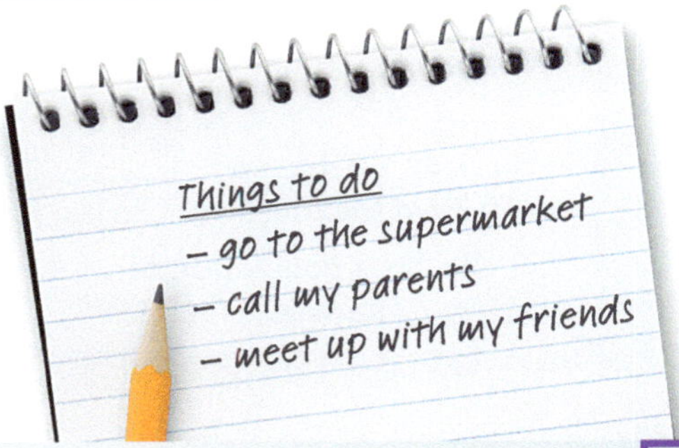
Things to do
– go to the supermarket
– call my parents
– meet up with my friends

Personal Best Write about the town or city you live in.

7B The daily commute

Learning Curve

1 Is traffic a problem in your town/city? How do most people travel to work?

2 Look at the pictures in exercise 4. In pairs, use the words in the box to describe them.

> traffic jam   drive   rush hour   commuter   passenger   car park
> platform   take the train   parking space   public transport

In picture a, people are driving to work, but there's a really bad traffic jam.

Personal Best

Go to Vocabulary practice: transport, page 148

3 7.8 Look at exercise 4. Which cities do pictures a–c show? Watch or listen to the first part of *Learning Curve* and check.

a ________   b ________   c ________

Skill listening for facts and figures

We often have to listen for specific information.

- Before you listen, focus what type of information you need to listen for. For example, is it a number, a person, a time, a place, etc?
- Listen for 'clues'. For example, if the information is an age, you might hear 'old' or 'years'.
- Write the exact word(s) you hear. Then read the sentences to make sure they make sense.

4 **A** Read the Skill box. Match the types of information in the box with the gaps in the text.

> a specific time   a verb (x2)   a noun   an adjective (x2)   a period of time (x2)   a number (x2)

B 7.8 Watch or listen again and complete the text with the correct words.

Commuting around the world

The global average commuting time is [1] ________, but it is much worse in some cities.

1-50012

a

The average journey time is [2] ________.

Rush hour is between [3] ________ and 9.30 in the morning.

This city has a population of [4] ________ people.

b

Companies employ 'pushers' to [5] ________ passengers onto trains.

They wear [6] ________ gloves as a sign of respect to passengers.

[7] ________ passengers use the train system every day.

c

Seven million [8] ________ come into this city every day.

24% of people have [9] ________ about a parking space in the last year.

Car parks are so [10] ________ that people can lose their cars.

5 7.9 Watch or listen to the second part of the show. How do Mike, Sandra and Lorena get to work/university?

Mike

Sandra

Lorena

6 **A** Read questions 1–8. What kind of information do you need to answer them?

1 How long does Mike's journey take in total? *a period of time*
2 What time does he usually leave his house? __________
3 What causes him problems on his commute? __________
4 Which city is Sandra in? __________
5 How often does she usually travel with Bonnie? __________
6 How far is it to Sandra's work? __________
7 How long does it take Lorena to walk to university? __________
8 How much does she spend on public transport? __________

B 7.9 Watch or listen again. Answer the questions.

7 Discuss the questions in pairs.

1 How do you get to work/university/class?
2 How long does it take you?
3 What time do you set off?
4 Do you ever have any problems?
5 Who do you travel with?
6 How does the journey make you feel?

8 7.10 Listen to the sentences from the show. When are the /t/ sounds in **bold** pronounced?

1 What time do you se**t** off?
2 My bigges**t** problem is pedestrians.
3 I'm here in fron**t** of our building in New York.
4 Today, I'm jus**t** listening to my car radio.

Listening builder final /t/ sound

English speakers don't often pronounce the /t/ sound at the end of a word when the next word begins with a consonant. If the next word begins with a vowel sound, they link the sounds together.

I get‿off the train. *I ge(t) to chat with my good friend.*
There's still a lot‿of traffic. *She doesn'(t) drive.*

9 7.11 Read the Listening builder. Listen and complete the sentences.

1 The __________ __________ to get to work is to drive, __________ __________ is impossible.
2 I __________ __________ at 8.00 and __________ __________ me over an hour.
3 The traffic __________ __________ completely, so we __________ __________ and walked.
4 It's the __________ __________ in the world for commuting, but they __________ __________ buy a car.
5 I __________ __________ taking the metro. I feel __________ __________ __________ people come out of the station.

10 **A** In pairs, prepare a talk of 1–2 minutes about the transport system in your city or country. Use the ideas in the boxes.

the type of transport people use	the cost and frequency of public transport	the problems commuters have	suggestions for people visiting your city or country

B Work with another pair. Take it in turns to listen, then ask at least one question.

Personal Best Write a paragraph about the advantages and disadvantages of one type of transport.

7C A life in three cities

1 A Look at the pictures. Try and answer the questions in pairs.

1 Who is the person?
2 What is her job?
3 Which film has she been in?
4 What nationality is she?

B Read the introduction in the text and check your answers.

A TALE OF THREE CITIES

She won an Oscar for her first film, *12 Years a Slave*, in 2013. Since then, the Kenyan actress Lupita Nyong'o has become a Hollywood superstar and appeared on red carpets and magazine covers all over the world. We look at the three cities which have shaped this talented actress.

MEXICO CITY

Lupita was born in 1983 in Mexico City, where her father was working at a university. The family returned to Kenya when she was just a few months old, but at the age of 16, Lupita went back to Mexico for a year to learn Spanish. She's spoken Spanish since 1999, and has even given TV interviews in Spanish.

NAIROBI

Lupita went to school in Nairobi, and this is where she first started acting. Her first big performance was at the age of 14 when she played Juliet in *Romeo and Juliet*. One of her happiest memories is of climbing the mango trees in her grandmother's village and eating the fruit straight from the branches!

NEW YORK

Lupita has lived in Brooklyn, New York, since 2013, and this is now her home. When she isn't working, she spends her time doing yoga and cooking her favourite dishes like *enchiladas verdes*. She also loves travelling into Manhattan on the subway to go shopping, just like anyone else in New York! The big question is: Where next for Lupita?

2 Read the rest of the text. Are the sentences true (T) or false (F)?

1 Lupita has been very famous since 2013. ____
2 She has had an interest in acting for over ten years. ____
3 She has spoken Spanish since she was a small child in Mexico. ____
4 She has lived in New York for most of her life. ____

3 Look at sentences 1–4 in exercise 2. Choose the correct options to answer the questions. Then read the Grammar box.

1 Are the situations in the sentences finished? *yes / no*
2 Which tense are the verbs in? *present continuous / present perfect*
3 When do we use the word *since*? *for a point in time / for a period of time*
4 When do we use the word *for*? *for a point in time / for a period of time*

Grammar present perfect with *for* and *since*

For situations that started in the past and continue in the present:

*I**'ve worked** as an actress **for** twenty years.* *She **hasn't seen** me **since** 2010.*

Look! We use ***for*** for a period of time and ***since*** for a point in time:

*I've had this car **for six months**.* *I've had this car **since February**.*

Personal Best

Go to Grammar practice: present perfect with *for* and *since*, page 125

4 A 7.13 **Pronunciation:** *for and since* Listen and repeat the sentences. Pay attention to the rhythm. Are *for* and *since* stressed or unstressed words?

1 She's lived in New York since 2013.
2 She hasn't been to Mexico for a few years.

B 7.14 Underline the stressed words in the sentences. In pairs, practise saying them. Listen, check and repeat.

1 I've lived in this house for six years.
2 She's known him since 1995.
3 I haven't seen him for months.
4 They've had the car since March.

Go to Communication practice: Student A page 162, Student B page 170

5 7.15 Listen to the conversation and answer the questions.

1 Where do you think the people are?
2 How do Laura and Pete know each other?
3 What is Jess's job?
4 What do Laura and Jess discuss at the end?
5 Do you think connections are important to find a good job?

6 A Complete the questions with the past simple or present perfect form of the verbs in brackets.

1 Where ________ Laura and Pete ________? (meet)
2 How long ________ Jess ________ in LA? (be)
3 How long ________ Jess ________ in Toronto? (live)
4 How long ________ Jess ________ scripts for TV and films? (write)
5 What ________ she ________ before she was a writer? (do)
6 How long ________ Laura and Pete ________ the idea for the TV comedy series? (have)

B 7.15 Listen to the conversation again. Ask and answer questions 1–6 in pairs.

7 A Complete the circles with information about you.

- the name of an important friend
- the name of your street
- your occupation (job/student, etc.)
- a hobby you enjoy
- an important possession
- a place you want to visit
- something you use every day
- something you are frightened of

B In pairs, ask and answer the question *How long have you ...?* with a suitable verb and the information in the circles. Try to give more information.

A *How long have you known Martin?*
B *I've known him since we were at secondary school together. We were in the same class.*
A *How long have you had your phone?*
B *I've had it for six months. It was a birthday present from my brother.*

Personal Best Think of someone you know well and write a paragraph about his/her life. Try and use the present perfect with *for* and *since*.

7D I think it's a great idea

1 Look at the pictures in exercise 2. Discuss the questions in pairs.

1 How often do you use your mobile phone each day?
2 Do you call people when you are in the street? If so, who?
3 Do you use your phone on public transport? If so, what for?
4 Do you send messages when you go out with friends? If so, how often?
5 Do you think we use our phones too much? Why/Why not?

2 **A** Read the title of the essay. What does the verb *ban* mean?

a make something illegal ☐ b make something easier ☐

B Read the essay. Does Kai agree or disagree with the question?

Is it time to ban smartphones in public?

Kai Meng

Smartphones are amazing inventions and help us in lots of different ways, but I'm worried that we use them too much. Every day, I see hundreds of people using their phones in the city and it's causing some serious problems.

Firstly, I believe smartphones can be dangerous. When people are walking in the street and sending messages at the same time, or if they're listening to music with headphones, they don't concentrate on the traffic and it's much easier for them to have an accident.

The second reason is that I think speaking on phones in public is annoying. If you're on a train or in a restaurant, you don't want to hear someone else's conversation. In my opinion, people should wait to call their friends and colleagues in private unless it's a real emergency.

Finally, banning smartphones in public is a good idea because it would make people more sociable and talk more. Even when some people meet up with their friends, they spend half the time checking their phones and going on social media. If they didn't have their phones, they'd talk to each other more and they'd have a much better time.

In conclusion, although there are lots of advantages of smartphones, I think we should ban them in public. Personally, I think this would be safer for pedestrians, nicer for passengers on public transport and would help us to communicate with each other more.

3 Answer the questions about the essay. Then read the Skill box.

1 How many reasons for banning smartphones does Kai give? What are they? Which paragraphs are they in?
2 What is the purpose of paragraph 1? *to introduce the topic / to summarize all his reasons*
3 What is the purpose of the final paragraph? *to introduce the topic / to summarize all his reasons*

Skill **writing an essay**

In essays, we discuss a topic and give our point of view.

- Organize your ideas into paragraphs (introduction, reasons and conclusion).
- Explain the reasons for your opinions in separate paragraphs. Give examples or evidence to support them.
- Use sequencers, like *firstly*, *the second reason*, *finally* and *in conclusion* to help readers.

4 Look at the pictures. In pairs, think of some reasons why we *shouldn't* ban smartphones in public.

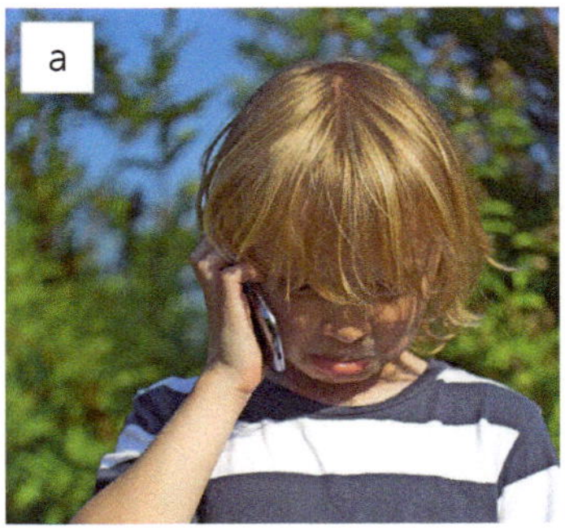
a

b

c

5 A Match the halves to make sentences. Did you have similar ideas?

1 We can check emails, read documents
2 I believe this is very important
3 Personally, I love being able to watch
4 In my opinion, smartphones
5 They make our lives safer, more
6 Secondly, smartphones make
7 In conclusion, I don't think we should
8 The first reason is that phones help us
9 The last reason is that they are
10 Modern technology has changed

a the way we communicate.
b have made our lives better in three different ways.
c stay in touch with each other.
d for our safety.
e us work more efficiently.
f and organize meetings outside the office.
g lots of fun and keep us entertained.
h films or play games when I'm on the train.
i ban smartphones in public.
j efficient and even more fun.

B Which sentences come from:
the introduction? ________ paragraph 3? ________ the conclusion? ________
paragraph 2? ________ paragraph 4? ________

6 A In pairs, use the sentences in 5A to help you write an essay against banning smartphones in public.

B Which essay is more convincing: Kai's or the one you wrote in exercise 6A? Do you think we should or shouldn't ban smartphones in public?

7 Read the essay in exercise 2 again. Underline any phrases Kai uses to give his opinion.

Text builder giving opinions

We use a variety of phrases to give our opinions:
I (don't) think/believe (that) ... *I'm worried/delighted (that) ...* *... is a good/bad idea.*
In my opinion/view, ... *Personally, ...* *I would(n't) say (that) ...*

8 Read the Text builder. In pairs, give your opinions about ideas 1–5. Explain your ideas.

1 I *think* / *don't think* public transport should be free for everyone because ...
2 Children playing computer games is a *good* / *bad* idea because ...
3 In my opinion, learning English *is* / *isn't* very difficult because ...
4 Personally, I *watch* / *don't watch* too much TV because ...
5 I *would* / *wouldn't* say that we eat less healthily than our parents because ...

9 A PREPARE Choose an essay title and decide if you agree or disagree with it. Give three reasons with examples and evidence to support them.

- Should universities be free for everyone?
- Do we need to ban fast-food restaurants?
- Should people who live in cities be allowed to keep pets?
- Do we need shops now that we can buy everything online?

B PRACTISE Write an essay giving your opinion. Use the Skill box and Text builder to help you.

C PERSONAL BEST Swap essays with another student and correct any mistakes. Is his/her essay convincing? How could he/she improve it?

Personal Best Write an essay with the opposite point of view to the one in exercise 9.

UNIT 8

Food for thought

LANGUAGE *too, too many, too much* and *(not) enough* ■ food and drink

8A Sweet but dangerous

1 Put the words in the box in the correct columns. Can you add two more words to each column?

beef cabbage peach salmon strawberry prawns lamb aubergine

fruit	vegetables	meat	fish and seafood

Personal Best

Go to Vocabulary practice: food and drink, page 149

2 Ask and answer the questions in pairs.

1 What did you have for breakfast?
2 What did you have for dinner last night?
3 What food do you eat if you want a snack?
4 What would you cook for a romantic dinner?
5 Are you allergic to any food?
6 Do you think you have a healthy diet? Why/Why not?

3 Look at the picture of the breakfast. Do you think it's healthy? How much added sugar do you think it contains? Read the text and check.

Most of us know that too much sugar isn't good for us. We know that we shouldn't eat lots of chocolate or drink too many fizzy drinks. But how much do we really know about the other food we eat?

Australian film-maker, Damon Gameau, decided to investigate the 'hidden' sugar in food. He spent 60 days only eating products advertised as 'healthy', such as low-fat yoghurt, cereal bars, fruit juices and sports drinks. But instead of feeling healthier, Damon gained 8kg in weight and started to have health problems. The reason? The high levels of sugar that manufacturers add to many food products to make them taste better. The breakfast pictured here looks good, but the juice, cereal and yoghurt actually contain fourteen teaspoons of extra sugar!

Damon says that food companies are not honest enough about the amount of sugar that they add to products; their marketing makes us believe we're eating and drinking healthily, when really, we are not. The World Health Organization recommends a daily limit of 25g (about six teaspoons) of sugar. That means there's enough sugar in three quarters of a can of cola for one day.

After Damon's experiment finished, he returned to his usual diet of fresh fruit, vegetables, meat and fish. His weight went down and his health problems disappeared. He still enjoys a little chocolate from time to time, but he finds that most processed food now tastes too sweet.

So next time you're in the supermarket, remember to check how much sugar is in that packet of 'healthy' cereal before you buy it!

4 Tick (✓) the best title for the article. Explain your answer.

1 Is sugar good or bad for you? ☐
2 How to lose weight in 60 days ☐
3 The truth about sugar and processed food ☐
4 Five unhealthy foods to avoid ☐

5 Discuss the questions in pairs.

1 Did the text surprise you? Why/Why not?
2 Do you think people in your country eat too much sugar?
3 How often do you check how much sugar is in the products you buy?
4 Should the government do anything about sugar in food? If so, what?

6 A Complete the sentences with the words in the box. Check your answers in the text.

too too much too many not enough

1 We shouldn't drink _________ fizzy drinks.
2 _________ sugar isn't good for us.
3 Food companies are _________ honest enough.
4 There's _________ sugar in three quarters of a can of cola for one day.
5 Most processed food tastes _________ sweet.

B Match the words from sentences 1–5 with the definitions. Then read the Grammar box.

1 *too / too much / too many*
2 *enough*
3 *not enough*

a less than necessary
b more than necessary
c the right amount

Grammar ***too, too many, too much* and *(not) enough***

More than necessary:
*It's **too** noisy. I can't concentrate.*
*You put **too much** milk in my coffee!*
*There are **too many** people on the bus.*

The right amount:
*We have **enough** eggs to make a cake.*
*Is the room warm **enough** for you?*

Less than necessary:
*I **don't** have **enough** time.*
*The car **isn't** fast **enough**.*

Personal Best

Go to Grammar practice: *too, too many, too much* and *(not) enough*, page 126

7 A 8.3 **Pronunciation:** *too much sugar* Listen and repeat the sentence from the text. Pay attention to the sounds in **bold**: /uː/, /ʌ/ and /ʊ/.

T**oo** m**u**ch s**u**gar isn't good for us.

B 8.4 How do you say the words? Listen, check and repeat.

c**oo**k s**ou**p c**u**p f**oo**d en**ou**gh p**u**t bl**oo**d sh**ou**ld **u**se

8 8.5 How do you say the questions? Listen, check and repeat. Ask and answer the questions in pairs.

1 Do you have enough time to cook dinner every night?
2 Do you think good food is too expensive?
3 Do you spend too much time using social media sites?
4 Do you think you have too many clothes?
5 Is your internet connection fast enough for you?
6 Do you know anyone who drinks too much coffee?

9 8.6 Listen to a conversation. Tick (✓) the food that the restaurant needs to buy.

meat: lamb ☐ chicken ☐ beef ☐ turkey ☐
fish/seafood: salmon ☐ prawns ☐ tuna ☐
fruit: peaches ☐ pears ☐ coconuts ☐ strawberries ☐ pineapples ☐
vegetables: peppers ☐ lettuces ☐ cucumbers ☐ tomatoes ☐ aubergines ☐

Go to Communication practice: Student A page 162, Student B page 170

10 A Complete the sentences with your own ideas. Compare them in pairs.

1 I don't spend enough time on _________.
2 I spend too much money on _________.
3 I worry about _________ too much.
4 Sometimes, I'm too _________.
5 I have too many _________.
6 I don't think I'm _________ enough.

B Tell the rest of the class about your partner.

He doesn't spend enough time on his homework.

Personal Best Write a list of ingredients for three of your favourite dishes.

8B Ice-cream university

1 Look at the title of the article and the pictures. Discuss the questions in pairs.

1 Where do you think the university is?
2 Who do you think goes on courses here?
3 Would you like to learn how to make ice-cream?
4 What's your favourite ice-cream flavour?

Skill scanning for specific information

To find a specific piece of information in a text quickly, you should scan for it.

- Identify the key word(s) in the question for the information you need.
- Quickly look for the key words in the text. You can use your finger to help you.
- Stop when you find the key word. If the information you need isn't there, continue scanning until the key word appears again.

2 Read the Skill box. Scan the text and answer the questions. The key words are underlined.

1 What is *gelato*?
2 When did the museum open?
3 How much does a one-day course cost?
4 When was the Gelato University founded?
5 What is the average age of students at the university?

3 Underline the key words in the questions. Scan the text again to answer them.

1 How many students attend the university every year?
2 What languages are lessons taught in?
3 What happens if you make *gelato* using too much sugar?
4 What is the right temperature for *gelato?*
5 How much is a visit to the museum?

4 Read the text in detail. Match the headings in the box with the paragraphs A–E.

The secret of good *gelato* | A city to study in | If you just want a taste | A course for everyone | A mix of students

Text builder linkers to contrast information

but: *There are courses that last up to five weeks,* ***but*** *I'm going to try the one-day course.*
however: *There are courses that last up to five weeks.* ***However****, I'm going to try the one-day course.*
although: ***Although*** *there are courses that last up to five weeks, I'm going to try the one-day course.*
I'm going to try the one-day course, ***although*** *there are courses that last up to five weeks.*

5 **A** Read the Text builder. Underline examples of *but*, *however* and *although* in the text. In pairs, discuss what information is contrasted.

B Complete the sentences with *but*, *however* and *although*. Which paragraphs do they go with?

1 ________ *gelato* is Italian, it has an international reputation.
2 It's a complicated process, ________ after a few hours, I have a litre of pink ice-cream.
3 It's only four euros for children under thirteen. ________ , they must be accompanied by an adult.
4 I'm really looking forward to this course, ________ I've never been a 'good student'.
5 There's even a course to become a professional *gelato* taster. ________ it sounds like the dream job, I don't think I could eat ice-cream 365 days a year!

6 Discuss the questions in pairs.

1 Apart from English, are you studying anything else at the moment?
2 What courses would you like to do if you had the time and the money?
3 If you could start your own business, what would it be?

ICE-CREAM UNIVERSITY

A ________

The city of Bologna in Italy is home to the oldest university in the world, founded in 1088. The list of former students includes artists, politicians, poets and even film directors. However, what a lot of people don't realize is that Bologna is also home to another, much newer, university. I've signed up for a course, although I'm not going to study Law or Engineering. I'm going to learn how to make *gelato* – Italian ice-cream. Welcome to Gelato University!

GELATO UNIVERSITY CARPIGIANI

B ________

The Carpigiani Gelato University was founded in 2003, and every year it attracts more than 6,000 students who want to learn how to make the perfect ice-cream. However, it isn't just about making ice-cream. Students all have the same dream of starting their own *gelato* business, so lessons include how to write a business plan, how to market your product, even how to design your own *gelateria* – or ice-cream shop. There are courses that last up to five weeks, but I'm going to try the one-day course, which costs about 100 euros.

C ________

In my class of 20, there are students from all over the world, and although my lessons are in English, there are also classes in Italian, Spanish, Chinese and other languages. The average age of the students is about 35, but company director Robert from LA is planning to move into the *gelato* business at the age of 72! 'You're never too old to try new things,' he says.

D ________

Back in the classroom, and today we're making strawberry *gelato*. However, before we start, there's a Science lesson. There's a lot of Chemistry and Mathematics, and a calculator is essential. If there's too much sugar in the mix, it won't freeze. If there isn't enough air, it will be too heavy. And it has to be served at the right temperature (5–10° C), which is much warmer than normal ice-cream.

E ________

If you're interested in *gelato*, but you haven't got the time or the money to do a course, the university also has its own Gelato Museum, opened in 2012. For five euros, you can visit the museum, discover the history of *gelato*, the technology behind it, and – of course – taste some of the different flavours! And if you're wondering how my strawberry *gelato* tasted, it was delicious!

Personal Best Write a paragraph about your school or university. Remember to use linkers to contrast information.

8C You must eat your vegetables

1 A 8.7 Look at the pictures of school lunches. Which countries do you think they are from? Listen and check.

a

b

c

B 8.7 Match the adjectives in the box with the pictures. Listen again and check.

healthy crunchy sweet spicy salty tasty

Personal Best

Go to Vocabulary practice: adjectives to describe food, page 150

2 Discuss the questions in pairs.

1 Did you ever have school lunches? If so, what were they like?
2 Which dishes from your childhood did you love/hate? Why?

3 Look at the pictures. Do you recognize the man? In pairs, answer the questions. Read the text and check.

1 What is the man's job?
2 Which country is he in?
3 Why is he in this country?
4 Why does he look disappointed?

THE FOOD REVOLUTION THAT FAILED

British celebrity chef, Jamie Oliver, has tasted failure for the first time with his American TV show, *Jamie's Food Revolution*. One of the biggest health problems in the USA is obesity and Jamie thought that he could help by changing what children ate … but he found that it wasn't so easy.

In the USA, more than 32 million children eat in school cafeterias every day. Unfortunately, the meals aren't always very healthy and some children don't have to eat fruit or vegetables. Instead, many choose hamburgers and pizzas with sweet drinks like chocolate milk.

Jamie decided to change the menu at a school in Los Angeles. The cooks made different meals, including vegetarian curry, fresh salads and spicy chicken noodles. However, Jamie's experiment failed and most children threw his new recipes in the bin. With hungry children and angry parents, hamburgers and pizzas were soon back on the menu.

However, it isn't all bad news. Although Jamie's idea didn't work, things have started to change. New laws say that all schools have to serve healthier food. School meals mustn't contain too much salt, and cafeterias must offer two vegetables a day … but there's still some work to do. According to the rules, tomato sauce on pizzas counts as 'one vegetable'!

4 Discuss the questions in pairs.

1 What do you think about Jamie's experiment?
2 Why do you think it failed?
3 What would you think if he tried to change school meals in your country?

5 A Match the halves to make sentences. Check your answers in the text.

1 Children **don't have to** — a serve healthier food.
2 All schools **have to** — b offer two vegetables a day.
3 School meals **mustn't** — c eat fruit or vegetables.
4 Cafeterias **must** — d contain too much salt.

B Answer the questions about the words in **bold** in sentences 1–4. Then read the Grammar box.

1 Which words mean 'there is a rule to do this'? ________ ________
2 Which words mean 'this isn't necessary'? ________
3 Which words mean 'this is not allowed'? ________

Grammar *must(n't)* and *(not) have to*

Obligation:
*You **must** start school at 9.00 a.m.*
*Do they **have to** wear a uniform?*

Prohibition:
*Students **mustn't** use a calculator in the exam.*

Not necessary:
*You do**n't have to** do the course, but you can if you want.*

Go to Grammar practice: *must(n't)* and *(not) have to*, page 127

6 Choose the correct options to complete the hotel rules. Would you like to stay in this hotel? Why/Why not?

HOTEL RULES

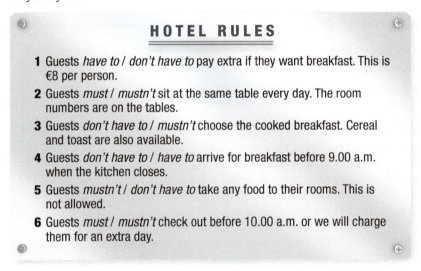

1 Guests *have to* / *don't have to* pay extra if they want breakfast. This is €8 per person.
2 Guests *must* / *mustn't* sit at the same table every day. The room numbers are on the tables.
3 Guests *don't have to* / *mustn't* choose the cooked breakfast. Cereal and toast are also available.
4 Guests *don't have to* / *have to* arrive for breakfast before 9.00 a.m. when the kitchen closes.
5 Guests *mustn't* / *don't have to* take any food to their rooms. This is not allowed.
6 Guests *must* / *mustn't* check out before 10.00 a.m. or we will charge them for an extra day.

7 A 8.10 **Pronunciation:** sentence stress Listen to the sentences. Underline the stressed words.

1 People must carry an identity card at all times.
2 You don't have to buy a ticket when you get on the bus.
3 People mustn't use their mobile phones on public transport.
4 Children have to stay at school until the age of 18.
5 Parents don't have to send their children to school. They can educate them at home.
6 Everyone has to vote in national elections.

B 8.10 Say the sentences, paying attention to the stress in each one. Listen again, check and repeat.

8 In pairs, decide if the sentences in exercise 7A are true in your country.

Go to Communication practice: Student A page 163, Student B page 171

9 A In pairs, imagine you are the managing directors of a new company. Write a list of rules that will keep your employees happy and productive and make your company successful. Think about these factors:

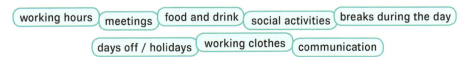

working hours | meetings | food and drink | social activities | breaks during the day | days off / holidays | working clothes | communication

B Tell the rest of the class your rules.

Personal Best Write a list of rules in your place of work or university. How could you change them to make them better?

Learning Curve

8D First dates

1 In pairs, look at the pictures of restaurants. Decide which are the best places for the situations in the box.

> business meeting first date meeting up with friends
> birthday celebration lunch on your own family meal

a

b
Hopeful
Enthusiastic

c

d

2 Discuss the questions in pairs.

1 How would you feel if you had a first date?
2 Where would you go on a first date?
3 Who would you ask for advice about a first date?

3 8.11 Watch or listen to the first part of *Learning Curve*. Are the sentences true (T) or false (F)?

1 Jack feels shy about asking Eleanor out on a date. ____
2 Jack met Eleanor while he was studying at university. ____
3 He invites Simon to try his new dish and he wants his advice. ____
4 Simon thinks Jack should take Eleanor to a fish-and-chip restaurant. ____
5 Jack rings Eleanor to ask her out on a date. ____

4 8.11 Use the words in the box to complete what Jack and Simon said. Watch or listen again and check.

> dish great be in sounds
> new Would that interested
> you trying a Thanks out

Jack
Simon

Conversation builder making and responding to invitations

Inviting:
Would you like to …?
Would you be interested in …?
Do you want to …?
Do you fancy …?
I was wondering if you'd fancy …

Accepting:
I'd love to. Thank you.
Thanks, that sounds great!
That's very kind of you.
That would be lovely.
Fantastic.

Refusing:
That's really nice of you, but I'm sorry, I can't.
I'm afraid I already have plans.
I really appreciate the invite, but …
Sorry, I think I'm busy that evening.

5 Read the Conversation builder. In pairs, take turns to invite your partner for a coffee one day this week. Refuse the first time but when he/she invites you for a coffee on a different day, accept.

6 **A** 8.12 Watch or listen to the second part of the show. Where do Jack and Eleanor decide to go for their date?

B 8.12 Complete the conversation with the words in the box. Watch or listen again and check.

appreciate like fancy sorry want kind

Eleanor

Jack I was wondering if you'd [1]_________ having dinner with me at my restaurant?
Eleanor Oh, that's right, you're a chef. Thanks, that's very [2]_________ of you.
Jack Great. I know it's short notice, but, would you [3]_________ to come tonight? I have a new, special dish.
Eleanor Did you say tonight? That's really nice of you, but I'm [4]_________, I can't. I already have plans.
Jack Well, do you [5]_________ to go out at the weekend? Perhaps tomorrow?
Eleanor Er, I would. I really [6]_________ the invite, but, I'm going to go visit my granddad.

7 8.13 Listen and repeat the phrases when you hear the beeps. Do Eleanor and Jack sound polite?

Skill sounding polite

It's important to sound polite in English, especially when you say something negative.
- Use intonation to express yourself. Flat intonation can sound rude.
- Apologize before you say something negative.
- Use longer phrases and give explanations.

8 **A** 8.14 Read the Skill box. Listen to six conversations and tick (✓) the response which sounds more polite: a or b.

1 Tom, could you help me with this box? It's really heavy. a ☐ b ☐
2 Hi, do you fancy seeing a film tonight? a ☐ b ☐
3 So, what did your boss think of the designs? a ☐ b ☐
4 Would you like to get a coffee after class? a ☐ b ☐
5 Wow! That new jacket looks great on you. a ☐ b ☐
6 Would you be interested in seeing my band play tomorrow evening? a ☐ b ☐

B 8.15 Listen and repeat the polite responses. Explain why they are more polite.

Go to Communication practice: Student A page 163, Student B page 171

9 **A** PREPARE In pairs, look at the diagram and discuss what you could say at each stage. You can make notes.

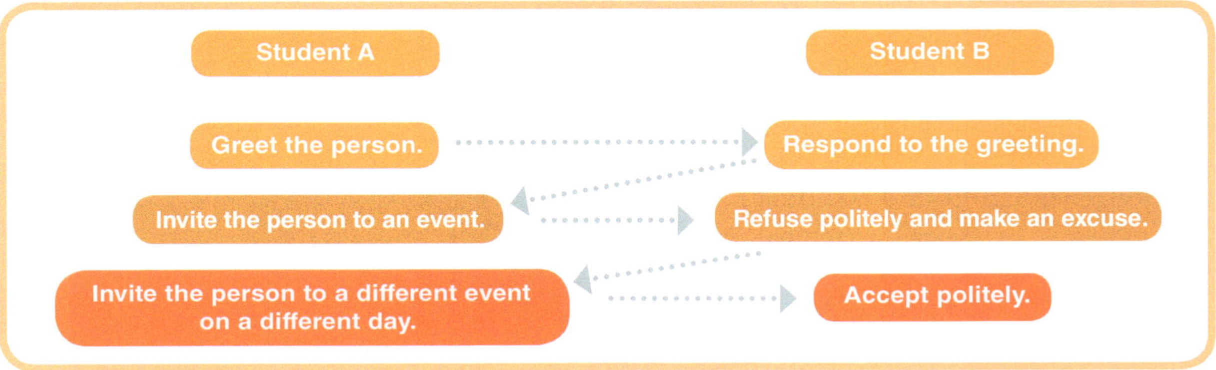
Student A
Student B
Greet the person.
Respond to the greeting.
Invite the person to an event.
Refuse politely and make an excuse.
Invite the person to a different event on a different day.
Accept politely.

B PRACTISE Repeat your conversation until you can say it without looking at the diagram or your notes.

C PERSONAL BEST Work with another pair. Listen to their conversation. Did they use the same language as you? Was their conversation polite? In what way?

Personal Best Write another dialogue using the diagram in exercise 9A, but use different phrases.

Grammar

1 Cross (**X**) the sentence which is NOT correct.

1 **a** I've just called Claude. ☐
b I've called Claude 10 minutes ago. ☐
c I called Claude 10 minutes ago. ☐

2 **a** I have to wear a suit at work. ☐
b I must wear a suit at work. ☐
c I haven't to wear jeans at work. ☐

3 **a** I've worked here since January. ☐
b I've worked here for five months. ☐
c I've worked here since five months ago. ☐

4 **a** This restaurant is too crowded. ☐
b This restaurant isn't quiet enough. ☐
c This restaurant is too much crowded. ☐

5 **a** I've seen the film yet. ☐
b I saw the film last week. ☐
c I've already seen the film. ☐

6 **a** You have too many clothes in the wardrobe. ☐
b You don't have space enough for your clothes. ☐
c You don't have enough space in the wardrobe. ☐

7 **a** I haven't seen my parents for a month. ☐
b I didn't see my parents since last month. ☐
c I haven't seen my parents since last month. ☐

8 **a** You mustn't walk on the grass. ☐
b You have to walk on the path. ☐
c You must to walk on the path. ☐

2 Use the words in brackets to write sentences that mean the same as the first sentence.

1 It isn't necessary for Sofia to take the train.
Sofia ________ take the train. (have)

2 I saw her five minutes ago.
I ________ her. (just)

3 I went to the shops this morning.
I ________ to the shops. (already)

4 We've had the car since March.
We ________ six months. (for)

5 We need more bread.
We ________ bread. (enough)

6 She hasn't visited me for years.
She ________ 2012. (visited)

7 The coffee has more milk than I wanted.
There's ________ in my coffee. (too)

8 You're not allowed to use your phone in here.
You ________ your phone in here. (use)

3 Choose the correct options to complete the text.

Don't look down!

The city of Dubai [1]*built / has built* over 200 skyscrapers [2]*for / since* 2000 and the Burj Khalifa is the tallest of these. It's 830 m high, with 163 floors and has an incredible 24,000 windows … which all [3]*have / must* to be cleaned! The highest part of the building is [4]*too / too much* difficult for people to clean, and machines are used. However, a team of 36 men clean the rest of the building. We talk to Bibek Thapa from Nepal, who has [5]*just / yet* finished cleaning for the day.

What's the hardest part about the job?

I've climbed [6]*enough mountains / mountains enough* in Nepal not to be afraid of heights. The worst thing for me is the sun. Sometimes it's [7]*too / too much* hot and we [8]*have to / mustn't* wear protective clothes.

What's it like in bad weather?

We don't work when there's [9] *too many / too much* wind or dust because it's so dangerous.

Do you need any special equipment?

We use lots of safety equipment, obviously, but we [10]*have to / don't have to* use any special cleaning chemicals. We just use soap and water, like when you clean windows at home.

Vocabulary

1 Match the words with the definitions.

rush hour fresh set off coconut raw pedestrian crossing turkey give someone a lift litter bin commuter

1 to take someone to a place in your car ________
2 a place for rubbish when you're in the street ________
3 a person who travels to work ________
4 a large bird we can eat ________
5 a large fruit from a palm tree ________
6 to leave your house to go somewhere ________
7 food that is not cooked ________
8 a place where you can cross the road safely ________
9 the busiest time of day on the roads ________
10 food that was prepared recently ________

2 Circle the word that is different. Explain your answer.

1	passenger	platform	pedestrian	commuter
2	sour	sweet	bitter	crunchy
3	drive	ride	go by	traffic
4	beef	lamb	prawns	turkey
5	tunnel	bridge	bike lane	litter bin
6	delayed	signpost	statue	pavement
7	tuna	peach	pineapple	strawberry
8	tasty	burnt	healthy	delicious

3 Choose the correct word to complete the sentences.

1 My bus never ________ on time.
  a arrives b gets c drives
2 Is the fish ________? It doesn't smell very good.
  a fresh b tasty c healthy
3 You should ________ now or you'll be late.
  a arrive b set off c drive
4 We're having ________ for dessert.
  a flour b lettuce c apple pie
5 My car is in the garage, so I can't ________ to work.
  a ride b drive c arrive
6 A: What's on the pizza?
  B: There's tomato sauce, peppers, and ________ .
  a flour b tuna c cereal
7 There are no ________ on this road – it's so dark!
  a traffic lights b street lights c signposts
8 The doctor said I shouldn't eat ________ food.
  a fresh b salty c disgusting

4 Complete the conversations with the words in the boxes.

parking space benches car park
apartment block public transport

Jo Is your new [1] ________ near the city bridge?
Lee No, it's next to the square with the fountain and all the [2] ________ to sit on.
Jo That's a great area! Do you get a [3] ________ for your car?
Lee Yes, but I use [4] ________ to get to work because my office doesn't have a [5] ________.

fresh delicious prawns spicy vegetarian

Kim Don't forget you have to cook [6] ________ food for my parents. They don't eat meat.
Jon I know. I'm going to cook a curry.
Kim Don't cook a curry! It will be too [7] ________ for them! Why don't you cook the *paella* you made last week? It was [8] ________! I loved it.
Jon But that had [9] ________ in it!
Kim Oh, yeah. Can't you make it without them? Just add lots of [10] ________ vegetables.

Personal Best

Lesson 7A
Write a question with *yet*, and an answer with *just*.

Lesson 8A
Name five fruits.

Lesson 7A
Name five city features you usually see in the street.

Lesson 8A
Write one sentence using *enough*, and another with *too*.

Lesson 7B
Name four ways of going to work.

Lesson 8B
Write a sentence using *although*.

Lesson 7C
Write a question with *how long*, and an answer with *since*.

Lesson 8C
Name five adjectives to describe food.

Lesson 7C
Write three sentences about yourself or your family using *for*.

Lesson 8C
Write three rules you have at home.

Lesson 7D
Give three expressions for giving your opinion.

Lesson 8D
Give two expressions for accepting an invitation, and two for refusing.

UNIT 9 Money and shopping

LANGUAGE *used to* ■ money verbs

9A He used to be poor

1 **A** Look at the title of the text and the pictures. Discuss the questions in pairs.

1 Have you ever been to a Zara shop?
2 What does Zara sell?
3 Who is the man?
4 What does the title of the text mean?

B Read the introduction and check your answers.

FROM ZERO TO ZARA

Today, he's one of the richest men in the world with a global business that is worth billions of dollars, but he used to be a poor boy from Galicia, in the north of Spain. This is the story of Amancio Ortega, the founder of the clothes company, Zara.

ZARA

Amancio was born in 1936. His father was a railway worker and didn't earn much money. The family sometimes couldn't afford food and his mother used to ask for credit at the grocery store, but one day they said no. That was the moment Amancio decided to leave school and get a job. He was just 14.

Amancio's first job was in a shirt shop. He used to fold the shirts and deliver them to customers on his bike. Then he moved to another shop, where he learned a lot about the industry. Clothes used to be quite expensive and there wasn't much choice, so customers didn't use to buy many. Amancio realized that if he could produce more attractive clothes more cheaply, people would spend more money.

So, at the age of 27, and with just a little money that he'd saved, Amancio started his own business making pyjamas, which he sold to local shops. After borrowing some money from a bank, he began making other types of clothes and the business grew. In 1975, Amancio opened his first Zara shop and the company soon opened more shops in Spain.

Today, you can find Zara and the other fashion companies Amancio owns in 88 different countries around the world, but he still lives in Galicia, where he grew up.

2 Order the events from 1–8. Read the text and check.

a ☐ He worked in a shirt shop.
b ☐ Zara expanded around the world.
c ☐ He left school.
d ☐ The first Zara shop opened.
e ☐ He started to produce other types of clothes.
f ☐ Amancio was born in northern Spain.
g ☐ He used his own money to start a business.
h ☐ He asked the bank for some money.

3 What do you think Amancio Ortega is like? Why?

4 **A** Match the halves to make sentences. Check your answers in the text.

1 Amancio decided to
2 His mother used to
3 Customers didn't use to
4 He used to

a ask for credit.
b buy many clothes.
c leave school.
d be a poor boy from Galicia.

B Look at sentences 1–4 again and answer the questions. Then read the Grammar box.

1 Are the sentences about the past, the present or the future? ________
2 Which sentence is an action that only happened once? ____ Which tense is it? ________
3 Which sentence is a situation that was true in the past, but isn't true now? ____
4 Which sentences are actions that happened more than once in the past? ____ ____

Grammar *used to*

Actions that happened regularly in the past, but don't happen now:
*How **did** you **use to get** to school?*
*We **used to walk** to school. We **didn't use to take** the bus.*

Situations that were true in the past, but aren't true now:
*What **did** she **use to be** like?*
*She **used to be** quite shy. She **didn't use to be** very confident.*

Look! We use the past simple for an action that only happened once.
*I **went** to the shops yesterday.* NOT ~~*I used to go to the shops yesterday.*~~

Go to Grammar practice: *used to*, page 128

VISA
MasterCard

5 9.2 **Pronunciation:** *used to/use to* Listen to the sentences. How do you say the words in **bold**? Do they sound different? Listen again and repeat.

1 His family **used to** be poor.
2 He didn't **use to** earn much money.
3 Did he **use to** work from home?

Go to Communication practice: Student A page 163, Student B page 171

6 Match the words in the box with definitions 1–6. Look at the highlighted words in the text on page 76 to help you.

be worth   earn   can afford   spend   save   borrow

1 have enough money to buy something ________
2 not use money and keep it in a bank ________
3 use money to buy something ________
4 have a value of a certain amount of money ________
5 take money from someone but return it later ________
6 make money from work ________

Go to Vocabulary practice: money verbs, page 151

7 Discuss the questions in pairs.

1 What do you spend your money on?
2 Do you find it difficult to save money?
3 Do you own your home or do you rent it?
4 Which professions earn the most money?
5 Have you ever borrowed money from a bank?
6 Do you have a car? How much is it worth?
7 Do you think footballers get paid too much money?
8 Do you ever waste money on things you don't need?

8 **A** 9.4 Listen to five people talking about their childhood. Match the topics in the box with the speakers.

bedtime   money   toys   holidays   food

1 Rachel ________ 2 Angus ________ 3 Freddy ________ 4 Lucy ________ 5 Sam ________

B 9.4 Complete the sentences with the past simple or *used to* form of the verbs in brackets. Listen again and check.

1 The first book I ________ was *Northern Lights*. (buy)
2 Our parents ________ about us. (not worry)
3 We ________ for dinner every Sunday night. (go out)
4 My granddad always ________ me a story in bed at night. (read)
5 I ________ a Buzz Lightyear toy for my birthday one year. (get)

9 **A** In pairs, talk about your childhood. Use the topics in the boxes or your own ideas.

bedtime   clothes   food   holidays   money   music   school   toys and games   TV

I used to go to bed at 7.00 p.m. every night. What time did you use to go to bed?

B Tell the class some things that you found out about your partner.

He/She used to ...   *He/She didn't use to ...*

Personal Best Write ten sentences about you with the verbs from the Vocabulary practice.

Learning Curve

9B What a bargain!

1 Match the words in the box with pictures a–f.

discount	till	shopping centre	cash	queue	receipt

a

ROXY

b

HARVEY NICHOLS
SALE

c

d

UP TO 50%
UP TO 30%

e
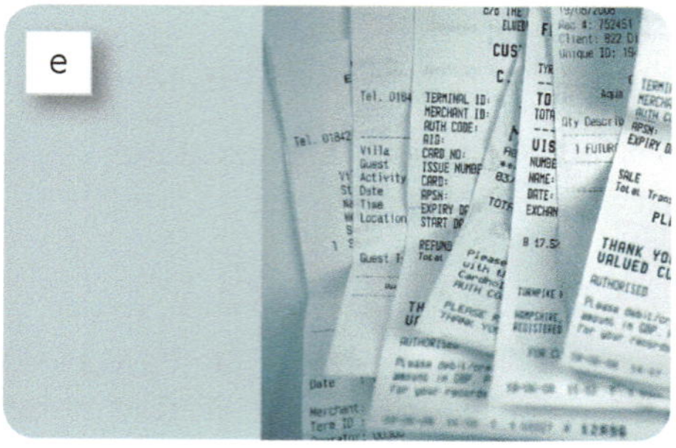

f

Personal Best

Go to Vocabulary practice: shopping, page 151

2 Discuss the questions in pairs.

1 Do you prefer to shop in shopping centres, department stores, small independent shops or online? Why?
2 Have you ever found a bargain in the sales? If so, what was it?
3 Do you always try on clothes in the changing rooms before you buy them? Why/Why not?
4 How long do you keep a receipt after you have bought something? Why?
5 Do you ever go window-shopping? Why/Why not?

3 ▶ 9.7 Watch or listen to the first part of *Learning Curve*. Tick (✓) the best summary of what Ethan says.

a Shopping in the past was very different. ☐
b Shopping centres have a long history. ☐
c Shopping centres are the best place to find bargains. ☐

4 ▶ 9.7 What do sentences 1–6 refer to: *Trajan's Market* (TM), or *Grand Bazaar* (GB)? Watch or listen again and check.

1 It is over 600 years old. ____
2 Today it's a museum. ____
3 It has about 5,000 shops. ____
4 It has about 250,000 visitors per day. ____
5 It's almost 2,000 years old. ____
6 People used to live there. ____

5 **A** Tick (✓) Kate's opinion of the Grand Bazaar.

a She thinks it's an interesting place for tourists. ☐
b She thinks it's a good place to go shopping. ☐
c She prefers modern shopping malls. ☐

B Can you remember what words she used to give this opinion? Read the Skill box.

Ethan

Skill identifying attitude and opinion

It's often important to understand what someone's personal opinion is.

- Listen for phrases that we use to give opinions: *I think ..., I'd say ..., to be honest ...*, etc.
- Listen for adjectives that describe feelings: *boring, excited, upset, annoyed, pleased*, etc.
- Listen for verbs that express attitude: *look forward to, prefer, love, have to*, etc.

6 9.8 Watch or listen to the second part of the show. Match the reasons for going to a shopping centre in the box with the three people.

see a film | return something to a shop | meet up with friends

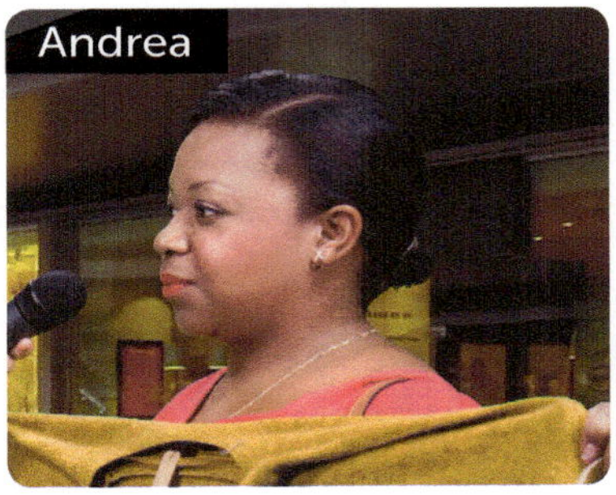
Andrea

Lohi

Joan

7 A 9.8 Watch or listen again. Are the sentences true (T) or false (F)?

1 Andrea is annoyed that her friends aren't coming. ____
2 She doesn't like queues. ____
3 Lohi is surprised at the size of the shopping centre. ____
4 He thinks he made a mistake shopping there. ____
5 Joan was angry because she couldn't exchange her jumper. ____
6 She's pleased with her new jumper. ____

B Can you remember the words and phrases that helped you to answer the questions?

8 Discuss the questions in pairs.

1 When did you last go to a shopping centre?
2 Did you buy anything? If so, how did you pay?
3 What were the last clothes you bought?
4 Did you try them on?

9 9.9 Read what Andrea said. Can you understand it without the missing words? Listen and complete the sentences.

[1] ________ , I'm supposed to be meeting up with some friends, but [2] ________ , they [3] ________ , just texted me to say they're not coming. I'd say it's a bit rude really, but I can't do anything, so I'm just [4] ________ looking around, window-shopping, [5] ________ ?

Listening builder filler expressions

Fillers are words and phrases that speakers say to give themselves time to think. They don't really mean anything:

***So**, I bought this jacket, **like**, a week ago, **I mean**, I wanted to **kind of** return it and, **er**, get a refund.*
***Well**, I don't have the receipt, **you see**, because I **sort of** lost it.*

10 9.10 Read the Listening builder. Listen to the conversation and answer the questions.

1 What is Jason doing at the shopping centre?
2 Which filler expressions do you hear?

11 In pairs, discuss how shopping has changed from the past. Use the topics in the boxes or your own ideas.

size of shops | opening hours | location | customer service | choice | quality of products | ways to pay | prices

I think the quality of clothes used to be much better.

Personal Best Use your ideas from exercise 11 to write a paragraph about how shopping has changed.

9C Going, going, gone!

Nick

1 Ask and answer the questions in pairs.

1 Have you ever been to an auction? Where was it?
2 Have you ever bought anything on an online auction website?
3 What did you buy? How much did you pay?

2 9.11 Look at the pictures. In pairs, match four of the prices in the box with the items that were sold at auctions. Listen and check.

$5,000 $100,000 $1.8m $4.6m $75m $120m

a

b

c

d

3 9.11 In pairs, try to complete the sentences. Listen again and check.

1 *The Scream* **was painted** in ________ **by** Edvard Munch.
2 This version **is thought** to be ________ **by** many experts.
3 The jacket **was worn by** Michael Jackson in the music video for ________.
4 It's **made** of red and black ________.
5 The Aston Martin car **was driven by** Sean Connery in the ________ films.
6 Another car from the films **was stolen** in ________.
7 Vegemite **is eaten by** millions of ________ every day.
8 This piece of toast **was given** to Niall Horan from ________ on an Australian TV show.

4 Look at the words in **bold** in exercise 3. Answer the questions. Then read the Grammar box.

1 Which grammar structure is used in the sentences? ________
2 Which sentences are in the present tense? ________ Which are in the past tense? ________
3 How do we make this structure? The verb ________ + the ________ of the main verb.
4 Which word do we use before the people who do/did the action? ________
5 What is more important in the passive: the people who do/did the action or the action? ________

Grammar the passive

Present passive
*Where **are** the cars **made**?*
*They **are made** in Italy.*
*They **aren't made** anywhere else.*

Past passive
*When **was** the book **written**?*
*It **was written** in 1957.*
*It **wasn't published** until 2015.*

Look! To say who does/did the action we use ***by***.
*The cars are made **by factory workers**.* *The book was written **by Harper Lee**.*

Go to Grammar practice: the passive, page 129

Personal Best

5 **A** 9.13 **Pronunciation:** sentence stress Listen and repeat the sentence. Pay attention to the underlined stressed words.

The picture was painted in 1945.

B 9.14 Underline the stressed words. Listen, check and repeat.

1 These clothes were worn by Lady Gaga.
2 These peaches are grown in Brazil.
3 The salmon is cooked with lemon.
4 The car was driven by Lewis Hamilton.
5 These watches are made in Switzerland.
6 The bridge was opened in 2010.

Go to Communication practice: Student A page 163, Student B page 171

6 Look at the picture and the title. What do you think the text is about? How much is the box worth? Read the text and check.

FAMILY FINDS 'LOST' TREASURE AT FATHER'S HOME

This beautiful wood and gold box was made in Japan in 1640. It is one of ten boxes that were made in Kyoto by Kaomi Nagashige, a well-known Japanese artist. However, this box was thought to be lost. In fact, the Victoria and Albert Museum in London had spent over fifty years searching for it. Unknown to the museum, the box was just one kilometre away in a Kensington house. It was bought by a French engineer for £100 in 1970 and, amazingly, it was used as a table for his television! After he died, his family decided to sell it and it was identified by art experts as one of the lost Japanese boxes from 1640. It went to auction, and was sold to the Rijksmuseum in Amsterdam for £6.5 million – making the family millionaires. ■

7 **A** Use the words to make passive questions.

1 what / the box / make of ? ______
2 where / the box / make ? ______
3 when / the box / make ? ______
4 who / the box / buy / by / in 1970 ? ______
5 how much / the box / buy / for ? ______
6 what / the box / use / for ? ______
7 who / the box / identify / by ? ______
8 who / the box / sell / to / for £6.5 million? ______

B Ask and answer the questions in pairs.

8 Discuss the questions in pairs.

1 Do you think the box is really worth so much money?
2 How would you feel if you were the family of the French engineer?
3 What is your most important possession? Would you ever sell it?

9 Answer the quiz questions in pairs.

Quiz Time

1 Where are roubles used as money?
2 Who was *The Alchemist* written by?
3 When was penicillin discovered?
4 Which city in the USA is known as 'The Big Apple'?
5 How many Harry Potter films were made?
6 Which languages are spoken in Canada?

10 **A** In pairs, write five quiz questions with the passive form of the verbs in the boxes.

invent | make | sing | direct | wear | write | paint | record | know | discover | use | win

B Swap quizzes with another pair and answer the questions.

Personal Best Write about an important possession and say how much it is worth to you.

9D I'd like a refund

1 What are the advantages and disadvantages of online shopping? Discuss the questions in pairs.

1 How often do you buy things online?
2 What do you prefer to buy in shops? Why?
3 Have you ever had a problem with something you bought online?

2 Match the problems in the box with pictures a–e.

The wrong size was sent. It was broken or damaged. Part of the order was missing. The order arrived late / didn't arrive. I was charged too much.

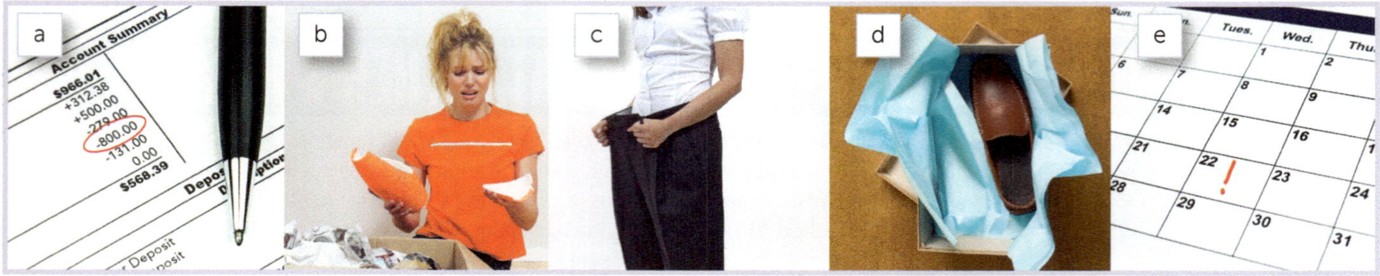
a
Account Summary
$966.01
+312.38
+500.00
-279.00
-800.00
-131.00
0.00
$568.39
b
c
d
e
Tues.
Wed.
Thu.

3 Read the email and answer the questions.

1 What are the three problems with Valerie's order?
2 What did she pay extra for?
3 What does she want the company to do?
4 Would you use this company?

To: info@phonetastic.com
Subject: Problems with my order (P389746-D)

Dear Sir/Madam,
I am writing to complain about the problems I have had with my online order (P389746-D).
I ordered a red X3 smartphone from your website on 14 January and I paid $4.99 extra for next-day delivery. I waited for one week, but nothing arrived, so I contacted your customer service team and I was told that it was on its way. However, the phone was only delivered yesterday – two weeks after I ordered it. Apart from the late delivery, there are two other problems with the phone. Firstly, it is the wrong colour. The phone I was sent is black – not red. And secondly, the screen is cracked. I have attached a photo so you can see what I mean. Because of these problems, I wish to return the phone and I would like a full refund, including the extra delivery charge.
I look forward to hearing from you soon.
Regards
Valerie Lemoir

4 **A** Is the style of the email formal or informal? Why?

B Order the different parts of the email. Then read the Skill box.

a ☐ say what she wants the company to do
b ☐ complain about the late delivery
c ☐ give the reason for writing
d ☐ close the email
e ☐ explain the other problems
f ☐ include a short and accurate subject line

Skill writing a formal email

We often write formal emails to people who work for other companies and organizations.

- Use a formal greeting: *Dear Sir/Madam, Dear Mrs Jones*
- Order your paragraphs: reason for writing, explaining the situation, what you want to happen
- Avoid contractions: *I am writing* ... NOT ~~*I'm writing*~~ ...
- Use formal expressions: *I contacted* ... NOT ~~*I called*~~ ...
- Use passives to avoid being personal: *I was told* ... NOT ~~*They told me*~~ ...

5 Choose the correct options to complete the reply from Suleiman.

To: valerie.lemoir@mailshop.com
Subject: RE: Problems with my order (P389746-D)

[1]*Hi Valerie / Dear Ms Lemoir*
I am writing [2]*with regard to / about* your email of 29 January.
Firstly, [3]*I'm very sorry about / please accept my apologies for* the problems you experienced with our online ordering system, which was [4]*unacceptable / really bad*. Unfortunately, [5]*the wrong software was installed / they installed the wrong software* and this has caused some unexpected problems.
Therefore, I [6]*would be very happy to refund / don't mind refunding* the money, including all delivery costs that [7]*you were charged / we charged you*. Please [8]*tell me / advise me of* a suitable date for our delivery team to collect the phone. [9]*In addition to this / Also*, I would like to offer you a $50-voucher to spend on any product at Phonetastic. I hope this is satisfactory, and we look forward to you shopping with us in future.
[10]*Cheers! / With kind regards*,

Suleiman Malik
Customer Services Manager

6 How did Suleiman try to solve the problem? Do you think Valerie will use the company again?

7 **A** Complete the sentences from Valerie's email with the words in the box. Check your answers in her email.

delivered delivery order ordered

1 I am writing to complain about the problems I have had with my online ________ ...
2 I ________ a red X3 smartphone from your website on ...
3 However, the phone was only ________ yesterday – two weeks after I ordered it.
4 Apart from the late ________ , there are ...

B How does Valerie repeat her ideas without repeating the exact words?

Text builder noun forms of verbs

No change:	*order → order*	**Noun ends in -*sion*:**	*decide → decision*
Noun ends in -*ment*:	*argue → argument*	**Noun ends in -*ation*:**	*inform → information*
Noun ends in -*y*:	*deliver → delivery*		

8 Read the Text builder. Complete the sentences with the noun form of the verbs in brackets.

1 There's a problem with the ________ on this credit card. (pay)
2 We have received your ________ for the job. (apply)
3 In ________, this is a serious problem. (conclude)
4 I didn't receive an ________ for their mistakes. (apologize)
5 He hasn't given me an ________ yet. (answer)

9 **A** **PREPARE** Choose a problem with an online order. Make notes about the details of the problem and what you want the company to do (e.g. contact you/exchange/refund).

missing part

arrived 3 days late

wrong colour

wrong product delivered

B **PRACTISE** Use the Skill box to write a formal email complaining about the order. Repeat your ideas in different ways using noun and verb forms of words.

C **PERSONAL BEST** Swap emails with your partner. Tick (✓) three sentences you think are very good. Suggest three ways to improve his/her email.

Personal Best Write the company's reply to your partner's email from exercise 9.

UNIT 10

Sport and fitness

LANGUAGE past perfect ■ sports and competitions

10A Winning is everything

1 10.1 Listen and match the speakers with pictures a–c.

a

b

c

2 10.1 Complete the sentences with the words in the box. Listen again and check.

beat	win	match	race	umpire	athlete	medal	trophy	score	crowd

1 The ________ is almost over. In one minute, Real Madrid will ________ the game and the ________. But wait. What's this? Here come Arsenal. The ball goes to Walcott. He has to ________ a goal, now. He does!

2 Serena Williams to serve. Was that out? She looks at the ________. You can hear the ________ cheering. They're sure Serena is going to ________ her sister, Venus.

3 Here they come, the end of the 100 m ________, and Bolt is going to win the gold ________ again. Yes, he's done it. What an amazing ________!

Personal Best

Go to Vocabulary practice: sports and competitions, page 152

3 Discuss the questions in pairs.

1 Do you prefer to watch or take part in sports?
2 Have you ever won a medal or a trophy?
3 Would you like to be a professional athlete?
4 How have sports changed over the last 100 years?

4 Read the text. What are the names of the athletes in the pictures?

a
b
c
36
d

THE TOUGHEST RACE EVER?

There are some difficult events in the Olympic Games, but nothing compares with the 1904 Olympic Marathon. One athlete almost died and the race ended in a public scandal.

The marathon started on an incredibly hot day in St Louis, in the USA, and there were lots of cars and horses on the dusty roads. One athlete, William Garcia, started coughing after he'd breathed in too much dust. It was so bad that he had to give up the race and was taken to hospital. Another runner, Len Tau from South Africa, eventually finished in ninth place, but he was disappointed because some wild dogs had chased him for over a mile in the opposite direction during the race!

Meanwhile, the first athlete to cross the finish line was an American, Fred Lorz. The crowd thought a local athlete had won so they started celebrating, but actually, Lorz had cheated. He'd felt ill during the race and had travelled 11 miles in a car! Fortunately, a spectator had seen Lorz getting out of the car one mile before the finish line and told the referee, so Lorz didn't win the gold medal.

The next runner to finish was another American, Tom Hicks. Hicks hadn't felt well either so his friends had given him a drink of eggs mixed with some chemicals to help him. However, this had made him feel even worse and, in the end, his friends had helped him walk the final part of the race. Even though he hadn't run the whole marathon on his own, the organizers presented Hicks with the gold medal after the hardest marathon of all time.

5 **A** Read the sentences. Tick (✓) the action that happened first: **a** or **b**?

1 a ☐ William Garcia **started** coughing after b ☐ he'**d breathed** in too much dust.
2 a ☐ Len Tau **was** disappointed because b ☐ some wild dogs **had chased** him for over a mile.
3 a ☐ The crowd thought a local athlete **had won**, so b ☐ they **started** celebrating.
4 a ☐ Even though he **hadn't run** the whole marathon, b ☐ the organizers **presented** Hicks with the gold medal.

B Look at the verbs in **bold** in exercise 5A and answer the questions. Then read the Grammar box.

1 What tense are the actions that happened first? *past simple / past perfect*
2 What tense are the actions that happened later? *past simple / past perfect*
3 How do we form the past perfect? ________ + ________

Grammar past perfect

An action that happened before another action in the past:
*I **had forgotten** my keys so I couldn't open the door.*
***Had** you **eaten** anything before you went swimming?*
*I explained to my boss that I **hadn't finished** the report.*
*When I got to the party, my friend **had gone**.*

Personal Best

Go to Grammar practice: past perfect, page 130

6 10.6 **Pronunciation:** *'d /hadn't* Listen to the sentences. How do you say *'d* and *hadn't?* Listen again and repeat.

1 He'**d** breathed in too much dust.
2 He **hadn't** run the whole marathon on his own.

7 **A** Complete the sentences with the past perfect form of the verbs in brackets.

1 They ________ before the game. (not warm up)
2 I knew they ________! (cheat)
3 She ________ a rugby match before. (not see)
4 We celebrated because he ________ a goal. (score)

B 10.7 In pairs, say the sentences. Pay attention to the *'d/hadn't* contractions. Listen, check and repeat.

Go to Communication practice: Student A page 164, Student B page 172

8 10.8 Complete the text with the correct form of the verbs in brackets. Use the past simple or past perfect. Listen and check.

Who's the twelfth man?

There are eleven players in a football team, but in this team photo of Manchester United there are twelve – so who's the twelfth man? The team [1] ________ (be) very excited after they [2] ________ (travel) to Germany for their Champions League match against Bayern Munich. The players [3] ________ (line up) for a photo when suddenly Karl Power [4] ________ (run) onto the pitch dressed in the Manchester United kit and [5] ________ (stand) next to them. Even though some of the players [6] ________ (notice) Karl, the photographer still [7] ________ (take) the photo. Karl then [8] ________ (go) back to his seat to watch the match. Unfortunately, Manchester United [9] ________ (lose), but Karl was happy because he [10] ________ (meet) his heroes!

9 **A** In pairs, write as many sentences as you can about the pictures. Use the past simple and past perfect.

He was very disappointed because he'd lost the match.

a

b

c

B Tell the class your most interesting sentence. Who has the most original explanation?

Personal Best Write about an occasion when you did something that you had never done before.

10B Rock 'n' roll on wheels

1 Look at the pictures and the title of the text on page 87. Answer the questions.

1 What are the Paralympic Games?
2 Have you ever seen a wheelchair rugby match?
3 Would you like to take part in a game?
4 What kind of person do you think Laura is?

Skill finding information in a text

When we want to find information in a longer text, we need to know where to look.
- Read the text quickly and understand the general topic of each paragraph.
- Read the question carefully and underline any key words.
- Match the question with the paragraph that has the information you need.
- Read this paragraph in detail to answer the question.

2 Read the Skill box. Then read the text quickly and match paragraphs A–G with topics 1–7.

1 how it feels to play wheelchair rugby ____
2 how to find out more about the sport ____
3 creating interest in disabled sports ____
4 Laura's physical appearance ____
5 media interest in wheelchair rugby ____
6 the origins of the sport ____
7 the rules of wheelchair rugby ____

3 **A** Read the questions. Underline the key words and match them with paragraphs A–G.

	Paragraph	Answer
1 How long does it take Tim to cross the court?	____	________
2 Which movie did wheelchair rugby appear in?	____	________
3 What other wheelchair sports are there?	____	________
4 When was wheelchair rugby invented?	____	________
5 What is the official wheelchair rugby organization?	____	________
6 Where does Laura have a bandage?	____	________
7 How many players are on a wheelchair rugby team?	____	________

B Read the paragraphs and answer the questions.

4 Did you know anything about wheelchair rugby before you read the article? Would you like to watch a match?

5 Find the highlighted words in the text.

1 Which words come before nouns?
2 Which words come at the start of a sentence?

Text builder giving examples

Listing examples:
I'd like to visit countries in south-east Asia, ***like*** *Thailand and Vietnam.*
You shouldn't eat unhealthy food, ***such as*** *pizzas or hamburgers.*

Giving an example phrase:
She's had problems at work. ***For example,*** *she arrived late every day last week.*

Look! We can also use ***for instance*** instead of *for example* with no change in meaning:
She's had problems at work. ***For instance****, she arrived late every day last week.*

6 Read the Text builder. Complete the sentences with your own ideas. Compare your sentences in pairs.

1 Cheating has become very common in some sports. For example, ...
2 My country has produced some famous sportspeople, like ...
3 Some sports can be quite dangerous, such as ...

7 **A** In pairs, choose an interesting sport. Prepare a short talk about it. Use the ideas in the boxes.

where it is played | the rules | how popular it is | famous players | how it feels to play | media interest

B Tell another pair about your sport. Would you like to try this sport?

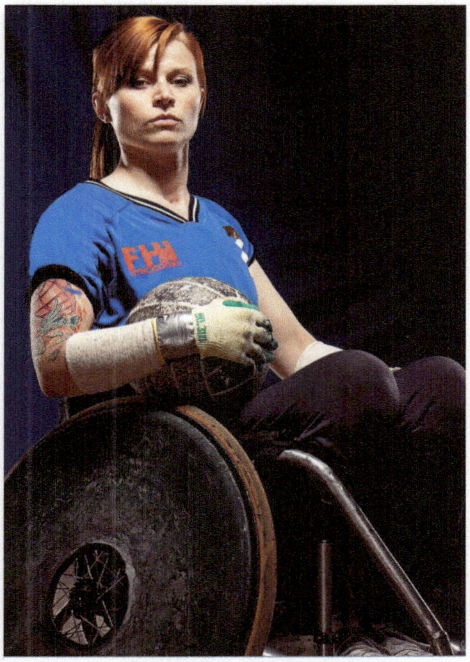

Sports interview:

Tim White meets wheelchair rugby player, Laura Sabetta

A
The first thing I notice about Laura Sabetta is her arms. They're almost as big as my legs. The next thing I notice is a bandage on her arm. 'I often get injuries because we play to win,' the Argentinian athlete explains, '… it's rugby, after all.'

B
Wheelchair rugby has always been a tough, physical sport. Invented in Canada in 1977, it was first called 'Murderball'. As the sport's popularity grew, the name changed to the more serious 'wheelchair rugby'. It was a new name, but the game was just as violent.

C
People who have never played the sport might think of it as a fun way to spend an afternoon, but it's exhausting. Laura gives me a special wheelchair and I move slowly onto the court. I wear gloves, but it's very hard work pushing the chair using only my arms. Wheelchair rugby is played on a basketball court, which measures 28 x 15 metres, and it takes me over three minutes to cross it. Meanwhile, Laura has already finished warming up.

D
I'm soon happy to join the spectators and watch the match. Wheelchair rugby is a mix of basketball, rugby and ice hockey. Two teams of four players throw and carry a volleyball, trying to score goals. Players score when their wheels cross the line at the end of the court while holding the ball in their hands.

E
Wheelchair rugby's popularity exploded after it featured in the 2005 movie *Murderball*. Many of its players are now big names in Paralympic sports, like the movie's star, Mark Zupan. The sport is now played in more than 25 countries, such as Japan and the USA. So, however you look at it, wheelchair rugby is big news.

10
AUSTRALIA
6

F
This places lots of responsibility on the players, as Laura explains. 'There are lots of sports opportunities out there for people who need a wheelchair, such as skiing, tennis and sailing. The important thing is making sure people know about them so they can take part. We also need fans. We want big crowds watching the game. That's why I'm doing this interview!'

G
Getting involved is easy. There's plenty of information online. For example, there's the website of the International Wheelchair Rugby Federation at www.iwrf.com. It's also quite easy to find a match in most large towns if you just want to watch. Many people only watch the sport once every four years at the Paralympic Games, but as Laura tells me, 'For people like me, this isn't a hobby. Since I lost the use of my legs, it's been my life.'

Personal Best Write five more questions about the wheelchair rugby interview.

10C He said it had changed his life

1 Match the words in the box with the parts of the body.

chest	knee	shoulder	elbow	neck	wrist

1 ________ 3 ________ 5 ________
2 ________ 4 ________ 6 ________

Personal Best

Go to Vocabulary practice: parts of the body, page 153

1
2
3
4
5
6
HIGH-INTENSITY TRAINING
GET FIT WITH THREE MINUTES OF EXERCISE PER WEEK

2 **A** Look at the poster. Discuss the questions in pairs.

1 How much exercise do doctors recommend you do each week?
2 Is it possible to get fit doing three minutes of exercise per week?
3 What do you think 'high-intensity training' is?

B 10.10 Listen to an interview and check your answers.

3 Discuss the questions in pairs.

1 How much exercise do you do per week? What do you do?
2 Do you believe that high-intensity training works? Why/Why not?
3 Would you like to try high-intensity training? Why/Why not?

4 **A** 10.10 Complete the sentences about what Carlos and Vicky said. Listen again and check.

1 Carlos said that in HIT you used almost all your ________.
2 Carlos said two years ago he had weighed almost ________ kg.
3 Carlos said he was eating more ________ and ________ now.
4 Carlos said that he had lost ________ kg.
5 Carlos told Vicky that first she would do some gentle cycling to ________.
6 Vicky told Carlos she was going to try ________ seconds of high-intensity cycling.

B Look at the sentences 1–6 again and answer the questions.

1 Which two verbs do we use to report what someone says in the past? ________ ________
2 Which verb do we use when we say who the person is talking to? ________
3 Is it always necessary to use *that* with these verbs? *Yes / No*

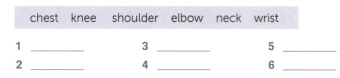

5 **A** 10.11 Listen carefully to what Carlos and Vicky said. Write the verbs they used.

1 In HIT, you ________ almost all your muscles.
2 Well, two years ago I ________ almost 100 kg.
3 Oh, and I ________ more fruit and vegetables now.
4 Of course – 75 kg. I ________ 25 kg.
5 OK, so first you ________ some gentle cycling to warm up.
6 Thanks, Carlos. Well, I ________ 20 seconds of high-intensity cycling now.

B Compare the verbs in exercise 5A with the verbs in exercise 4A. How have they changed? Then read the Grammar box.

1 present simple → *past simple*
2 past simple → ________
3 present continuous → ________
4 present perfect → ________
5 *will* → ________
6 *am/are/is going to* → ________

Grammar reported speech

Direct speech:	Reported speech:
*'I **play** tennis.'*	*She said (that) she **played** tennis.*
*'Vicky **tried** HIT.'*	*He said (that) Vicky **had tried** HIT.*
*'It's **raining**.'*	*They said (that) it **was raining**.*
*'She **hasn't arrived** yet.'*	*You said (that) she **hadn't arrived** yet.*
*'I'**ll help** you.'*	*You said (that) you **would help** me.*
*'We'**re going to call** you.'*	*They said (that) they **were going to call** me.*
*'Ravi **can't come** to work.'*	*She said (that) Ravi **couldn't come** to work.*

Look! We use ***told*** to say who the person talked to: *She **told me** (that) she played tennis.*

Personal Best

Go to Grammar practice: reported speech, page 131

6 10.13 Match the sentences in the box with the people. Listen and check.

I go to the gym to meet my friends. I'll tell my husband because he needs to lose weight.
I can't do HIT at my age! I've tried it, but I hurt my shoulder.

Rosa
Kurt
Barry
Jamila

7 10.14 **Pronunciation:** weak form of *that* Listen to the sentences. Underline the stressed words. How do we pronounce *that*? Listen again, check and repeat.

1 Carlos said that HIT was very popular.
2 He told me that I should ask some other people what they think.

8 A Complete the sentences using the information from exercise 6.

1 Rosa said that ______________________.
2 Kurt told Vicky that ______________________.
3 Barry told her that ______________________.
4 Jamila said that ______________________.

B 10.15 In pairs, practise saying sentences 1–4. Pay attention to the pronunciation of *that*. Listen, check and repeat.

9 In pairs, ask and answer the question *What did … say?* Use reported speech to answer the questions.

A *What did José say?* **B** *He said that he …*

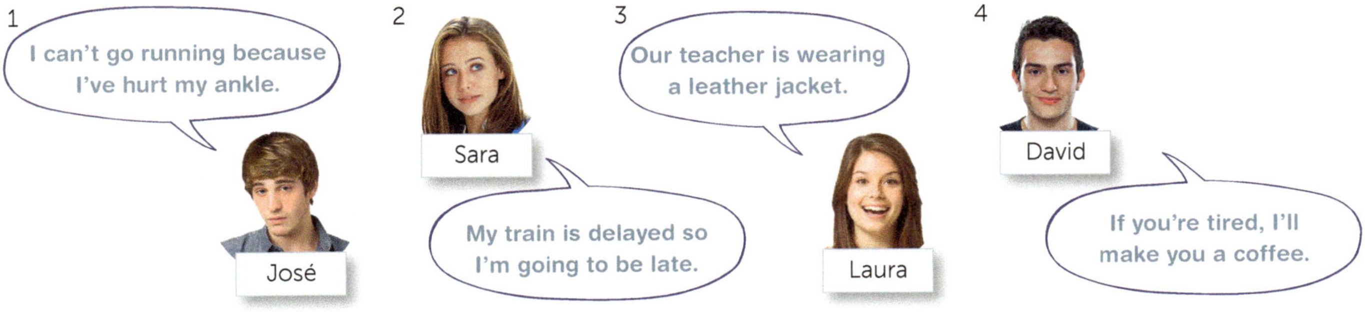
1
I can't go running because I've hurt my ankle.
José
2
Sara
My train is delayed so I'm going to be late.
3
Our teacher is wearing a leather jacket.
Laura
4
David
If you're tired, I'll make you a coffee.

Go to Communication practice: Student A page 164, Student B page 172

10 A In pairs, ask and answer the questions. Make notes of your partner's answers.

1 Have you ever run a long distance?
2 What was the first film you saw at the cinema?
3 What are you going to do this weekend?
4 Can you play any unusual sports?
5 What series are you watching on TV at the moment?
6 What are you doing after the lesson today?

B Work with another student. Report what your first partner said about questions 1–6.

Personal Best Think of a news story or an interview with a sportsperson. Write what the person said.

Learning Curve

10D Could you tell me ...?

1 Discuss the questions in pairs.

1 What are the best ways to keep fit?
2 Have you ever thought about joining a gym?
3 What would be important for you if you joined a gym?
4 Look at the webpage. Would you join this gym? Why/Why not?

2 ▶ 10.16 Watch or listen to the first part of *Learning Curve*. Why does Marc want to join the gym?

3 ▶ 10.16 Watch or listen again and complete the webpage with the correct information.

OUR CENTERS | GYM FACILITIES | SWIMMING POOL | FITNESS CLASSES | MEMBERSHIP | TIMETABLE

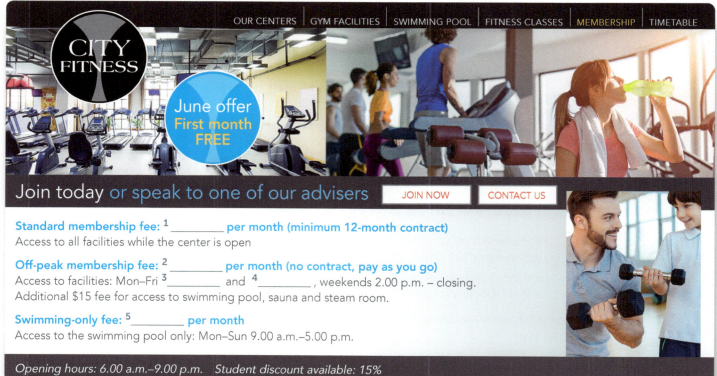

CITY FITNESS
June offer
First month FREE

Join today or speak to one of our advisers   JOIN NOW   CONTACT US

Standard membership fee: [1] ________ **per month (minimum 12-month contract)**
Access to all facilities while the center is open

Off-peak membership fee: [2] ________ **per month (no contract, pay as you go)**
Access to facilities: Mon–Fri [3] ________ and [4] ________ , weekends 2.00 p.m. – closing.
Additional $15 fee for access to swimming pool, sauna and steam room.

Swimming-only fee: [5] ________ **per month**
Access to the swimming pool only: Mon–Sun 9.00 a.m.–5.00 p.m.

Opening hours: 6.00 a.m.–9.00 p.m.   Student discount available: 15%

4 ▶ 10.17 Match the halves to complete Marc's enquiries. Listen and check.

1 Could I speak to someone
2 Could you tell
3 Could you give me some
4 I'd like to ask about
5 Just one more
6 So can I double-check

a the cost, please?
b information about that?
c thing.
d off-peak membership.
e about joining the gym?
f me about the cost?

Conversation builder making enquiries

Starting enquiries politely:
Could I speak to someone about ...?
Could you give me some information about ..., please?
Excuse me, I was hoping you could help me.

Asking for additional information:
I'd also like to ask about ...
I was told ... Is that true?
Just one more thing. Do you ...?
Can I double-check? Do you ...?

5 Read the Conversation builder. Choose three subjects in the boxes. In pairs, make enquiries about City Fitness. Use the information on the webpage to answer.

student discount | June offer | opening hours | how to join | swimming-only membership

6 A 10.18 Watch or listen to the second part of the show. Does Marc decide to join the gym?

B 10.18 Are the sentences true (T) or false (F)? Watch or listen again and check.

1. Marc thought Taylor worked at a different centre. ____
2. Taylor likes this centre because it's small. ____
3. The receptionist told Marc about all the facilities. ____
4. Taylor offers Marc a free training session as a special offer. ____
5. Marc wants to start training slowly. ____

7 10.19 Listen and repeat the receptionist and Taylor's phrases when you hear the beeps. How are they helpful to Marc?

Skill being helpful

There are different ways to be helpful in English, especially with colleagues and customers.

- Use friendly intonation to show you are happy to help.
- Make offers and suggestions: *Would you like me to ...? Shall I ...? I'll ... if you want.*
- Check the person is satisfied: *Does that sound OK? Is there anything else I can help you with?*

8 A Read the Skill box. Are phrases 1–6 answers to questions (A), offers and suggestions (O) or checking the customer is satisfied (C)?

1. The nearest one is on the corner of Sutton Street. ____
2. Do you have any other questions? ____
3. I think it costs about $20 to the city centre. ____
4. I'll just print you a map of the area. ____
5. Would you like me to write that down for you? ____
6. Is there anything else you'd like to know? ____

B 10.20 Listen and repeat phrases 1–6. Pay attention to the intonation.

Go to Communication practice: Student A page 164, Student B page 172

9 Discuss the questions in pairs.

1. Have you ever worked with customers or the public? What did you do?
2. What's the most difficult thing about working with customers or the public?
3. Have you ever had a bad experience with customer service? What happened?
4. Can you think of a good experience with customer service? What happened?

10 A PREPARE Choose one of the situations. Use the phrases and your own ideas to prepare questions.

Travel agent

Holidays in the USA
Best city to visit
Cost of flights

Pharmacist

Medicine for the flu
How often to take it
Other advice to feel better

Sports shop assistant

Running shoes
Best type for long distance
Colours and sizes

B PRACTISE In pairs, make enquiries using your questions. Your partner should try to answer your questions and be as helpful as possible.

C PERSONAL BEST Were you a satisfied customer? What could your partner do differently to be more helpful? Choose another situation and make more enquiries.

Personal Best Write down five questions you could ask in a restaurant.

Grammar

1 Cross (**X**) the sentence which is NOT correct.

1 **a** I used to have a bike, but then I sold it. ☐
b I had a bike, but then I sold it. ☐
c I used to have a bike, but then I used to sell it. ☐

2 **a** Cervantes wrote Don Quixote. ☐
b Don Quixote was written by Cervantes. ☐
c Cervantes was written Don Quixote. ☐

3 **a** He'd gone home because he'd forgotten his wallet. ☐
b He went home because he'd forgotten his wallet. ☐
c He'd forgotten his wallet, so he went home. ☐

4 **a** Emma said, 'I'll be on time.' ☐
b Emma told me she would be on time. ☐
c Emma said me she would be on time. ☐

5 **a** She didn't used to do much exercise. ☐
b She didn't do much exercise. ☐
c She didn't use to do much exercise. ☐

6 **a** The radio was invented by Marconi. ☐
b The radio is invented by Marconi. ☐
c Marconi invented the radio. ☐

7 **a** He was late because he had missed the bus. ☐
b He missed the bus, so he was late. ☐
c He had been late so he had missed the bus. ☐

8 **a** Pete said he was seeing the film before. ☐
b Pete said he had seen the film before. ☐
c Pete said, 'I've seen the film before.' ☐

2 Use the words in brackets to write sentences that mean the same as the first sentence.

1 Someone stole my car last week.
My car ________ someone last week. (stolen)

2 Neil said, 'I haven't been to Greece.'
Neil said that ________ to Greece. (been)

3 When I was young I played the piano.
I ________ the piano. (used)

4 They make Vespas in Italy.
Vespas ________ in Italy. (are)

5 We ate our soup. Then he brought the drinks.
When he brought the drinks, we ________ our soup. (had)

6 Kelly said, 'I don't need any help.'
Kelly ________ any help. (me)

7 I didn't take an umbrella and I got wet.
I got wet because I ________ an umbrella. (took)

8 I wasn't a very shy child.
When I was a child, I ________ very shy. (be)

3 Complete the text with the correct form of the verbs in brackets.

HOW NOT TO LOSE YOUR PET

Fumie Takahashi, a 64-year-old woman from Japan, was very happy when the police [1] ________ (tell) her that they [2] ________ (find) her pet parakeet, Piko Chan. But what was amazing was that the bird [3] ________ (tell) the police its own address!

Mrs Takahashi [4] ________ (use / have) another parakeet, but it escaped and flew away. So, when she bought Piko Chan, she taught it to repeat her street name and house number. Last Sunday, Piko Chan escaped, too, when the door to its cage [5] ________ (leave) open. It flew to a nearby hotel and after a few hours, it [6] ________ (take) to the police station by a guest.

The police [7] ________ (say) that the bird [8] ________ (be) silent for two days and they hadn't known what to do with it. Eventually, however, Piko Chan surprised them all when it [9] ________ (tell) them where it [10] ________ (live).

If Piko Chan escapes again, it'll probably be found even more quickly. Its photo has appeared in newspapers all over Tokyo, and Mrs Takahashi recently took the bird to a press conference, where it told journalists its address again.

Vocabulary

1 Put the words in the box in the correct columns.

receipt till ankle crowd knee refund
medal queue referee cheek beat chin

the body	sports	shopping

2 Complete the conversation with the correct words.

Lena These jeans look amazing! Where is the [1]c *hanging* r*oom* ?
Peter Over there, but can you [2]a _______ to buy them? I didn't think you had much money at the moment.
Lena Probably not. I don't [3]g _______ p _______ until the end of the month. Can I [4]b _______ some money from you?
Peter You already [5]o _______ me 50 euros!
Lena I'll [6]p _______ b _______ all the money at the end of the month. I promise.
Peter OK, [7]t _______ o _______ the jeans. If they [8]f _______ you, I'll think about it.
Lena Thanks Peter! There's a 70% [9]d _______ on them today, they're a real [10]b _______.
Peter OK, Lena.

3 Circle the word that is different. Explain your answer.

1	win	draw	lose	score
2	earn	borrow	lend	pay back
3	bargain	queue	discount	the sales
4	return	exchange	deliver	refund
5	finger	thumb	chest	hand
6	medal	umpire	trophy	race
7	knee	elbow	shoulder	forehead
8	shopping centre	department store	supermarket	changing room

4 Choose the correct word to complete the sentences.

1 I _______ my parents $100.
a refund b owe c pay back

2 We _______ them 2–1.
a won b scored c beat

3 I'm not buying anything. I'm just _______ .
a spending b getting paid c window shopping

4 You can only use your _______ to move the ball.
a brain b heart c foot

5 Here's your change and here's your _______ .
a cash b refund c receipt

6 There was a _______ of 60,000 at the game today.
a spectator b crowd c athlete

7 How much do you _______ in your job?
a earn b be worth c borrow

8 You need to _______ before a match.
a cheat b give up c warm up

9 Look how long the _______ is!
a queue b till c bargain

10 The day after the marathon, my _______ were so tired!
a back b bones c muscles

11 When I was younger it was easy to touch my _______ , but now I can't.
a toes b fingers c thumb

Personal Best

Lesson 9A Name five things you can do with money.

Lesson 10A Write a sentence using the past perfect.

Lesson 9A Write two sentences about your grandparents using *used to*.

Lesson 10A Name three things you can win.

Lesson 9B Name five things you usually see in a shopping centre.

Lesson 10B Write a sentence with *for example*, and another with *such as*.

Lesson 9C Write a sentence in the present passive, and another in the past passive.

Lesson 10C Name five parts of the body that we have two of.

Lesson 9D Name five nouns ending in *-ion*.

Lesson 10D Give a phrase to start an enquiry, and another to ask for additional information.

Lesson 9D Write an expression to start a formal email, and another to end it.

Lesson 10D Give an expression to check someone is satisfied.

UNIT 11

At home

LANGUAGE *-ing*/infinitive verb patterns ■ household objects

11A Dream home

1 Look at the picture. Would you like to live somewhere like this? Why/Why not?

2 Read the text and answer the questions.

1 Where is the house?
2 Who are the people in the picture?
3 Why do they live there?

Living the dream

Have you ever imagined escaping city life and moving to a desert island? Well, meet the family who did just that.

Karyn von Engelbrechten wanted to travel the world after she became tired of her three-hour commute to London, where she worked as an IT manager. She left her job and her home and, with husband Boris and their three children, decided to start a new adventure.

They bought some land on a tiny island in the South Pacific and started to build a house with materials they found on the island. Everything was done by hand. They learned to cut down trees to make floors and doors. Electricity was generated using solar panels and rainwater was collected so the family had water in the bathrooms and kitchen. They even started growing their own fruit and vegetables.

Now the family runs their home as a guesthouse for other travellers. If you don't fancy swimming in the beautiful clear ocean, you can sit on the balcony and enjoy watching whales and turtles. The kitchen is basic, but it has most things you'd need, like a fridge-freezer and oven.

There's no air-conditioning, but the bedrooms are cool and comfortable with extra blankets and duvets in the wardrobe for the colder months. From the house, steps go down to your own private beach, or if you're feeling brave, you can explore the island.

It sounds like paradise, but there are some disadvantages. Apart from the fruit and vegetables that Karyn and Boris grow, when they need to buy food the nearest shop is a three-hour boat trip away. The island is also quite near a volcano and they often have earthquakes and tropical storms. And their eldest son, Jack, has gone to school in New Zealand because he missed being with other children his own age.

However, if you're tired of your daily routine, the message is clear – follow your dreams!

3 Which of these things does the house have? *Yes* (✓), *No* (**X**) or *Don't know* (**?**). Read the text again and check.

1 air-conditioning ☐	3 central heating ☐	5 freezer ☐	7 washing machine ☐	9 oven ☐
2 blankets ☐	4 dishwasher ☐	6 wardrobe ☐	8 duvets ☐	10 taps ☐

Personal Best

Go to Vocabulary practice: household objects, page 154

4 **A** Ask and answer the questions in pairs.

1 Do you have a fridge or fridge-freezer at home?
2 How often do you use your washing-machine?
3 How often do you use your iron? Do you like ironing?
4 Do you have a carpet or rugs at home? What colour are they?
5 Do you have a big wardrobe? Is it organized or messy?
6 Do you sleep with a sheet, a blanket or a duvet?
7 Do you have a microwave oven? How often do you use it?
8 Do you use central heating or air-conditioning at home? How often?

B Tell the class some things you found out about your partner.

5 **A** Choose the correct form of the verbs to complete the sentences. Check your answers in the text.

1 Have you ever **imagined** *to escape / escaping* city life?
2 Karyn von Engelbrechten **wanted** *to travel / travelling* the world.
3 She **decided** *to start / starting* a new adventure.
4 You can sit on the balcony and **enjoy** *to watch / watching* whales and turtles.

B Answer the questions about the verbs in **bold** in sentences 1–4.

1 Which form of the verb comes after *imagine* and *enjoy? Infinitive with to / -ing* form
2 Which form of the verb comes after *want* and *decide? Infinitive with to / -ing* form

6 **A** Find examples of the verbs in the box in the text. Put them in the correct column.

manage start learn fancy need miss

Verbs followed by *-ing*	Verbs followed by the infinitive with *to*

B Which verb can be followed by both the infinitive with *to* and the *-ing* form? ________
Now read the Grammar box.

Grammar ***-ing*/infinitive verb patterns**

Verbs followed by the *-ing* form:	*She **enjoys living** in the city.*
Verbs followed by the infinitive with *to*:	*I **want to live** in a bigger house.*

Look! Some verbs can be followed by both the infinitive and *-ing* forms:
*It's started **to rain**. = It's started **raining**.*

Personal Best

Go to Grammar practice: *-ing*/infinitive verb patterns, page 132

7 11.4 **Pronunciation:** sentence stress Listen and underline the stressed words in the sentences. How is *to* pronounced? Listen, check and repeat.

1 Karyn wanted to travel the world.
2 She enjoys watching whales and turtles.

8 **A** Complete the sentences with the correct form of the verbs in brackets.

1 She's planning ________ Science. (study)
2 My doctor suggested ________ less coffee. (drink)
3 I haven't forgotten ________ the customer. (call)
4 Do you fancy ________ tonight? (eat out)
5 We can't afford ________ on holiday. (go)
6 We should spend more time ________ together. (talk)

B 11.5 In pairs, practise saying the sentences. Pay attention to the sentence stress. Listen, check and repeat.

Go to Communication practice: page 174

9 **A** Complete the questions with the correct form of the verbs in brackets.

1 Imagine ________ (design) your dream house. What would you want it ________ (be) like?
2 Do you expect ________ (work) in the same job all your life? Are you planning ________ (change) jobs soon? What do you hope ________ (do) in the future?
3 Do you enjoy ________ (travel)? Have you arranged ________ (go) anywhere soon?
4 Do you like ________ (live) in your house? What would you like ________ (change) about it?
5 Would you like ________ (live) abroad in the future? Where do you fancy ________ (live)?
6 At what age do you think you will stop ________ (work)? What will you spend your time ________ (do) when you retire? Do you think you will miss ________ (work)?

B Ask and answer the questions in pairs.

Personal Best Write a description of a room in your house including all the things inside it.

Learning Curve

11B The truth about housework

1 Look at the picture. Have you ever seen a kitchen like this? If so, where?

2 Complete the man's list of jobs with the words in the box.

do (x3) clear take out load mop water

1	________ the washing up	3	________ the ironing	5	________ the table	7	________ the rubbish
2	________ the dishwasher	4	________ the washing	6	________ the plants	8	________ the floor

Personal Best

Go to Vocabulary practice: housework, page 155

3 Complete the table about you. In pairs, compare your tables and explain your answers.

Housework I hate doing	Housework I don't mind doing	Housework I enjoy doing

4 A 11.7 In pairs, decide if the sentences are true (T) or false (F). Watch or listen to the first part of *Learning Curve* and check.

1 It's a fact that everyone hates doing housework. ____
2 The majority of us usually prefer to do other activities in our free time. ____
3 Today, robots that can do the housework for us really exist. ____
4 Robots will never have arms and legs. ____
5 In Japan, there's a robot which can pick up heavy things. ____

B 11.7 Watch or listen again. Write down the key words that Simon or Kate use that helped you check the answers.

Skill understanding and interpreting information

It's helpful to notice key words and phrases before you listen.

- Look at the questions and underline any key words or phrases.
- Think about other words or phrases that speakers could use to give this information.
- As you listen, pay attention to all the words and phrases you have noticed or thought of.

5 **A** Look at the underlined key words in questions 1 and 2 and think about what words and phrases Julie might use. Underline the key words in questions 3–6.

B 11.8 Watch or listen to the second part of the show. Choose the correct options.

1 What does Julie prefer doing at the weekends?
  a She prefers spending time with her children.
  b She prefers going shopping.
  c She prefers doing housework.
2 Why does she want her children to do housework?
  a She has too much work.
  b So they learn to do things on their own.
  c Because it's healthier than videogames.
3 Why did Axel buy a cleaning robot?
  a He wants more time for himself.
  b The salesman offered him a good price.
  c He has injured his back.
4 What does he say about his dishwasher?
  a It's broken.
  b He prefers doing the washing by hand.
  c It works very well.
5 Why does Roberta buy the 'Mop It' robot?
  a It's better at cleaning than she is.
  b Her friend has one.
  c There was a discount.
6 How does housework help her?
  a It's a way to do exercise.
  b It helps her to relax.
  c She saves money.

Julie

Axel

Roberta

6 Discuss the questions in pairs.

1 Do you share the housework equally at home?
2 Who does the most housework? Why?
3 Did you do housework when you were a child?
4 Do you think doing housework is good for you?

7 11.9 Read and listen to the phrases from the programme. Which words are missing? Why didn't the speakers use them?

1 Just doing a bit of dusting in the studio.
2 Kate, anyone there with an opinion?
3 Makes the floor look good.
4 It does a better job than I can. So exciting!

Listening builder omission of words

Speakers sometimes don't say all the words in a sentence because they think the meaning is obvious without them, or because they don't want to repeat words or phrases.

Pronouns: *No, (I) don't really like cleaning.*
Articles: *(The) Dishwasher's broken.*
***be* and auxiliary verbs:** *(It's) Time for spring cleaning.*
There is/are: *(Is there) Anyone there with an opinion?*
Avoid repeating words: *It does a better job than I can (do).*
Phrases: *Anyway, (let's go) back to Kate.*

8 **A** 11.10 Read the Listening builder. Read and listen to the conversation. Which words are missing?

Karim Hi, Maya. 1 ________ You there?
Maya 2 ________ In the living room. 3 ________ Just clearing the table.
Karim 4 ________ Coffee's ready. 5 ________ Want some?
Maya No, thanks. 6 ________ Already had three 7 ________ today.

B 11.11 Listen and check.

9 In pairs, discuss the statement: 'People only notice housework when it isn't done.'

Personal Best Write a short conversation about housework where the speakers omit words.

11C Technology you can wear

1 Discuss the questions in pairs.

1 Do you find it difficult to decide what to wear each day?
2 How often do you buy new clothes?
3 What are your favourite clothes in your wardrobe?

2 Label the picture with the materials in the box.

cotton leather wood denim wool metal

1 ______
2 ______
3 ______
4 ______
5 ______
6 ______

Personal Best

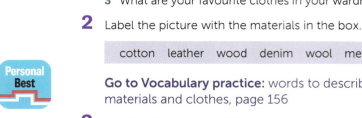

Go to Vocabulary practice: words to describe materials and clothes, page 156

3 In pairs, describe the different types of clothes.

what you're wearing now | what you wear at the weekend | what you'd wear at a wedding | what you'd wear to a party | what you'd wear to a job interview | what you'd wear on a first date

4 Look at pictures a–c. What do they show? Read the text and match them with descriptions 1–3.

WEARABLE TECHNOLOGY

a
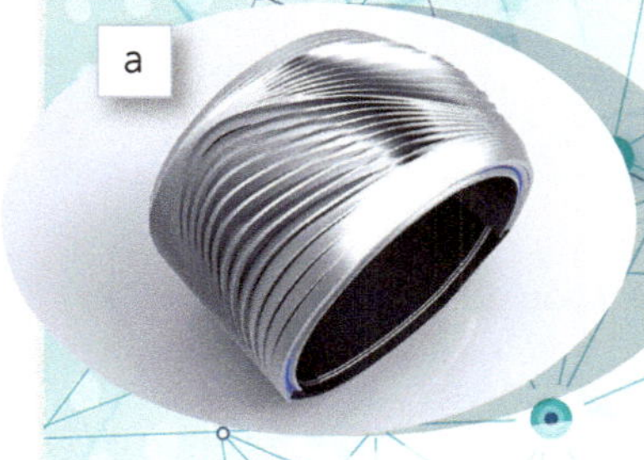

b

c

Our houses are full of technology, but how much do we have in our wardrobes? You might think you don't have any, but get ready for that to change. Experts predict that the amount of money we spend on wearable technology will reach $74 billion a year by 2025. You're probably already familiar with smart watches and fitness bracelets, but what are some of the other things coming our way?

1 MATERIAL THAT CAN COMMUNICATE

In the USA, Google and Levi's® are developing a new kind of material that is touch-sensitive, like the screen on a smart phone. The material is made by mixing thin metal wires with cotton, denim or silk. Designers can then use this material to create interactive areas on clothes and furniture. Soon people will be able to control machines just by touching their trouser legs!

2 ACCESSORIES THAT CONTROL YOUR TEMPERATURE

Have you ever been in a place where half the people are complaining about the cold, and the other half are too hot? The solution is *Wristify*, a bracelet which can heat or cool your skin at the touch of a button. It's perfect for a trip to the gym, a day at the beach, or for keeping you warm at home, so the bracelet could also save you money on energy bills. The design isn't finished yet, but here's what the final product might look like.

3 CLOTHES THAT CHARGE YOUR PHONE

Pauline van Dongen is an exciting new designer who specializes in wearable technology, and uses both traditional and new materials to create amazing clothes. Her stylish T-shirts and jackets have solar panels, which can charge a mobile phone in just a few hours ... when the sun is shining, of course.

5 Discuss the questions in pairs.

1 Which idea do you think is the most useful? Why?
2 Would you buy any of these inventions? Why/Why not?
3 Can you think of other types of wearable technology?

6 Complete the sentences with the articles *a*, *an*, *the* or – (no article). Check your answers in the text.

1 The amount of money we spend on wearable technology will reach $74 billion ____ year.
2 People will be able to control ____ machines just by touching their trouser legs!
3 The solution is *Wristify*, ____ bracelet which can heat or cool your skin.
4 Perfect for a trip to ____ gym...
5 ... or for keeping you warm at ____ home.
6 ____ bracelet could also save you money on energy bills.
7 Pauline van Dongen is ____ exciting new designer.
8 ... when ____ sun is shining, of course.

7 Match sentences 1–8 in exercise 6 with rules a–h. Then read the Grammar box.

a We use *a*/*an* to talk about a person or thing for the first time. ____
b We use *the* when we have already mentioned the person or thing before. ____
c We don't use an article to talk about things in general (plural or uncountable nouns). ____
d We use *a*/*an* to talk about a person's job. ____
e We use *a*/*an* in some measurement expressions. ____
f We use *the* if there is only one of the thing. ____
g We use *the* with specific places in a town. ____
h We don't use an article with some places we go to regularly. ____

Grammar articles

a/*an*	*the*	No article
*I live in **a** tall block of flats.*	*I live in a modern flat. **The** flat is in ...*	*They're interested in sports cars.*
*Eric is **an** architect.*	*The address is on **the** internet.*	*I got to work at about 9.00.*
*We go on holiday twice **a** year.*	*I'll meet you in **the** park.*	

Personal Best

Go to Grammar practice: articles, page 133

8 A 11.15 **Pronunciation:** *the* Listen and repeat the phrases. Match the words in **bold** with the sounds /ðə/ and /ðiː/. Why does the pronunciation change?

1 **the** amount of money we spend on technology ____ 2 **the** screen on a smartphone ____

B 11.16 Practise saying the words in pairs. Pay attention to the pronunciation of *the*. Listen, check and repeat.

the solution the answer the office the USA the internet the sun the hour the gym

Go to Communication practice: Student A page 165, Student B page 173

9 11.17 Complete the text with *a*, *an*, *the* or – (no article). Listen and check.

A BRIGHT IDEA

Christina Mercando is [1]____ businesswoman and [2]____ inventor. She started [3]____ company in [4]____ USA called Ringly. Her first product is [5]____ ring that connects to your smartphone. When [6]____ phone receives [7]____ text or email, [8]____ ring lights up. [9]____ idea came to Christina when she was having [10]____ dinner with friends. She didn't want to miss any important calls on her phone, but she didn't want to put her phone on [11]____ dinner table. It's [12]____ common problem for [13]____ women who keep [14]____ phones in their handbags or purses, where they may not hear them. [15]____ rings are made in China, and Christina has calls with the factory once [16]____ week. It's [17]____ exciting time for Christina and [18]____ future is definitely bright!

10 In pairs, take turns to talk about these things. Remember to use the correct articles.

types of food and drink you hate
a machine that you couldn't live without
the places you went to yesterday
what you have in your bedroom
some clothes you want to buy but can't afford
how often you charge your mobile phone

Personal Best Think of an idea for another piece of wearable technology. Write about how it could work.

11D House swap

1 Discuss the questions in pairs.

1 Have you ever done a house swap or stayed in someone else's house on holiday?
2 What are the advantages and disadvantages of a house swap?
3 How would you feel about letting strangers stay in your home?

2 Describe the pictures. Which home would you prefer to stay in? Why?

a

b

3 Read the description on a house swap website. Which home from exercise 2 does it describe?

Homes away from home | Two-bedroom flat in central London, United Kingdom

About our home

Our home is an attractive two-bedroom flat, right in the centre of London. It's a 20-minute walk from the London Eye, where you can see amazing views of the River Thames and the city.

The main bedroom has its own bathroom and a double bed with plain white cotton sheets. Although the second bedroom is slightly smaller, it's bright and has two comfortable single beds. There's a fashionable leather sofa and two large armchairs in the modern living room. The spacious up-to-date kitchen includes everything you'll need, with an electric oven, fridge-freezer, dishwasher and a new Italian coffee machine. Glass doors open from the kitchen onto a gorgeous sunny balcony, where you can have a relaxing breakfast.

The flat is on a peaceful street, but it's just a few minutes away from shops, cafés and some excellent restaurants. The underground station is also close by, so this is an ideal place if you want to explore all of London's attractions.

7 reviews
★★★★
2 bedrooms
Sleeps 4
2 bathrooms

4 A Read the text again. Find words which mean the same as adjectives 1–6.

1 big ________ ________
2 beautiful ________ ________
3 quiet ________ ________
4 very good ________ ________
5 light ________ ________
6 modern ________ ________

B How does the writer make the text interesting? Read the Skill box.

Skill making writing interesting

We can use different techniques to make our writing more interesting.

- Use a variety of adjectives to describe things: *a* ***gorgeous***, ***sunny*** *balcony*
- Use synonyms to avoid repeating words: *two* ***large*** *armchairs, the* ***spacious*** *kitchen*
- Use linkers to give reasons and results (*so, because, that's why*), to contrast information (*but, although, however*) or add information (*and, also, too, as well*).
- When you describe a place, use *where* and an example of what you can do: *a balcony, where you can have a relaxing breakfast*

5 In pairs, rewrite the sentences to make them more interesting.

1 The house is very pretty. It has a pretty garden.
The house is very pretty and it has a gorgeous garden.

2 The flat is quite small. It's a good place to stay. It's in the centre of the city centre.
____

3 There's an old living room. It has an old fireplace. You can keep warm in the winter.
____

4 The building has a quiet roof terrace. You can enjoy nice views of the countryside.
____

5 If the weather is nice, you can sit in the big garden.
____

6 Complete the phrases with the adjectives in brackets in the correct order. Check your answers in the text.

1 an ______ ______ flat (two-bedroom, attractive)
2 ______ ______ ______ sheets (cotton, plain, white)
3 a ______ ______ sofa (fashionable, leather)
4 a ______ ______ coffee machine (Italian, new)

Text builder adjective order

When we use more than one adjective to describe a noun, they go in a specific order:
opinion size shape age colour nationality material (noun)
She has long blond hair. NOT ~~*She has blond long hair.*~~
It's an interesting Chinese painting. NOT ~~*It's a Chinese interesting painting.*~~

7 Read the Text builder. Put the words in the box in the correct columns.

blue Dutch glass green large leather Mexican old
round small square stylish unusual young

opinion	size	shape	age	colour	nationality	material

8 Complete the sentences with the adjectives in brackets in the correct order.

1 We live in a ______ ______ ______ house in the country. (stone, beautiful, old)
2 It's got ______ ______ floors, and is warm and cosy. (wooden, attractive)
3 There's a ______ ______ ______ rug on the floor. (square, wool, large)
4 You can relax on one of our ______ ______ ______ armchairs. (leather, old, comfortable)
5 Outside, there's a ______ ______ garden. (long, beautiful)
6 Near the house, there's a ______ ______ restaurant. (Indian, fantastic)

9 Write descriptions of three items you own, using as many adjectives as possible. Compare with a partner.

I have a beautiful old brown leather armchair.

10 **A** **PREPARE** Plan a description of your home for a house-swap website. Write notes for three paragraphs:

Paragraph 1: the type of home it is and where it is
Paragraph 2: description of the rooms and what is in the rooms
Paragraph 3: description of the local area and what is nearby

B **PRACTISE** Write your description. Remember to make your writing interesting and order adjectives correctly.

C **PERSONAL BEST** Swap your text with a partner. After reading the description, would you like to stay there? How could he/she make the description more interesting?

Personal Best Write a short description of a place you know well, such as where you work or study, a restaurant or a shop.

UNIT 12

People and relationships

LANGUAGE defining relative clauses ■ relationships

12A Bring your parents to work

1 Match the words in the box with the definitions.

colleague	neighbour	parents-in-law	boss
flatmate	employee	business partner	relative

1 someone who manages you at work ______
2 your husband's/wife's mother and father ______
3 someone who works for you ______
4 someone in your family ______
5 someone who works with you ______
6 someone who lives near you ______
7 someone who shares a flat with you ______
8 someone who owns a company with you ______

Personal Best

Go to Vocabulary practice: relationships, page 157

2 Choose three of the relationships from exercise 1 and write down the names of people you know. Tell your partner about them.

3 Read the text and answer the questions.

1 Which company introduced the idea of a *Bring Your Parents To Work Day?*
2 How many people in the USA take part in the *Take Your Child To Work Day?*
3 What does the company say the benefits of the day are?
4 How many companies now have a similar day?
5 What does Martin Richards' daughter do at work?

Would you bring your parents to work?

How would you feel about bringing your mum or dad into work with you? Would you be worried about the things that they might say to your boss? Or nervous that they might start showing embarrassing photos of you as a child to the colleague who sits next to you? Well, get ready for *Bring Your Parents To Work Day*, an event which is already becoming popular in some American companies and which could be coming your way soon!

The company where it all started, LinkedIn, realized that there are a lot of parents who don't understand what their children's jobs involve. There is already a national *Take Your Child To Work Day* for workers who want to take their sons and daughters to their places of work, and more than 37 million Americans take part every year. So why not do the same thing for parents? LinkedIn's argument is that employees who are supported by their family are happier and more productive. Now, there are more than 80 companies in 18 countries that organize an annual event for parents to get to know how their kids spend their time at work.

So what do the parents think of it? Martin Richards has just spent a day at the office where his daughter and son-in-law work. 'For me, it was a great opportunity to see how digital marketing works, to meet some of Imogen's co-workers, and – best of all – to spend a day with my eldest daughter!'

4 Discuss the questions in pairs.

1 As a child, did you ever visit the place where your parents worked? Was it a useful experience?
2 How would you feel if you brought your parents to your work? Why?
3 Do you think people's jobs have changed a lot in the last thirty years? If so, how?

5 A Complete the sentences with *who*, *which* and *where*. Check your answers in the text.

1 Get ready for *Bring Your Parents To Work Day*, an event _________ is already becoming popular in some American companies.
2 There is already a national *Take Your Child To Work Day* for workers _________ want to take their sons and daughters to their places of work.
3 Martin Richards has just spent a day at the office _________ his daughter and son-in-law work.

B Look at sentences 1–3 and answer the questions. Then read the Grammar box.

1 Which word do we use to give information about: people? _________ things? _________ places? _________
2 In which sentences can we use *that* instead? ____ ____

Grammar **defining relative clauses**

To give information about people:	*I'm going to see my cousin* ***who*** *lives in Greece.* *All the employees* ***that*** *work in Sales have a meeting.*
To give information about things:	*The company sells machines* ***which*** *are made in Japan.* *It looks like the shirt* ***that*** *my flatmate bought last week.*
To give information about places:	*That's the restaurant* ***where*** *my brother-in-law works.*

Personal Best

Go to Grammar practice: defining relative clauses, page 134

6 A 12.3 **Pronunciation:** sentence stress Listen to the sentences and underline the stressed words. When do we stress *who*?

1 Who do you live with?
2 The man who works in the bank.

B 12.4 Match the halves to make sentences. Listen, check and repeat. Pay attention to the sentence stress.

1 A remote control is something which
2 A flight attendant is someone who
3 A nursery is a place where

a young children go.
b you use to turn on the TV.
c works on a plane.

7 A Write definitions with *who*, *which* or *where*.

1 something / use to see small things
____
2 a place / buy newspapers and magazines
____
3 someone / collects the rubbish
____
4 an animal / very slow and lives in trees
____
5 a person / plays an instrument in the street
____
6 a building / horses sleep and eat
____

a
b
c
d
e
f
NEWS

B In pairs, match definitions 1–6 with pictures a–f. Do you know the names of these things in English?

Go to Communication practice: Student A page 165, Student B page 173

8 Complete the sentences so that they are true for you. Compare your sentences in pairs.

1 I like going on holiday to places where ...
2 Most of my friends are people who ...
3 I like TV programmes that ...
4 I wouldn't want to live in an area where ...
5 The worst kind of boss is someone who ...
6 I don't like food which ...

Personal Best Write about a friend, a relative or a colleague. Use relative clauses to describe him/her.

12B In our lifetime

1 In pairs, write down five activities that take up most time in a typical day.
sleeping, working ...

2 Look at Figure 1 on page 105. Answer the questions.

1 What are the top five activities in the pie chart?
2 Are they similar to your list in exercise 1?
3 What information does the pie chart show?
4 Does anything surprise you?

Skill interpreting data

Many texts include graphs and charts to show information more clearly.

- Read any words on the graphs like the title, the key and the horizontal and vertical axes.
- Look at the data and think about the information it shows.
- When you read a paragraph, look at the graph or chart it describes again and see how the words relate to the data.
- Use information in the text and the graphs and charts to answer the questions.

3 **A** Read the Skill box. Look at Figures 2 and 3. What do they show?

B Choose the correct options to complete the information about Figures 2 and 3.

1 We spend *more* / *less* time at work than in the past.
2 Over the last twenty years, there *has* / *hasn't* been a big change.
3 The total time spent on housework by men and women has *decreased* / *increased*.
4 Men do *more* / *less* housework now than in 1965.

4 Read the text and look at Figures 1–3. Tick (✓) the best summary of the text.

1 We have a lot more time to spend with friends and family than in the past. ☐
2 We worked more in the past, but we were happier. ☐
3 We have very busy lives and not much time to do the important things. ☐

5 Read the text and look at Figures 1–3 again. Are the sentences true (T) or false (F)?

1 On average, people live to be 76 years old. ____
2 In 1900, people worked 60 hours a week. ____
3 We spend about a third of our lives sleeping. ____
4 We spend two and a half years in the shower. ____
5 People who work in big cities spend less than a year in their cars. ____
6 We spend a lot of free time using technology. ____

6 Do you think the information is correct for people in your country? Why/Why not? Discuss in pairs.

Text builder expressing approximate quantities

Approximately:	*In a typical lifetime, we spend* ***around*** *91,000 hours at work.*
	People sleep for ***about*** *eight hours a day.*
	That means we spend ***roughly*** *three and a half years of our lives studying.*
More than:	*... just* ***over*** *two years to spend with family and friends.*
The same/more:	*You can say goodbye to* ***at least*** *another year of your life.*
Less than:	*... which is* ***nearly*** *ten and a half years.* *We spend* ***almost*** *four years using our phones.*

7 Read the Text builder. Write sentences about how much time you spend doing the activities in the boxes. Use words to express approximate quantities.

sleeping | working | studying | watching TV | going on social media | driving/travelling | talking on the phone | doing exercise | eating and drinking

Where does the time go?

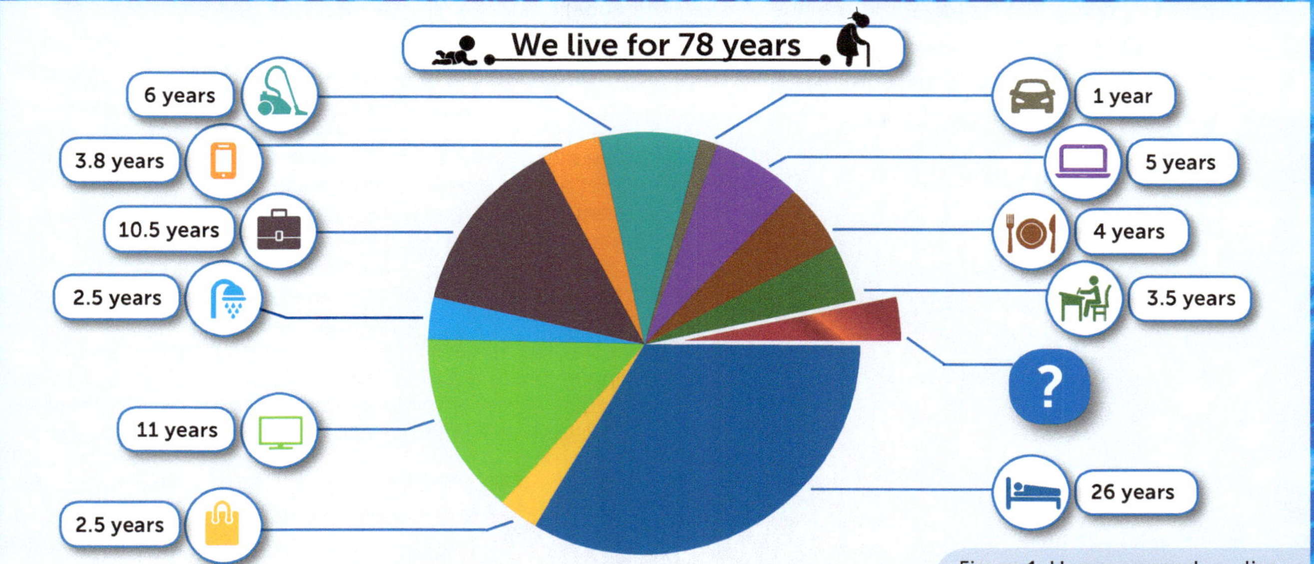
We live for 78 years
6 years
3.8 years
10.5 years
2.5 years
11 years
2.5 years
1 year
5 years
4 years
3.5 years
?
26 years
Figure 1 How we spend our lives

We have more free time than ever before. In many countries, the average working week is now under 40 hours, far shorter than it was for our parents and grandparents before us. So why do our lives feel so busy, and where does our time go?

Figure 2

Time spent at work (hours per week)
65
60
55
50
45
40
35
30
1900
1925
1950
1975
2000
2015

People sleep for about eight hours a day, which means we spend 26 years in our beds over an average lifetime of 78 years. We spend another eleven years watching TV and, depending on where you live, two years of that can be spent just watching the adverts!

In a typical lifetime, we spend around 91,000 hours at work, which is nearly ten and a half years. And do you drive to work? If so, you can say goodbye to at least another year of your life – even more if you work in a big city like Istanbul or Rio de Janeiro and have to sit in traffic jams every day.

In many countries, the law requires young people to stay in education until they're at least 16 years old. Many carry on to further education at university or college. That means we spend on average 31,000 hours – roughly three and a half years of our lives – studying. Two and a half years of our lives are spent in the bathroom – brushing our teeth, using the toilet, having a shower and getting ready to go out. Shopping uses up another two and a half years and we spend at least another four years eating.

The introduction of modern appliances, such as dishwashers, washing machines and microwaves, means that, overall, we spend less time on cooking and cleaning than our parents did. Women still do most of the housework, but men are sharing domestic tasks more than they used to.

Figure 3

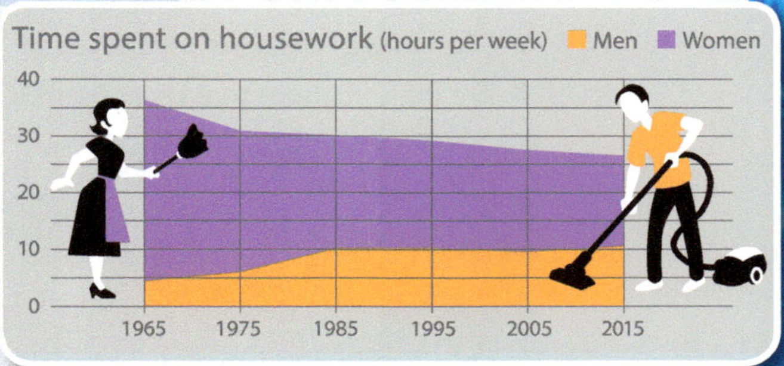
Time spent on housework (hours per week)
Men
Women
40
30
20
10
0
1965
1975
1985
1995
2005
2015

In recent years, the big change in how we spend our time is technology. We spend an average of five years online and almost four years using our phones, and those numbers are growing every year. If you add up all that time, it leaves you with just over two years on average to spend with family and friends, to see the world and to achieve your dreams. So, what are you waiting for? The clock is ticking!

Personal Best Make a pie chart and write about how you spend your time at the weekend.

12C Long-distance love

1 Look at the pictures and the title. Answer the questions in pairs. Then read the text and check.

1 What do you think the text is about?
2 Where do you think the man is?
3 Where do you think the woman is?
4 How do you think they keep in contact?

The *ultimate* long-distance relationship

Having a long-distance relationship isn't easy. Keeping in touch takes extra effort and not having your partner around when you need support can be difficult. So it's hard to imagine what life is like for Amiko Kauderer, whose boyfriend, Scott Kelly, is often not even on the planet with her. That's because Scott is an astronaut who spends months floating 400 km above The Earth on the International Space Station!

Amiko works at NASA, which is how she got to know Scott. They met a few times, and after talking 'for hours and hours' one evening, Scott finally asked her out. They've now been together for several years. However, Scott's job means he is often away. His first trip to the Space Station lasted six months. After that he lived in space for a whole year to find out what would happen to the human body on a journey to Mars.

On his first trip, it wasn't easy for Amiko to keep in touch. Emailing involved a six-hour delay, but now it's almost instant and it's also possible to videochat once a week. But there are some things that it isn't possible to do. 'One of the things I miss most is holding hands,' says Amiko. 'We can connect on phone calls. I can upload pictures, but you can't upload human touch.'

Other couples might have broken up in such a situation, but not Scott and Amiko. 'We really appreciate a challenge because we know, at the end of it, we can say "Yeah, we did that".'

So whenever you think your love life is difficult, just think of Amiko and Scott!

2 A Match sentences 1–5 with pictures a–e.

1 Amiko **got to know** Scott at a friend's house. ____
2 They **fell in love** at first sight. ____
3 Scott **asked** Amiko **out** on a date. ____
4 **Keeping in touch** now is easier than it was. ____
5 They **broke up**, but **got back together** in the end. ____

B Are the sentences true (T) or false (F)? Check your answers in the text.

a

b

c

d

e

Personal Best

Go to Vocabulary practice: relationship verbs, page 157

3 Choose the correct words to complete the sentences. Check your answers in the text.

1 *To have / Having* a long-distance relationship isn't easy.
2 ... after *to talk / talking* 'for hours and hours' one evening, Scott finally asked her out.
3 He lived in space for a whole year *to find out / finding out* what would happen to the human body.
4 It's also possible *to videochat / videochatting* once a week.

4 Look at sentences 1–4 from exercise 3 again. Complete the rules with the *-ing* form or infinitive with *to*. Then read the Grammar box.

1 We use ________ after an adjective.
2 We use ________ as the subject/object of a sentence.
3 We use ________ after a preposition.
4 We use ________ to say why we did something.

Grammar uses of the *-ing* form and the infinitive with *to*

***-ing* form of the verb:**
After a preposition: *I'm interested **in learning** languages.*
Subject/object of a sentence: ***Breaking up** with someone is hard.* *I hate **breaking up** with someone.*
Infinitive with *to*:
After an adjective: *It's **difficult to meet** new people in this city.* *It's **important to keep** in touch.*
To express a purpose: *I went to Juan's house **to talk** to him.*

Personal Best

Go to Grammar practice: uses of the *-ing* form and the infinitive with *to*, page 135

5 **A** 12.7 **Pronunciation:** word stress Listen to the words and underline the stressed syllables. Listen again, check and repeat.

1 distance 2 relationship 3 imagine 4 happen

B 12.8 Underline the stressed syllables in the words below. Listen, check and repeat.

important colleagues impossible except technology better afraid probably

6 **A** 12.9 Write the infinitive with *to* or the *-ing* form of the verbs in brackets. Listen and check.

1 It's very important ________ with your colleagues at work. (get on)
2 ________ in love at first sight is impossible, except in films. (fall)
3 You can use technology ________ in touch, but meeting face to face is better. (keep)
4 You shouldn't be afraid of ________ someone out. They'll probably say yes! (ask)

B In pairs, practise saying sentences 1–4. Say if you agree or disagree with the sentences.

Go to Communication practice: Student A page 165, Student B page 173

7 Complete the text with the infinitive with *to* or the *-ing* form of the verbs in the box.

arrive choose say make show

HOW TO SUCCEED ON A FIRST DATE

1 ________ a nice place to meet is the first thing you need to think about.
2 You should wear nice clothes ________ a good impression.
3 It's important ________ on time.
4 Don't be afraid of ________ the real you.
5 Before ________ goodnight, tell him/her that you enjoyed the date.

8 In pairs, think of more advice for how to succeed on a first date. Use the ideas in the boxes.

be polite | don't talk too much | ask questions | keep eye contact | laugh | listen | smile | tell a joke | relax

A *I think it's important to be polite.* **B** *Yes, but being polite isn't the most important thing ...*

Personal Best Write a paragraph about a couple you know. Explain how they met and their relationship.

Learning Curve

12D Thanks a million!

a

b

c

d

1 A Look at the pictures. How are the people celebrating their birthdays?

B Answer the questions.

1 How important are birthdays to you? Why?
2 How did you celebrate your last birthday?
3 What's the best birthday present you've ever received? Why?
4 Have you ever had a surprise birthday party? Did you enjoy it?

2 12.10 Watch or listen to the first part of *Learning Curve*. Are the sentences true (T) or false (F)?

1 Today is Simon's birthday. ____
2 Everyone has forgotten about his birthday. ____
3 Simon has a tennis match today. ____
4 Kate gives Simon a present. ____
5 Simon will pay to post the parcel. ____
6 Simon's parents always call him in the morning. ____

3 A 12.10 Watch or listen again. Match the phrases 1–5 with the reasons a–e.

1 That's very kind of you.
2 Thanks a lot.
3 Thanks so much!
4 Thanks a million!
5 I will, thanks.

a Kate gives Simon a cup of tea.
b Kate offers to make Simon a tea.
c Simon says he'll pay at the post office.
d Simon agrees to post a parcel.
e Kate wants Simon to say hello to his parents for her.

B Look at phrases 1–5 again. Answer the questions.

1 Which phrases are polite responses to something small? ____ ____
2 Which phrases are to say thanks for something special or a big effort? ____ ____ ____
3 Can you think of any other ways to thank someone?

Conversation builder giving thanks

To be polite:	For a special favour:	To be more formal:
Thanks a lot.	*That's very kind of you.*	*I can't thank you enough.*
Thanks very much.	*Thanks a million.*	*I'm so grateful to you.*
Thanks.	*Thank you so much.*	*We really appreciate it.*

4 12.11 Read the Conversation builder. In pairs, read out the sentences and thank your partner in a suitable way. Listen and compare your answers.

1 Here's your T-shirt and $1 change.

2 We've decided to give you a 30% pay rise.

3 Here are some flowers. I know you've been ill.

4 The bus station? It's just across the road.

5 I've done all the shopping for you.

6 I cooked lamb curry. It's your favourite.

5 12.12 Watch or listen to the second part of the show. What other ways of thanking people do you hear?

6 12.12 Answer the questions. Watch or listen again and check.

1 Who cooked the food for the party? ________
2 Who sent flowers, chocolate and biscuits? ________
3 Did Kate organize the party on her own? ________
4 Whose parents arrive at the party? ________

7 12.13 Complete the sentences with the phrases in the box. Listen, check and repeat after the beeps.

it was easy | Glad you noticed | You're welcome | I had help | it isn't a problem

1 **Kate** Oh, and thanks again for taking this parcel.
Simon Right. Really, ________________ .
2 **Simon** And you look great, Pen. Is that a new dress?
Penny Thanks. ________________ !
3 **Kate** Jack, you really made a fantastic meal!
Jack Oh, come on, ________________ . I make this all the time.
4 **Simon** Lovely. I'm so grateful to you both!
Penny It was nothing. ________________ .
5 **Simon** That was a fantastic surprise. Kate, did you do all this by yourself?
Kate No, ________________ !

Skill responding modestly

We often respond to congratulations, thanks and compliments in a modest way.

- For congratulations, you can say it wasn't important or hard work, e.g. *It was nothing, I was just lucky.*
- For thanks, you can say it was something small or you enjoyed doing it, e.g. *No problem. It was a pleasure. You're welcome.*
- For a compliment, you can thank the person and say you are pleased, e.g. *Thanks. I'm glad you like it.* You can also say it isn't as good as the person thinks, e.g. *This old thing? I've had it for years.*

8 12.14 Read the Skill box. Match phrases 1–6 with responses a–f. Listen and check.

1 I can't thank you enough.
2 I love your new hairstyle.
3 This chicken is delicious.
4 You passed! Congratulations.
5 Thanks for looking after my children.
6 Well done on your promotion.

a Really? I thought it was a bit too spicy.
b Oh, it's just an internal one.
c Thanks. I'm glad you noticed.
d It was a pleasure. They're lots of fun!
e Thanks. The exam wasn't that difficult.
f It's no problem at all.

Go to Communication practice: Student A page 165, Student B, page 173

9 A PREPARE In pairs, look at the pictures and choose a situation. Prepare a short conversation between the people.

a

b

c
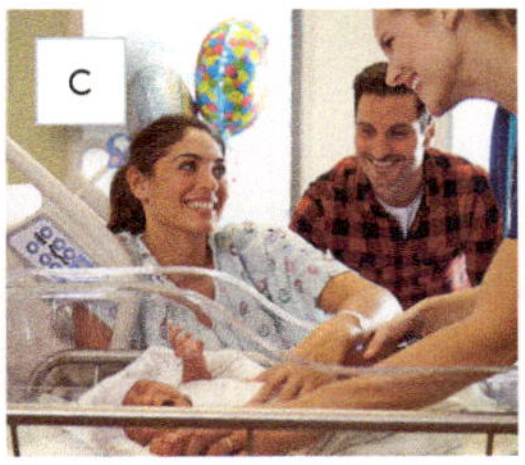

d

B PRACTISE Act out your conversation to another pair.

C PERSONAL BEST What was good about the other pair's conversation? What could they do better? Swap partners and prepare a conversation for another situation.

Personal Best Write a list of people you have thanked this week and explain why you thanked them.

Grammar

1 Choose the correct options to complete the sentences.

1 Keven has decided ________ his job.
   a leave
   b to leave
   c leaving
2 I normally go to ________ bed at 11.00 p.m.
   a a
   b the
   c – (no article)
3 Do you want ________ out tonight?
   a go
   b to go
   c going
4 My sister is ________ lawyer.
   a a
   b the
   c – (no article)
5 I'm meeting a colleague ________ has just left the company.
   a where
   b which
   c who
6 I phoned him ________ a meeting.
   a arrange
   b to arrange
   c arranging
7 This is the café ________ we said we would meet.
   a where
   b which
   c that
8 I'm keen on ________ to other countries.
   a travel
   b to travel
   c travelling

2 Complete the sentences with the correct form of the verbs in the box.

remember	take	buy	find
go	work	meet	write

1 I went to the library ________ a book about pets.
2 I'm not happy about ________ late this week.
3 He forgot ________ his girlfriend a birthday present.
4 I've finally finished ________ my essay.
5 I can't stand ________ trains. They're so crowded.
6 She's suggested ________ to the cinema tonight.
7 It's important ________ to turn off this machine when you leave.
8 ________ you is the best thing that has happened to me!

3 Choose the correct options to complete the text.

Stephanie is [1]*a / - / the* wedding planner and she is [2]*an / - / the* owner of *Blissful Days*, [3]*a / - / the* company based in Sydney, Australia.

How did you become a wedding planner?

I've always loved [4]*go / to go / going* to weddings. It's so exciting [5]*see / to see / seeing* everyone dressed up and enjoying such a wonderful day. But I noticed that some people couldn't enjoy it because they were worried about [6]*organize / to organize / organizing* everything. That's when I realized that I could start a company [7]*which / who / where* helps people to plan their weddings.

What advice can you give to couples planning a wedding?

First of all, you should agree on the guests [8]*which / who / where* you're going to invite. Once you know how many people will be there, you can find a place [9]*who / which / where* everyone will be comfortable. Send out invitations at least six months before the wedding, but expect about 20% of people not to be able to come. This can be more if the date of your wedding is on or near [10]*a / - / the* public holiday – so always check your dates carefully.

Vocabulary

1 Match the words in the box with the definitions.

oven	get back together	plain	do the washing
hang out the clothes	groom	stylish	iron
go out together	flatmate		

1 a machine you use to make clothes flat ________
2 a man who is going to get married ________
3 to start a relationship with someone ________
4 simple, with no pattern or design ________
5 someone who you live with ________
6 a machine which you use to cook food ________
7 to dry clothes after you wash them ________
8 to wash your clothes ________
9 fashionable and elegant ________
10 to return to a relationship with someone ________

2 Circle the words that are different. Explain your answers.

1	employer	classmate	colleague	business partner
2	break up	fall in love	go on a date	go out together
3	oven	dishwasher	wash basin	washing machine
4	mop	sweep	iron	vacuum
5	loose	wool	tight	casual
6	bride	girlfriend	stepsister	father-in-law
7	smart	cotton	denim	silk
8	sheets	pillow	duvet	iron
9	on well	married	in love	back together
10	wash up	lay the table	make the bed	load the dishwasher

3 Choose the correct word to complete the sentences.

1 My uncle's daughter is my ________ .
a niece b cousin c stepsister

2 I am ________ . I don't have any brothers or sisters.
a an only child b a single parent c a relative

3 I left my job because I ________ badly with my boss.
a got back b got on c went on

4 He ________ on a date!
a introduced b asked me out c kept in touch

5 The ________ is broken. Can you call a plumber?
a oven b tap c fridge-freezer

6 We need new ________ for the bed.
a rugs b carpets c sheets

7 I don't know him. He's a complete ________ .
a twin b enemy c stranger

8 It's really hot today. Can you ________ the plants?
a sweep b dust c water

4 Complete the conversation with the words in the box.

get to know break up vacuum introduce stylish do silk mop

Sue When did you 1 ________ with Harry?
Jo Two months ago.
Sue Let me 2 ________ you to Lee. I'm meeting him tonight.
Jo I can't. I've got to 3 ________ the carpets and 4 ________ the floor.
Sue You can do that any time!
Jo But I haven't got anything to wear. I need to 5 ________ the washing!
Sue Is your 6 ________ dress clean?
Jo Yes, it is.
Sue Well, that's really 7 ________ . Wear that! Come on, you should 8 ________ him. He's lovely!
Jo OK, I'll come with you.

Personal Best

Lesson 11A: Name five objects you find in a kitchen.

Lesson 12A: Write down five people and say how you are related to each of them.

Lesson 11A: Name five verbs which are followed by the *-ing* form.

Lesson 12A: Write three sentences with relative clauses and *who*, *which* and *where*.

Lesson 11B: Name five housework tasks you do at home.

Lesson 12B: Write three sentences using *roughly*, *at least* and *almost*.

Lesson 11C: Write a sentence with *a/an*, and another with *the*.

Lesson 12C: Write a sentence with the infinitive with *to*.

Lesson 11C: Use adjectives to describe two things you are wearing now.

Lesson 12D: Give three expressions to thank someone.

Lesson 11D: Describe a noun using three adjectives in the correct order.

Lesson 12D: Give an expression for responding modestly when someone thanks you.

1A Present simple

We use the present simple to talk about things that are always true.

My best friend is from Argentina. *He doesn't like tomatoes.*

We also use the present simple to talk about regular routines and habits.

I speak to my best friend every day. *We go for a coffee once a week.*

We form negatives and questions with *don't/doesn't* and *do/does* + the infinitive of the verb.

1.4	I / you / we / they	he / she / it
+	We **live** in Istanbul.	Carlos **lives** in Santiago.
–	They **don't live** in Quebec.	Megan **doesn't live** in Sydney.
?	**Do** you **live** in Shanghai?	**Does** she **live** in Cairo?
Y/N	Yes, I **do**. / No, I **don't**.	Yes, she **does**. / No, she **doesn't**.

We usually add ***s*** to the infinitive to make the third person singular (*he/she/it*) form.

Spelling rules for third person singular (*he / she / it*)
We usually add -***s*** to the infinitive. *live* ⇨ *lives*
When the infinitive ends in consonant + ***y***, we change the ***y*** to ***i*** and then we add -***es***. *study* ⇨ *studies*
When the infinitive ends in -***sh***, -***ch***, -***x***, -***s*** we add -***es***. *finish* ⇨ *finishes* *watch* ⇨ *watches*
Some verbs are irregular. *go* ⇨ *goes* *do* ⇨ *does* *have* ⇨ *has*

Look! The verbs *be* and *can* are irregular in the present simple.

I'm a generous person.	*David can swim well.*
You aren't late today.	*You can't use this computer.*
Are they good friends?	*Can you help us?*
Yes, they are.	*No, we can't.*

Adverbs and expressions of frequency

We use adverbs of frequency with the present simple to talk about habits and routines.

100% ——— 0%

always usually often sometimes hardly ever never

We put adverbs of frequency before the main verb.

I always see my friends after college. NOT ~~*Always I see my friends after college.*~~

But we put them after the verb *be*.

They're never late. NOT ~~*They never are late.*~~

We use *How often ...?* to ask questions about how frequently actions happen.

How often do you see your friends?

We can also use expressions of frequency such as *every day/week/month* or *once a week/month/year* to talk about regular routines.

We usually use expressions of frequency at the end of sentences.

I meet Julia once a week. NOT ~~*I meet once a week Julia.*~~

I speak to her every day. NOT ~~*I speak every day to her.*~~

1 Complete the sentences with the correct form of the verbs in brackets.

1 I ________ coffee. (not like)
2 ________ they ________ computer games with you? (play)
3 Luca ________ work at 6.00 p.m. (finish)
4 We ________ fun together. (have)
5 You ________ my best friend. (not know)
6 ________ Rohan ________ with you? (work)
7 Constanza is really shy. She ________ in class. (not speak)
8 My mum ________ a lot about her children. (worry)
9 ________ you________ me with this? (can / help)
10 Ravi ________ very patient. (not be)

2 Rewrite the sentences and questions with the adverbs of frequency in the correct place.

1 We have a coffee after our class. (sometimes)
____
2 Do you speak to your best friend every day? (usually)
____
3 My best friend is there for me, day or night. (always)
____
4 How do you talk to your best friend? (often)
____
5 My flatmates are in our flat. (hardly ever)
____
6 Luca works hard. (never)
____

3 Put the words in the correct order to make sentences and questions.

1 your / often / friends / do / see / how / you ?
____
2 usually / drink / doesn't / Luis / coffee
____
3 evening / Sandra / every / studies
____
4 me / friends / to / always / my / listen
____
5 day / we / home / every / at / cook
____
6 you / dentist / to / often / the / how / go / do ?
____
7 week / bedroom / a / tidy / times / I / my / three
____
8 often / on / you / how / holiday / go / do ?
____

◀ Go back to page 5

1C Present continuous

We use the present continuous to talk about things that are happening now.

My brother is having a shower right now.
Are you reading a good book at the moment?

We also use the present continuous to talk about things that are temporary.

I'm living at my parents' house for a few weeks.
She isn't working in the office this month.

We form the present continuous with the verb *be* + the *-ing* form of the main verb.

1.12	I	he / she / it	you / we / they
+	I'**m reading** a book.	Daniel'**s sleeping**.	We'**re** all **wearing** glasses!
–	I'**m not working** in the office today.	My cousin **isn't staying** with me this week.	We **aren't using** this room now.
?	**Am** I **dreaming**?	**Is** she **studying** French this month?	**Are** you **watching** TV?
Y/N	Yes, I **am**. / No, I'**m not**.	Yes, she **is**. / No, she **isn't**.	Yes, we **are**. / No, we **aren't**.

We usually add *-ing* to the infinitive to make the *-ing* form.

Spelling rules for the *-ing* form
We usually add ***-ing*** to the infinitive. *play ⇨ playing talk ⇨ talking*
When a verb ends in ***e***, we omit the ***e*** before adding ***-ing***. *take ⇨ taking live ⇨ living*
When a verb ends in consonant + vowel + consonant, we double the final consonant before adding ***-ing***. *sit ⇨ sitting plan ⇨ planning*

Look! We often use the present continuous with time expressions such as *now, today, this week/month/year, at the moment.*
I'm studying Economics at the moment.
Today, they aren't working very much.

Present continuous and present simple

We use the present simple to talk about things which are always true and the present continuous to talk about things that are temporary.

Rebecca lives in Buenos Aires, but this month she's living in New York.

We use the present simple to talk about things which happen regularly and the present continuous to talk about things that are happening now.

I usually take the bus to work, but today I'm taking a taxi.

However, there are some verbs which describe a state rather than an action. We don't normally use these verbs in the present continuous.

Maria hates the new TV series. NOT ~~*Maria is hating the new TV series.*~~
My teacher doesn't think it's correct. NOT ~~*My teacher isn't thinking it's correct.*~~
I have a hire car at the moment. NOT ~~*I'm having a hire car at the moment.*~~

State verbs	
Feelings	like, love, hate, want, prefer, need
Thoughts and opinions	know, believe, remember, forget, understand, think
States	be, exist, seem, look like, belong, own, have

1 Write sentences using the present continuous.

1 My sister / travel / in Asia / at the moment
____
2 Ivan / not work / this week
____
3 What / you / learn about / in your History class?
____
4 They / plan / a trip to Mexico
____
5 I / not shout
____
6 you / use / that chair?
____
7 she / wear / a scarf?
____
8 I / not go running / this month
____

2 Complete the sentences with the present continuous or present simple form of the verbs in brackets.

1 We can't have a picnic today. It __________ . (rain)
2 She often __________ her friends here. (meet)
3 Turn that music down! The children __________ . (sleep)
4 The trains are really busy because everyone __________ to work right now. (travel)
5 It's amazing how much she __________ her mum. (look like)
6 Can you turn off the TV, please, if you __________ it? (not watch)
7 He __________ a suit to work, except when he has an important meeting. (not wear)
8 I can't speak now as I __________ . I'll call you later. (drive)

3 Complete the text with the present continuous or present simple form of the verbs in brackets.

Ella Richards is the granddaughter of Keith Richards, who 1 __________ (play) guitar in the Rolling Stones. Ella is 18 and a model, and at the moment she 2 __________ (appear) in a series of adverts for a fashion company. She 3 __________ (live) at home, with her mum, dad and

younger brother, but this week she 4 __________ (work) in London, and she 5 __________ (stay) at her grandmother's house. In our photo, she 6 __________ (wear) a black dress with flowers, and she 7 __________ (carry) a handbag. She says that when she's older, she 8 __________ (want) to be a spy!

◀ Go back to page 8

2A Past simple

We use the past simple to talk about completed actions in the past.

I bought a new camera yesterday.
Emma didn't come to work last week.
Did you see Lucia at the party?

We form negatives and questions with *didn't* and *did* + the infinitive of the verb.

2.1	Regular verbs	Irregular verbs
+	We **walked** to school yesterday.	We **took** a lot of photos.
–	I **didn't study** Science at university.	He **didn't go** shopping last week.
?	**Did** he **use** his own camera?	**Did** you **meet** anyone interesting?
Y/N	Yes, he **did**.	No, I **didn't**.

We usually add *-ed* to regular verbs to make the positive form of the past simple.

Spelling rules for regular past simple positive forms
We usually add ***-ed*** to the verb. *play ⇨ played watch ⇨ watched*
When a verb ends in ***e***, we add ***-d***. *dance ⇨ danced live ⇨ lived*
When a verb ends in consonant + ***y***, we change the ***y*** to ***i*** and then we add ***-ed***. *study ⇨ studied*
When a verb ends in consonant + vowel + consonant, we double the final consonant and then add ***-ed***. *stop ⇨ stopped plan ⇨ planned*

Many common verbs have irregular past simple positive forms.

go ⇨ went have ⇨ had take ⇨ took

Look! The verbs *be* and *can* are irregular in the past simple.

I was at the party.	*We could see the house.*
She wasn't here.	*He couldn't come to class.*
Were you happy?	*Could you speak French when you were younger?*
Yes, I was.	*No, I couldn't.*

Time expressions

We often use time expressions with the past simple to say when an action happened. Time expressions can go at the end or at the beginning of sentences.

Last year, the president travelled to Europe.
The president travelled to Europe last year.
NOT ~~*The president travelled last year to Europe*~~.

2.2	Time expressions
at + times, *the weekend*	The train arrived **at 6 o'clock**. **At the weekend**, I went to the cinema.
in + seasons, months, years	They travelled **in the summer**. **In 2015**, we moved to Portugal.
last + *night / week / month / year*	**Last night**, I saw a good match on TV. We went there **last year**.
on + days, dates	What did you do **on Monday**? **On 4 July**, did you do anything special?
seconds, minutes, hours, days, weeks, months, years + ***ago***	**An hour ago**, Kevin was here. I saw him **three days ago.**
yesterday	I saw her **yesterday.**

1 Complete the sentences with the correct past simple form of the verbs.

1 They ________ to speak Spanish in Colombia. (learn)
2 ________ you ________ Hannah yesterday? (see)
3 We ________ this photo from the top of that building. (take)
4 I ________ to class last week. (not go)
5 ________ you ________ the film? (enjoy)
6 How annoying! Elise ________ her emails last night. (not check)
7 ________ Paula ________ to you on Monday? (speak)
8 I ________ in a restaurant five years ago. (work)

2 A Write past simple questions.

1 what / you / do / yesterday?
____
2 your sister / go / on holiday / with you / last year?
____
3 when / you / finish / the project?
____
4 you / have / a smartphone / ten years ago?
____
5 when / Mario / take / the photo?
____
6 where / be / you / on Monday / at 10.00 a.m.?
____

B Match answers a–f with questions 1–6.

a I finished it a few days ago. ____
b Yes, I did. It was quite expensive. ____
c I went to a friend's house and watched a film. ____
d I was in my car, driving to work. ____
e No, she didn't. She stayed at home. ____
f He took it last month when he was in Poland. ____

3 Choose the correct options to complete the sentences.

1 We didn't take any photos *on / in / at* the summer.
2 I bought this phone a few years *ago / last / past*.
3 We moved to a new flat *on / in / at* August.
4 Did you see Anton in town *yesterday / last day / day ago*?
5 The concert started *in / on / at* 9.00 p.m.
6 Monika and Julieta went to the cinema *in / at / on* Saturday.
7 Did your college course finish *in / on / at* 15 July?
8 They met in a café *ago / last / past* night.

◀ Go back to page 13

2C Question forms

When we ask for specific information, we use a question word such as *who*, *where*, *when*, *how* or *why*.

Where does Gupta live?	*She lives in New Delhi.*
How did they get here?	*They came by car.*
Why are you wearing a coat?	*I'm wearing it because I'm cold.*

When we ask for a *Yes* or *No* answer, we don't use a question word.

Do you like coffee?	*Yes, I do.*
Did the train arrive late?	*No, it didn't.*
Is Ling Mai from China?	*Yes, she is.*

With most verbs, we use an auxiliary verb.

2.9	question word	auxiliary verb	subject	main verb
	Where	**does**	your brother	**go** to university?
		Do	you	**remember** your primary school?
	How	**did**	your sister	**get** her first job?
		Did	Gustav	**see** you yesterday?
	Which book	**are**	you	**reading** at the moment?
		Is	Noelia	**looking** forward to the trip?

With the verb *be*, we don't use an auxiliary verb and the subject comes after *be*.

2.10	question word	*be*	subject	
	Where	**are**	you	from?
		Is	the meeting	in March?
	Why	**was**	the computer	broken?
		Were	you	at the party?

Look! We usually put prepositions at the end of questions, after the main verb.
Who did she get married to? NOT ~~*To who did she get married?*~~
What are you worried about? NOT ~~*About what are you worried?*~~

We use *how* in different ways when we ask questions.

How – to ask about the way of doing something
How do you travel to work?

How often – to ask about frequency
How often do you wash your hair?

How long – to ask about duration
How long is the film?

How old – to ask about age
How old were you when you moved here?

How much/many – to ask about quantity
How much money do you have?

How + adjective – to ask about a specific quality
How deep is the swimming pool?

1 Put the words in the correct order to make questions.

1 often / gym / how / you / the / go / do / to
________________________?

2 go / to / which / did / university / they
________________________?

3 weekend / go / where / at / you / the / did
________________________?

4 thinking / what / you / about / are
________________________?

5 whose / today / it / is / birthday
________________________?

6 to / work / how / get / she / does
________________________?

7 who / you / at / are / looking
________________________?

8 for / class / why / late / you / were
________________________?

2 Write questions for the answers.

1 He was born in Bela Horizonte in Brazil.
Where ____________________?

2 They grew up with their grandparents.
Who ____________________?

3 She met her husband at secondary school.
Where ____________________?

4 They have five children.
How many ____________________?

5 He retired because of bad health.
Why ____________________?

6 At the moment, he's working on a new project.
What ____________________?

3 A Put the words in the box into the correct place to complete the interviewer's questions.

you did it to with are

1 Where you from?
2 When you start singing?
3 What type of music do you listen?
4 Is difficult to write songs?
5 In the future, which musicians do you hope to work?
6 Do enjoy being famous?

B Match answers a–f with questions 1–6.

a I love all music – rock and pop, especially. ____
b I don't know. I just sing the songs. ____
c I was born in Puerto Rico, but I grew up in London. ____
d I'm planning on working with Shakira soon. ____
e Yes, I do. I love it! ____
f I started singing lessons when I was six years old. ____

◀ Go back to page 17

3A Comparatives, superlatives, *(not) as … as*

Comparatives

We use comparative adjectives + *than* to compare things.

Helen is taller than Jason.
The train is more expensive than the bus.

We can also use *less* + adjective + *than* to compare things.

Sofia is less tall than Helen. = Sofia is shorter than Helen.
The bus is less expensive than the train. = The bus is cheaper than the train.

(not) as … as

We use *as … as* with adjectives to say two things are the same.

Sofia is as tall as Jasmine. *The train is as fast as the bus.*

We use *not as … as* with adjectives to say two things are different.

Sofia isn't as tall as Helen. = Sofia is less tall than Helen.
The bus isn't as expensive as the train. = The bus is less expensive than the train.

Look! After comparatives or *(not) as … as*, we can use an object pronoun or a subject pronoun + auxiliary verb.
Marcos is faster than me. / Marcos is faster than I am.
Claudia is more relaxed than her. / Claudia is more relaxed than she is.

Superlatives

We use superlative adjectives to say that something is more than all the others in a group.

Helen is the tallest in her class.
The train is the most expensive way to travel in this city.

We can also use *the least* + adjective to say something is less than all the others in a group.

It's the least dangerous way to travel. = It's the safest way to travel.

Spelling rules for comparative and superlative adjectives
When an adjective is one syllable, we add ***-er*** / ***-est***. *fast ⇨ faster ⇨ fastest*
When a one-syllable adjective ends in consonant + vowel + consonant, we double the final consonant and add ***-er*** / ***-est***. *hot ⇨ hotter ⇨ hottest*
When an adjective ends in consonant + ***y***, we change the ***y*** to ***i*** and then we add ***-er*** / ***-est***. *easy ⇨ easier ⇨ easiest*
When an adjective is two or more syllables, we use ***more*** / ***most*** + adjective. *comfortable ⇨ more comfortable ⇨ most comfortable*
Some comparatives are irregular. *good ⇨ better ⇨ best* *bad ⇨ worse ⇨ worst* *far ⇨ further ⇨ furthest*

3.2	
Comparatives	Fish is **healthier than** meat. I'm much **more/less patient than** you.
(not) as … as	Melissa is **as friendly as** her sister. It is**n't as warm as** it was yesterday.
Superlatives	This is **the fastest** car in the world. I bought **the most/least expensive** phone in the shop.

1 Complete the sentences with the comparative or superlati form of the adjectives in brackets.

1 The Torre Latino is the ________ place for a view of Mexi City. (good)
2 I can't believe you're ________ than me! (old)
3 My flat is ________ from the park than yours is. (far)
4 I think Tokyo is the ________ city I know. (interesting)
5 Is Beijing ________ than Tokyo? (big)
6 Dubai is one of the ________ airports in the world. (busy)

2 Complete the second sentence with *(not) as … as* so it mea the same as the first sentence.

1 Your new flat is bigger than your old flat.
Your old flat is ______________ your new flat.
2 Moscow is more famous than São Paulo.
São Paulo is ______________ Moscow.
3 The metro and the bus are equally crowded.
The metro is ______________ the bus.
4 I think this part of town is livelier than the centre.
The centre is ______________ this part of town.

3 Look at the information. Write three sentences using the adjectives in the boxes.

Hotel Romeo €500 | Hotel Brooklyn €300 | Hotel Cruz €125

cheap expensive

1 Hotel Cruz is ________ hotel.
2 Hotel Romeo is ________ hotel.
3 Hotel Brooklyn is ________ Hotel Romeo, but it isn't as ________ Hotel Cruz.

1 March 10° | 2 March 15° | 3 March 25°

cold hot

4 1 March was ________ 2 March.
5 3 March was ________ day.
6 2 March was ________ 3 March, but it wasn't as ________ 1 March.

Mumbai | Madrid | Buenos Aires

busy quiet

7 Mumbai is ________ city.
8 Buenos Aires is ________ city.
9 Madrid isn't as ________ Mumbai, but it's ________ Buenos Aires.

◀ Go back to page 23

3C Past continuous

We use the past continuous to describe actions in progress at a particular time in the past.

I was sleeping at 7.00 this morning.
I was working at my desk when the telephone rang.

We form the past continuous with the past simple of the verb *be* + the *-ing* form of the main verb.

3.10	I / he / she / it	you / we / they
+	I **was watching** TV at 6.00 last night.	We **were walking** home when it started to rain.
–	It **wasn't raining** when I got to work.	The players **weren't playing** very well.
?	**Was** she **working** at this office when you met her?	**Were** you **living** here at the beginning of the year?
Y/N	Yes, she **was**. / No, she **wasn't**.	Yes, we **were**. / No, we **weren't**.

Past continuous and past simple

We use the past simple to describe completed actions in the past, for example a series of actions.

Yesterday, I woke up, I had breakfast and then I had a shower.

I woke up.
I had breakfast.
I had a shower.

We use the past continuous with the past simple to describe an action that was in progress when a completed action happened.

The action in progress can continue.
I was having breakfast when I heard the new song on the radio. = I continued having breakfast.

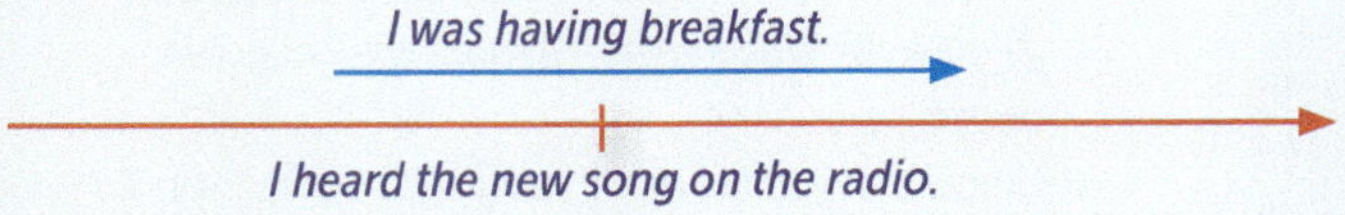
I was having breakfast.
I heard the new song on the radio.

Or the action in progress may stop.
I was sleeping when the telephone rang. = I stopped sleeping.

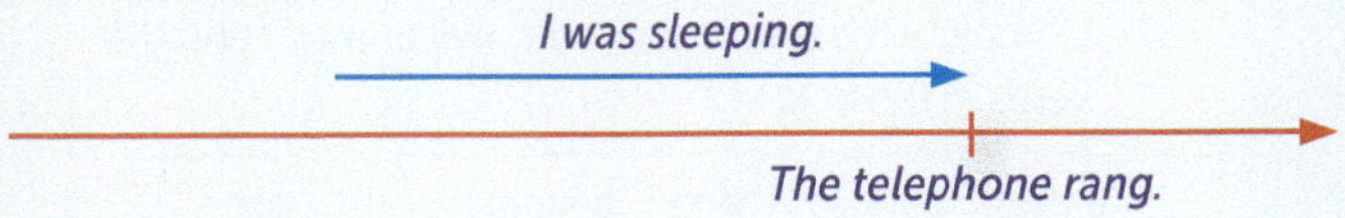
I was sleeping.
The telephone rang.

We can also use two past continuous verbs together to show that two actions were happening at the same time.

I was cooking while Steve was doing his homework.

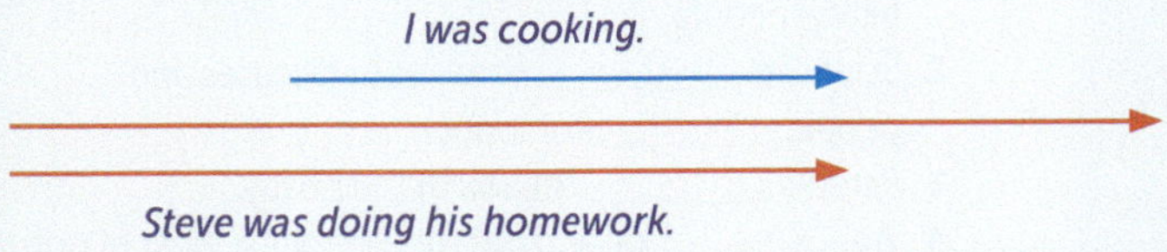
I was cooking.
Steve was doing his homework.

Look! We often use ***when*** and ***while*** in sentences with the past continuous.
I broke my leg while I was playing football.
I was playing football when I broke my leg.
While I was playing football, I broke my leg.

1 Complete the conversations with the past continuous form of the verbs in brackets.

1 A ________________ (you / watch) TV just now?
B No, I wasn't. It was the radio.
2 A Why didn't you see Paula and Mark?
B They ________________ (walk) the dog.
3 A Why was the boss angry with Nigel?
B He ________________ (not work) fast enough.
4 A Why didn't you play tennis yesterday?
B It ________________ (rain) all day.
5 A Did you ask Thomas to come to the party?
B Yes, I spoke to him while we ________________ (have) lunch.

2 Change one verb in each sentence to the past continuous.

1 We had dinner outside while we stayed in Rome.
____
2 When Lisa crossed the road, she dropped her phone and it broke.
____
3 We had dinner outside when it started to rain.
____
4 I didn't listen when the teacher told us about the exam next week.
____
5 While we sat in the taxi, we checked the address of the hotel.
____

3 Choose the correct form of the verbs to complete the text about a film of Alastair Humphreys' new adventure.

Into The Empty Quarter

In September 2012, Alastair Humphreys [1]*trained / was training* for an expedition to the South Pole. Unfortunately, he [2]*found out / was finding out* that the trip couldn't happen because there wasn't enough money. So he [3]*had to / was having to* find a new adventure quickly. One day, he [4]*was looking / looked* through his adventure books when he [5]*found / was finding* the answer – a book called 'Arabian Sands' about Wilfred Thesiger's journey across the Arabian desert in the 1940s. Alastair immediately [6]*contacted / was contacting* another explorer, Leon McCarron, and they started planning how to walk more than 1,600 kilometres across the desert. They [7]*began / were beginning* the journey in November 2012 and were home before the end of the year. But this time they [8]*filmed / were filming* all their adventures, too. *Into The Empty Quarter* is their story.

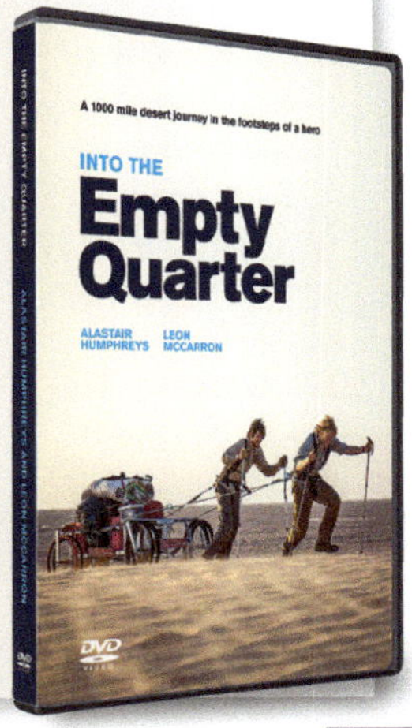
INTO THE
Empty Quarter
ALASTAIR HUMPHREYS
LEON MCCARRON
DVD

◀ Go back to page 27

4A *will, may* and *might* for predictions

We use *will* and *won't* (=*will not*) + infinitive to make predictions about the future. We usually use the contraction *'ll* after personal pronouns such as *I, he, she*, etc. and after *there*.

It'll be sunny tomorrow. *It definitely won't rain.*
There'll be lots of traffic tonight. *She won't be here on time.*

We often use *probably* to say that the prediction is less sure. *Probably* comes after *will* and before *won't*.

I'll probably go to the gym tonight.
You probably won't see Karen tomorrow.

We use *may* and *might* + infinitive to say that a prediction is possible. There is no difference in meaning between *may* and *might*.

He may be hungry when he gets home.
There might not be any food on the flight.

We don't use *may* or *might* to make questions.

Will the exam be difficult? NOT ~~*Might the exam be difficult?*~~

We can use *may* and *might* to reply to questions.

Will he get the job? *He might. I'm not sure.*
Will it rain tomorrow? *It might, or it might not!*

4.3	will	may	might
+	It'**ll rain** tomorrow.	It **may snow** tomorrow.	It **might be** windy.
–	She **won't pass** the exam.	Kelly **may not come**.	Jorge **might not arrive** on time.
?	**Will** she **be** the next president?		
Y/N	Yes, she **will**. / No, she **won't**.	Yes, she **may**. / No, she **may not**.	Yes, she **might**. / No, she **might not**.

Look! We often make predictions with *I think* ... or *I don't think* ... to show it is our opinion.
I think he'll win the race.
I don't think she'll lose her job. NOT ~~*I think she won't lose her job*~~.

1 Write sentences using the correct form of *will*, *may* and *might*.

1 It / probably / rain / tomorrow (will)
______
2 You / need / your car (may not)
______
3 I / don't think / we / see / you later (will)
______
4 We / have time / to get a coffee? (will)
______
5 She / come / to the meeting later (might)
______
6 They / probably / go / on holiday next year (won't)
______
7 I / think / there / be / lots of people / at the party (will)
______
8 What do you think / happen? (will)
______

2 Choose the correct words to complete the sentences.

1 They *will / might* go on holiday to France, but they haven't got much money so they *'ll / might* probably just stay at home.
2 I don't think that England *will / may* win the next World Cup. I'm sure it *will / may* be Germany.
3 I probably *won't / may not* come to the cinema, but I *'ll / may* be able to meet you afterwards. Can I text you later to let you know?
4 I'm sure *you 'll / might* pass your exam. *Will / Might* they tell you the result straight away?
5 It's certain that robots *will / may* become a part of all our lives. Who knows – a robot *will / may* even become president!
6 I know that *you 'll / might* really like Michael. You *'ll / might* meet him this weekend, although I'm not sure because his father's not well at the moment.

3 Complete the predictions with *will* or *won't* and the verbs in the box.

buy	choose	come	become	exist	use
go shopping	increase	live	understand		

What will the world be like in 2050?

1 The world's population ______ to more than nine billion people.
2 Scientists ______ more about diseases and people ______ for longer.
3 Parents ______ the sex of their baby.
4 We ______ oil and gas for electricity. Most of our energy ______ from solar power.
5 Some islands ______ anymore as sea levels increase. Some animals ______ extinct.
6 People ______ in the high street. Instead, they ______ everything online.

◀ Go back to page 31

4C *be going to* and present continuous

We use *be going to* + infinitive to talk about future plans.

What are you going to do tonight?
I'm going to watch a film on TV.

4.7	I	he / she / it	you / we / they
+	I'**m going to look** for a new job.	The company'**s going to move** to a new office.	We'**re going to design** a new product.
–	I'**m not going to take** the bus tomorrow morning.	Hans **isn't going to buy** a new car.	My friends **aren't going to visit** me next year.
?	**Am** I **going to work** harder next year?	**Is** she **going to study** Politics next year?	**Are** they **going to cook** dinner tonight?
Y/N	Yes, I **am**. / No, I'**m not**.	Yes, she **is**. / No, she **isn't**.	Yes, they **are**. / No, they **aren't**.

Look! When the main verb is *go*, we usually omit *to go*.
Are you going (to go) swimming tonight?
Maria is going (to go) abroad next year.

When we talk about arrangements with a fixed place and time, we often use the present continuous.

What are you doing tonight?
I'm meeting Charlie and Fiona in the town centre.

But it is also correct to use *be going to*.

What are you going to do tonight?
I'm going to meet Charlie and Fiona in the town centre.

Future time expressions

We often use future time expressions with *be going to* and the present continuous. The time expressions usually come at the beginning or at the end of a sentence.

Sandra is going to help us next week.
Next week, Sandra is going to help us.

4.8	
next + *week/month/year*, etc.	We're going to buy a new house **next year**.
In *... two days'/five years'* ***time***	**In three weeks' time**, we're meeting with our colleagues from Colombia.
tonight	What are you doing **tonight**?
tomorrow	I'm not going to do anything exciting **tomorrow**.
the day after tomorrow	Pierre is going to give a presentation at the conference **the day after tomorrow**.

1 Write sentences using *be going to*.

1 he / buy / some tickets for the football match
____
2 the actor / make / a new TV series / next year
____
3 they / go / to Spain / on holiday this year?
____
4 she / not use / an architect
____
5 where / you / sit?
____
6 he / ask / his manager about the problem
____
7 I / go / to the gym tonight
____
8 you / drive or get the bus?
____

2 Look at Kelly's diary. Make sentences using the present continuous.

9.00 a.m.	new manager (Josie) starts
10.00 a.m.	introduce Josie to the team
~~11.00 a.m.~~	~~visit the factory~~
1.00 p.m.	have lunch with Andy
2.00 p.m.	pick up new sofa!
~~6.30 p.m.~~	~~go to yoga class~~ cancelled

1 Kelly's new manager, Josie, __________ at 9.00.
2 At 10.00, Kelly __________ .
3 Is she __________ at 11.00? No, she isn't.
4 At 1.00, Kelly and Andy __________ together.
5 At 2.00, she __________ a new sofa.
6 She __________ her yoga class tonight. It's cancelled.

3 Choose the correct options to complete the sentences.

1 Hi, Bob. What ____ on 18 June next year?
 a you are going to do **b** are you doing **c** do you do
2 It's Mum's 70th birthday and we ____ a big party. You're invited!
 a 're having **b** have **c** 're going
3 The whole family ____ there, and lots of Mum's friends.
 a is being **b** is doing **c** is going to be
4 I'm sure everyone ____ a good time.
 a has **b** is having **c** is going to have
5 We want it to be a secret, so we ____ Mum.
 a are telling **b** don't tell **c** aren't going to tell
6 I ____ a big birthday cake for the party. Do you know a good cake shop?
 a 'm going to order **b** order **c** 'm order

◀ Go back to page 34

5A *should/shouldn't*

We use *should* and *shouldn't* + infinitive to ask for and give advice and recommendations.

Where should I go on holiday?
You should stay in this country.
You shouldn't go abroad. It's too expensive.

5.2	I / you / he / she / it / we / they
+	You **should see** a doctor.
–	Rachel **shouldn't drink** so much coffee.
?	**Should** I **buy** some new shoes?
Y/N	Yes, you **should**. / No, you **shouldn't**.

We often use *I think* and *I don't think* with *should* to show our opinion.

What do you think I should do?
I think you should stay in bed.
I don't think you should go out. NOT ~~*I think you shouldn't go out.*~~

Look! We can also use *ought to* and *ought not to* instead of *should* and *shouldn't* with no change in meaning.
You ought to speak to your boss. = You should speak to your boss.
Jorge ought not to go to bed so late. = Jorge shouldn't go to bed so late.

Other ways of giving advice or recommendations

When we want to give strong advice (or warnings) we use the imperative.
Whatever you do, don't go outside. It's freezing!

For recommendations, we use *why don't you ...?* or *you could* + infinitive.
Why don't you put a coat and hat on? It's cold outside.
You could stay inside, where it's nice and warm.

1 Complete the sentences with *should* or *shouldn't* and the verbs in brackets.

1 He looks really tired. I think he ________ to bed. (go)
2 There's a great new restaurant in town. You ________ it. (try)
3 You ________ so fast. You'll get a stomach ache. (not eat)
4 It's Andy's birthday. Do you think we ________ him a present? (buy)
5 She wants to get fit. She ________ a gym. (join)
6 We ________ so much salt on our food. It's not good for our health. (not put)
7 There's a lot of traffic. I don't think you ________ so fast. (drive)
8 They ________ to him like that. It's rude. (not talk)

2 Complete the sentences with the correct form of *should* and the verbs in the box.

buy	do	get up	lose	spend	study	talk	walk

1 **A** I'm always late for work.
B You ________ earlier.
2 **A** I haven't got much money at the moment.
B I don't think you ________ those shoes, then.
3 **A** These trousers don't fit me anymore.
B Do you think you ________ some weight?
4 **A** I want to improve my English.
B You ________ the summer in London.
5 **A** My brother wants to be an engineer.
B He ________ Maths and Physics at university.
6 **A** I'm feeling stressed at work at the moment.
B You ________ to your boss.
7 **A** You ________ home on your own at night.
B OK, I'll get a taxi.
8 **A** Do you think I ________ more exercise?
B Yes, definitely.

3 Put the words in the correct order to make sentences.

1 what / I / don't / do / I / should / know
____
2 before / to / the / ought / we / leave / house / 9.00
____
3 take / the / taxi / to / don't / a / airport
____
4 you / don't / homework / now / why / do / your?
____
5 job / for / Liam / another / look / could
____

◀ Go back to page 41

5C First conditional

We use the first conditional to talk about the result of a possible future action.

If you help me with my homework, I'll buy you a coffee.

There are two parts to a first conditional sentence: an *if* clause to describe the possible future action and the main clause to describe the result.

If it rains tomorrow, I'll take a taxi to the meeting.

if clause — main clause

We can put either clause first with no change in meaning. However, if we put the main clause first, we don't use a comma between the two clauses.

If I get ill on holiday, I'll feel miserable.
I'll feel miserable if I get ill on holiday.

We form the *if* clause with *if* + present simple and we form the main clause with *will* + infinitive.

5.11	*if* clause	main clause
+	**If** I **pass** my driving test,	I'**ll buy** a car.
–	**If** they **don't invite** me to the wedding,	I **won't buy** them a present.
?	**If** you **take** the medicine,	**will** you **feel** better?
Y/N	Yes, I **will**. / No, I **won't**.	

We can also use *may* or *might* + infinitive in the main clause to describe results that we are not sure about.

If I get the new job in Shanghai, I might move house.
She may come to the party if she finishes work early.

We use *can* + infinitive or *will be able to* + infinitive in the main clause to say that a result will be possible.

If I fix my bike, I can cycle to work.
He won't be able to make a cake if he doesn't buy some eggs.

Look! We can also use the imperative in the main clause to give people instructions for possible situations.
Please tell Carla about the new class if you see her tonight.
If you use this computer, don't press this button!

1 Choose the correct words to complete the sentences.

1 If she *passes* / *'ll pass* all her exams, her mum *is* / *will be* really proud.
2 If we *don't* / *won't* hurry up, we *miss* / *'ll miss* the bus.
3 I *am* / *'ll be* surprised if his flight *lands* / *will land* on time tonight.
4 If he *calls* / *will call*, *don't* / *won't* answer the phone.
5 I *tell* / *'ll tell* you a secret if you *promise* / *'ll promise* not to tell anyone.
6 She *is* / *'ll be* really disappointed if you *don't* / *won't* go to her party.
7 What *do* / *will* you say if he *asks* / *'ll ask* you to marry him?
8 If I *get* / *'ll get* lonely, *do* / *will* you give me a call?
9 He *'s* / *'ll be* really embarrassed if *he's* / *he'll be* late to his own wedding.
10 We *don't* / *may not* have time for lunch if the meeting *doesn't* / *won't* finish soon.
11 *Remind* / *Will remind* me if I *forget* / *'ll forget* to call the builder.
12 If you *don't* / *won't* leave now, I *call* / *'ll call* the police.

2 Write first conditional sentences.

1 I / write to you / if / I / have time
______
2 if / you / see him / you / give him this message, please?
______
3 she / not get her money back / if / she / lose the receipt
______
4 if / he / not get the job / he / be really miserable
______
5 if / you / not fix your car soon / the police / stop you
______
6 my mum / not forgive me / if / I / not remember her birthday
______
7 if / my phone/ ring / not answer it!
______
8 if / she / move to Italy / you / visit her?
______
9 if / you / go for a walk / it / help you to feel better
______
10 if / he / not get too nervous / he / do well in the exam
______
11 they / be late / if / they / not leave soon
______
12 if / I / stand here / you / take a photo of me?
______

◀ Go back to page 44

6A Present perfect with *ever* and *never*

We use the present perfect to talk about experiences in our lives.

I've read Don Quixote.
He hasn't been to the USA.
Have they done yoga?

We often use *ever* with questions and *never* instead of the negative to emphasize that we are talking about our lifetime.

Have you ever flown in a helicopter?
I've never eaten a hamburger!

We form the present perfect with the verb *have* and the past participle of the main verb.

6.3	I / you / we / they	he / she / it
+	I'**ve written** a novel.	Michelle **has been** to China.
-	They **haven't swum** in the river.	Claude **hasn't seen** my new car.
?	**Have** you **tried** this new drink?	**Has** he **worked** as a chef?
Y/N	Yes, I **have**. / No, I **haven't**.	Yes, he **has**. / No, he **hasn't**.

In regular verbs, the past participle is the same as the past simple form.

I cooked pasta yesterday. *I've never cooked dinner for her.*
He played tennis with her last week. *Have you ever played the saxophone?*

In some irregular verbs, the past participle is different from the past simple form. For a full list of irregular verbs, see page 175.

I ate toast for breakfast this morning. *Have you ever eaten Chinese food?*
I saw Roberta at Ruth's party. *I haven't seen that TV series.*

Look! We use *been to* to say that someone went somewhere and returned, and we use *gone to* to say that someone went somewhere and is still there.
She's been to Berlin. = She went and returned.
She's gone to Berlin. = She went and is there now.

Present perfect or past simple

We use the present perfect to talk about an experience in our lives and we use the past simple to talk about when a specific event happened.

I've met a film star.
I met George Clooney in Mexico two years ago.

We often start a conversation with the present perfect. When we ask for more information, or give details, we use the past simple.

Have you ever been to Australia?
Yes, I have. I went there in 2014.
Who did you go with?
I went with my friend, Ella.

1 Complete the table with the correct forms of the verbs.

	Infinitive	Past simple	Past participle
1	be		been
2	break	broke	
3		cried	cried
4		ate	eaten
5	drive	drove	
6	live		lived
7		sang	sung
8	speak	spoke	
9	stop		stopped
10	walk	walked	

2 Write sentences and questions in the present perfect.

1 you / ever / be / to New Zealand?
____
2 I / never / eat / fish and chips
____
3 she / walk / along the Great Wall of China
____
4 my uncle / not give up / smoking
____
5 you / ever / watch / the sun rise?
____
6 we / never / play / rugby
____
7 he / ever / ask / his boss for a pay rise?
____
8 my sister / try / to learn English
____

3 Choose the correct form (present perfect or past simple) to complete the conversation.

Rachel [1]*Have you ever learned / Did you ever learn* another language?
Sarah Yes, [2]*I have taught / I taught* myself Spanish about ten years ago.
Rachel So, [3]*have you ever been / did you ever go* to Spain?
Sarah No, but [4]*I've been / I went* to South America.
Rachel Really? When [5]*have you been / did you go* there?
Sarah Six years ago. [6]*I've been / I went* with John. It was our honeymoon.
Rachel Oh, lovely. [7]*Have you travelled / Did you travel* around a lot when you were there?
Sarah Yes, [8]*we've visited / we visited* Chile, Argentina and Brazil. It was amazing!

◀ Go back to page 49

6C Second conditional

We use the second conditional to talk about impossible or very unlikely situations.

If I went climbing in the mountains, I'd take a first aid kit. (but it's not likely that I'll go climbing in the mountains).

There are two parts to a second conditional sentence: an *if* clause to describe the situation and the main clause to describe the result.

If she had more money, she'd buy a new car.

if clause — main clause

We can put either clause first with no change in meaning. However, if we put the main clause first, we don't use a comma between the two clauses.

If he spoke German, he would apply for the job.
He would apply for the job if he spoke German.

We form the *if* clause with *if* + past simple, and we form the main clause with *would* + infinitive.

Look! We often use *were* instead of *was* in the *if* clause with *I/he/she/it*.
If he were a bit taller, the trousers would fit him.
I'd take a taxi if I were you.

6.10	*if* clause	main clause
+	**If** I **knew** the answer,	I**'d tell** you.
–	**If** you **weren't** so impatient,	you **wouldn't have** this problem.
?	**If** it **were** cheaper,	**would** you **buy** it?
Y/N	Yes, I **would**. / No, I **wouldn't**.	

We use *could* + infinitive or *would be able to* + infinitive in the main clause to say that a result would be possible.

If Alex didn't have so much work, he could go to the party.
Sara would be able to help us if she were here.

Second conditional or first conditional

We can sometimes use either the first conditional or the second conditional, but it depends on if we think a situation is a real possibility, or if we think it's very unlikely/impossible.

If I get the job, I'll be really happy. = a real possibility
If I got the job, I'd be really happy. = very unlikely
I'll meet you later if I don't have to work late. = a real possibility
I'd meet you later if I didn't have to work late. = impossible

1 Match the halves to make second conditional sentences.

1 If you had a daughter, ______
2 I would speak perfect English ______
3 Your computer wouldn't do strange things ______
4 If you told people about your website, ______
5 What would you do today ______
6 If I wrote a book, ______

a it would be much more popular.
b it would be about my childhood.
c if you weren't at work?
d if I came from the USA.
e what would you call her?
f if it didn't have a virus.

2 Choose the correct form of the verbs to complete the conversation.

AKIHABARA
GAMERS

A What [1]*did / would* you do if your company [2]*offered / would offer* you a job in Japan?
B If that happened, I [3]*thought / 'd think* about it. If they [4]*paid / would pay* me more money, I [5]*'ll / 'd* probably go.
A But [6]*wouldn't / didn't* you miss your family and friends if you went abroad?
B Yes, but they [7]*can / could* visit me if I was in Japan. It [8]*were / would be* a great opportunity if I went.
A I [9]*wouldn't / didn't go* ... not even if they [10]*doubled / would double* my salary!

3 Complete the sentences with the verbs in brackets so they are true for you. Use the second conditional if the situation is very unlikely. Use the first conditional if the situation is possible.

1 If it __________ (snow) this afternoon,
____ .
2 If I __________ (pass) my English exam,
____ .
3 If I __________ (see) my parents this evening,
____ .
4 If my computer __________ (stop) working,
____ .
5 If a reporter __________ (ask) me to appear on TV today,
____ .
6 If I __________ (go) out with my friends after class,
____ .

◀ Go back to page 53

7A Present perfect with *just, yet* and *already*

We often use the present perfect with *just*, *yet* and *already*.

Have you been to the new café yet?
Yes, I've just/already been there.
No, I haven't been there yet.

We use *just* to talk about something that happened very recently. *Just* comes before the main verb.

Is Andrea at home?
She's just gone to the shops, I'm afraid.

We use *yet* in negative sentences and questions to talk about something that we expected to happen before now. *Yet* comes at the end of the sentence or question.

Have you written the report yet?
I haven't finished it yet.

We use *already* to talk about something that happened before now or earlier than we expected. *Already* comes before the main verb.

Do you want to go out for lunch?
No, thanks. I've already eaten.

We form the present perfect with the verb *have* and the past participle of the main verb. For a full list of irregular verbs, see page 175.

7.2	I / you / we / they	he / she / it
+	I**'ve just seen** Claudia in the post office. We**'ve already heard** the news.	Kismet **has just bought** a new handbag. The train **has already left** the station.
-	They **haven't found** the keys **yet**.	He **hasn't paid** the bill **yet**.
?	**Have** you **been** to the shops **yet**?	**Has** she **spoken** to the police **yet**?
Y/N	Yes, I **have**. / No, I **haven't**. / **Not yet**.	Yes, she **has**. / No, she **hasn't**. / **Not yet**.

Look! In American English, we often use *just*, *yet* and *already* with the past simple.
I just finished my lunch.
Did Helena call you yet?
The supermarket didn't open yet.
We already gave him the papers.

1 Complete the conversation with the words in the box.

just already yet (x2)

A Watching TV again? What about your homework?
B I've ¹__________ done it.
A When did you do it?
B On the bus from school ... so now I'm watching the match.
A The match? Has it started ²__________?
B Yes! It's ³__________started, so you haven't missed anything ⁴__________.
A Great! Let me sit down. I want to watch this, too!

2 Choose the correct words to complete the sentences.

1 Shall we eat out tonight? They've *just / yet / already* opened a new restaurant near us.
2 A I have to clean the kitchen tonight.
  B Don't worry. I've *just / yet / already* cleaned it this week.
3 A Has Flora passed her driving test *just / yet / already*?
  B Yes, and she only had five lessons!
4 A Can I speak to Julia, please?
  B She was here a moment ago, but I think she's *just / yet / already* left the office.
5 Teresa hasn't booked her flight *just / yet / already*. It will be very expensive!
6 A Shall we watch *Titanic* tonight?
  B Do we have to? I've *just / yet / already* seen it about twenty times!
7 A Excuse me, where's the city centre?
  B Follow the new signposts. They've *just / yet / already* been put up to help tourists.
8 Have you used the new bike lane *just / yet / already?* It's much safer.
9 A I think we need to fill up the car with petrol.
  B It's OK. I've *just / yet / already* been to the petrol station today.
10 He only joined the company a year ago and they've *just / yet / already* promoted him twice!

3 Make sentences using *just*, *yet* or *already*.

1 she / not pack / her suitcase (yet)
____
2 the neighbours / send us / a party invitation (just)
____
3 the game / start (already)
____
4 you / speak / to Charles? (yet)
____
5 I / buy / a new flat (just)
____
6 I / have / three cups of coffee today (already)
____

◀ Go back to page 59

7C Present perfect with *for* and *since*

We use the present perfect with *for* and *since* to talk about a situation that started in the past and is still true now.

How long have you lived in Brazil? NOT ~~*How long are you living in Brazil?*~~
I've lived here all my life. NOT ~~*I'm living here all my life.*~~

We use *since* to refer to a fixed point in time in the past when the situation started.

I've worked for this company since 2010.
I haven't spoken to Farah since last summer.
Have you known Mark since you were a child?

We use *for* to refer to the period of time the situation has been true.

Youssef has been a teacher for two months.
This computer hasn't worked for years!
Has the building been here for a long time?

We use *How long ...?* to ask about the length of time a situation has been true.

How long have you known your boyfriend?
We've known each other since last March.
How long has he been a doctor?
He's been a doctor for about two years.

We form the present perfect with the verb *have* and the past participle of the main verb. For a full list of irregular verbs, see page 175.

7.12	**I / you / we / they**	**he / she / it**
+	I**'ve lived** in this part of the city **for** two years. They**'ve worked** together **since** 1990.	Sam**'s had** this car **for** over 20 years. It**'s been** much hotter **since** last weekend.
-	We **haven't spoken** to each other **for** a year. I **haven't swum** in the sea **since** I was a child.	Isabella **hasn't worn** her glasses **for** ages. He **hasn't driven** a car **since** he had the accident.
?	**How long have** you **known** her?	**How long has** he **been** a teacher?

Present perfect or past simple

We use the past simple to talk about completed actions in the past. We can often give the same information in two different ways.

a period of time / an unfinished action	**a point in the past / a completed action**
I've lived in Turkey for ten years.	I moved to Turkey ten years ago.
Jo has known me since I was 16 years old.	Jo met me when I was 16 years old.
How long have you worked here?	When did you start working here?
I haven't eaten meat since 2010.	I gave up meat in 2010.

We use the past simple to talk about a time period that started and finished in the past.

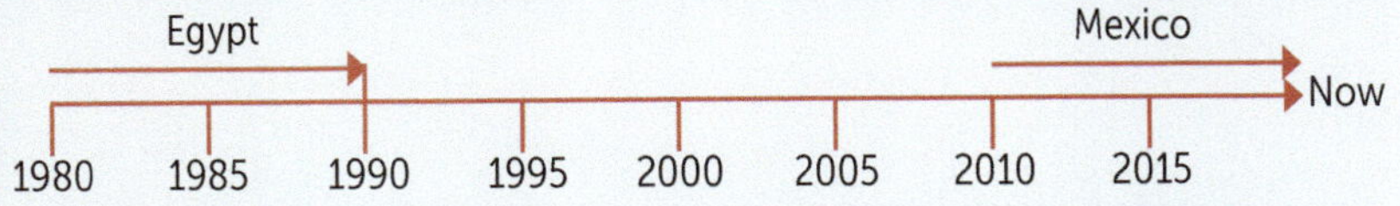

Egypt
Mexico
Now
1980
1985
1990
1995
2000
2005
2010
2015

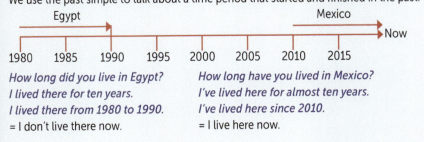

How long did you live in Egypt?
I lived there for ten years.
I lived there from 1980 to 1990.
= I don't live there now.

How long have you lived in Mexico?
I've lived here for almost ten years.
I've lived here since 2010.
= I live here now.

1 Put the times in the box in the correct column: *for* or *since*.

1997 9.30 a.m. a couple of hours a few seconds a fortnight a long time ages April five months he was a child I left university last night most of my life my accident seventeen years several weeks the middle of June the weekend three centuries Thursday

for	since

2 Write sentences using the present perfect form of the verbs in brackets. Write one sentence with *for* and one with *since*.

1 I moved to Istanbul in the middle of July. It's the middle of December now. (live)
I've lived in Istanbul for five months.
I've lived in Istanbul since the middle of July.
2 I bought my own car when I was 19. I'm 23 now. (have)
______
______
3 The last time I was on an aeroplane was in August. That was six months ago. (not be)
______
______
4 I met my best friend when I was five. I'm 22 now. (know)
______
______
5 I gave up English in 2005. That was ages ago. (not study)
______
______

3 Choose the correct form of the verbs to complete the sentences.

1 He *didn't speak* / *hasn't spoken* to his mum since he *got back* / *'s got* back from his holiday.
2 I *bought* / *'ve bought* this car in 2007, so I *'m having* / *'ve had* it for more than ten years now.
3 I'm a sales manager and I *worked* / *'ve worked* in this department for two years. Before that, I *worked* / *'ve worked* in marketing from 2012 to 2015.
4 We *knew* / *'ve known* each other for about ten years, in fact since we *met* / *'ve met* at university.
5 I *was* / *'ve been* worried about Frank since he *lost* / *'s lost* his job.
6 He *lost* / *'s lost* his phone this morning so I *'m not speaking* / *haven't spoken* to him for a few hours now.
7 I *lived* / *'ve lived* in Chicago for two years, but then I *moved* / *'ve moved* to Washington DC and I *lived* / *'ve lived* here since then.
8 Their wedding *was* / *has been* in May, so they *are* / *'ve been* married for nearly six months now.

◀ Go back to page 62

8A too, too many, too much and (not) enough

We use *too*, *too many* and *too much* to mean 'more than necessary' or 'more than is good'.

This exam is too difficult. There are too many questions!

We use *too* before adjectives and adverbs.

That restaurant is too expensive.
She works too hard.

We use *too many* before countable nouns.

I drink too many cups of coffee.

We use *too much* before uncountable nouns.

I eat too much chocolate.

We can also use *too much* after a verb without an object.

He worries too much.

We use *enough* to mean 'the right amount' or 'sufficient'. We can also use *not enough* to mean 'less than necessary' or 'less than is good'.

Is your coffee sweet enough? I didn't have enough sugar for everyone.

Enough comes before countable and uncountable nouns.

He doesn't eat enough vegetables.
Have we got enough time?

Enough comes after an adjective or adverb.

The information isn't clear enough.
He didn't sing well enough to win the competition.

We can also use *enough* after a verb without an object.

I didn't sleep enough last night.

8.2	too / too many / too much	(not) enough
Countable nouns	You shouldn't watch **too many films**.	We have **enough eggs** to make two cakes.
Uncountable nouns	Jen drinks **too much coffee** in the morning.	Do you have **enough money** to buy those shoes?
Adjectives	The train is **too crowded** at rush hour.	The soup is**n't hot enough**.

1 Choose the correct words to complete the sentences.

1 She eats *too much / too many* sweets.
2 They don't eat *enough vegetables / vegetables enough.*
3 Our flat is *too much / too* small for a party.
4 He has *too much / too many* sugar in his coffee.
5 Are you sure you're *fit enough / enough fit* to run a marathon?
6 You eat *too much / too many* junk food.
7 I don't have *enough money / money enough* to buy a new car.
8 These jeans are *too much / too* big for me now that I've lost weight.

2 Complete the sentences using *too, too many, too much* and *enough*.

1 You eat ________ takeaway meals. Don't you ever cook?
2 Don't cook the broccoli for ________ long.
3 My English isn't good ________ to have a conversation.
4 You drink ________ coffee. It isn't good for you.
5 I don't earn ________ money to buy a house.
6 I'm ________ tired to go out tonight.
7 My son spends ________ time playing computer games.
8 I have a stomach ache. I ate ________ cakes.

3 Rewrite the sentences using the words in brackets.

1 You should do more exercise. (enough)
You don't do enough exercise.
2 You eat more sugar than you should. (much)
____
3 She's too young to drive. (old)
____
4 It isn't quiet enough to work. (noisy)
____
5 We need more petrol. (enough)
____
6 There are more cars on the road than there should be. (too)
____

◀ Go back to page 67

8C *must(n't)* and *(not) have to*

We use *must* and *have to* to talk about obligations and rules.

You must always lock the door when you leave.
Amy has to wear smart clothes at work.

When we ask questions about obligations and rules, we usually use *have to*.

Do you have to start work early?
Why do we have to park the car here?

We use *mustn't* to talk about things that are not allowed. We call this prohibition.

I mustn't eat any chips. I'm on a diet.
You mustn't start the exam until I say.

We use *don't have to* to say that something isn't necessary.

You don't have to speak English for this job, but it's useful.
Kasim doesn't have to work today. It's a holiday.

8.9	I / you / we / they	he / she / it
have to	I **have to work** late tonight again, unfortunately. Do you **have to take** the train today? Yes, I **do**. / No, I **don't**.	Jackie **has to study** Maths at school. Does he **have to wait** for a long time? Yes, he **does**. / No, he **doesn't**.
must	We **must** all **eat** healthier food.	Karima **must do** her exams again.
not have to	You **don't have to pay** – it's free!	He **doesn't have to wear** a uniform at school.
mustn't	I **mustn't be** late for the meeting.	Luke **mustn't eat** too much salt.

Look! *Must* and *have to* often have a similar meaning.
I must go to the doctor.
I have to go to the doctor.
However, *mustn't* and *don't have to* have different meanings.
*You **mustn't walk** on the grass.* = it's not allowed.
*You **don't have to walk** on the grass – you can walk on the path.* = it's not necessary. You can choose.

1 Make sentences using the positive (+), negative (–) or question form (?) of *have to*.

1 What time / you / arrive / at the station (?)
____
2 My sister / study / English / at school (+)
____
3 You / show / your passport / to enter the country (–)
____
4 Lenny / cook / dinner / tonight (?)
____
5 We / finish / the project / until next week (–)
____
6 You / drive / on the left / in the UK (+)
____

2 Choose the correct words to complete the conversation.

A What's wrong, Urs?
B My brother [1]*mustn't / has to* go to the hospital tomorrow.
A Oh no! Why does he [2]*must / have to* go?
B It's nothing serious. He [3]*has to / mustn't* have a blood test.
A Does he [4]*have to / has to* spend the night there?
B No, he [5]*hasn't / doesn't*. The worst thing is he [6]*doesn't have to / mustn't* eat anything for 24 hours.
A I [7]*don't have to / mustn't* work tomorrow. I can give him a lift to the hospital, if you want.
B Thanks, Ada. That's great. He [8]*mustn't / must* be there at 10.00 a.m.
A That's fine.
B Great, he'll be happy he [9]*mustn't / doesn't have to* take the bus ... especially without any breakfast!

3 Look at the poster. Complete the rules for the swimming pool with the verbs in brackets.

City Centre Swimming Pool
Adults: £3.00
Children: Free

1 Adults ____________ (pay) to use the pool.
2 Children ____________ (pay) to go swimming.
3 You ____________ (eat) by the pool.
4 You ____________ (have) a shower before you swim.
5 You ____________ (run) near the pool.

◀ Go back to page 71

9A *used to*

We use *used to* + infinitive to talk about habits or situations that were true in the past, but aren't true now.

I used to cycle to school every day. = I don't cycle to school now.
I used to live in a small town. = I don't live there now.

We form the negative with *didn't* + *use to* + infinitive.

I didn't use to drink so much coffee. (=I drink a lot now).
She didn't use to like spicy food. (=She likes it a lot now).

We form questions with *did* + *use to* + infinitive.

Did you use to play in the school football team?
Why did you use to have two cars?

We can use the past simple instead of *used to*. The meaning is the same.

I used to have English classes at school = *I had English classes at school.*
She used to be shy when she was younger = *She was shy when she was younger.*

We don't use *used to* to talk about actions that only happened once.

I bought this shirt last year. NOT ~~*I used to buy this shirt last year.*~~
They started work at 9.00 this morning. NOT ~~*They used to start work at 9.00 this morning.*~~

9.1	I / you / he / she / it / we / they
+	I **used to like** reggae music when I was a teenager.
–	He **didn't use to be** as rich as he is now.
?	**Did** you **use to go** to the beach every day when you lived in Greece?
Y/N	Yes, I **did**. / No, I **didn't**.

Look! *Used to* only refers to the past. We use *usually* + present simple to talk about habits and situations which are true now.
Hande usually gets the bus to work.
He's not usually late for class.
How do you usually contact your family?

1 Read the text. Write sentences with *used to* or *didn't use to* and the verbs in brackets.

He used to be rich!
George Kaltsidis lives in a small house in the north of England. He drives an old Ford Fiesta and wears a second-hand watch. However, believe it or not, George used to be a millionaire and lived a life of luxury. He wasn't happy and last year he gave all his money away to charity. He's much happier now, he says. But what did his life use to be like?

1 He (live) in a small house. He (live) in an expensive apartment.
He didn't use to live in a small house. He used to live in an expensive apartment.
2 He (drive) an old car. He (have) a new BMW.
____
3 He (be) quite lonely because he (see) his family or friends very much.
____
4 He (wear) expensive clothes and he never (buy) second-hand things.
____
5 He (go) on luxury holidays, but he (enjoy) himself.
____

2 Complete the sentences with the positive, negative or question form of *used to* and the verbs in the box.

have (x2) do work argue go like be

1 They _________ a house in Spain, but they sold it last year.
2 _________ you _________ a lot of sport when you were younger?
3 I _________ to the gym, but now I usually go three times a week.
4 _________ you _________ a lot with your parents?
5 Where _________ you _________ before you got this job?
6 She _________ long hair, but now she prefers it short.
7 I _________ fish, but I love it now.
8 There _________ a park here before they built those houses.

3 Complete the sentences with *used to* or the past simple form of the verbs in brackets if *used to* is not possible.

1 Did you _________ a school uniform? (wear)
2 I _________ my arm when I was eight. I was ten. (not break)
3 I _________ quite naughty at school. (be)
4 My parents _________ a lot of money. (not earn)
5 I _________ a £50 note in the street one day. (find)
6 My grandma _________ listening to the radio. (love)
7 I _________ a lot of computer games when I was a teenager. (play)
8 The first film I _________ at the cinema was *Titanic*. (see)

◀ Go back to page 77

9C The passive

Sentences can be either active or passive.

Active: *My brother wrote this book.*
Passive: *This book was written by my brother.*

We use the active sentence to focus on the person who does the action.

My brother wrote this book.

We use the passive sentence to focus on the action itself or on the thing the action affects.

This book was written by my brother.

We also use the passive when we don't know who does/did the action or it isn't important.

These coffee machines are made in Italy.
My wallet was stolen yesterday.

We form the present simple passive with *am/is/are* + past participle of the main verb.
We form the past simple passive with *was/were* + past participle of the main verb.

Present passive: *Toyota cars are built in Japan.*
Past passive: *The buildings were destroyed five years ago.*

To say who does/did the action, we use *by*.

Lots of hotel towels are taken by tourists as souvenirs.
This building was designed in 1985 by a Chinese architect.

To form questions, we put the verb *be* before the subject.

Is your watch made of gold?
When was the book written?
Who was the music sung by?

9.12	Present passive	Past passive
+	The football matches **are played** in the evening.	The film **was directed** by Steven Spielberg.
–	The painting **isn't signed** by the artist.	Chess **wasn't invented** in Europe.
?	**Are** these biscuits **made** with butter?	**Were** the workers **paid** last month?
Y/N	**Yes**, they **are.** / **No**, they **aren't.**	**Yes**, they **were**. / **No**, they **weren't**.

1 Write sentences in the present or past simple passive.

1 English / speak / here (present)
English is spoken here.
2 This guitar / play / by Jimi Hendrix (past)
____
3 The soup / make / with fresh vegetables (present)
____
4 When / the photos / take? (past)
____
5 Who / the film / direct / by? (past)
____
6 credit cards / not accept / here (present)
____

2 Rewrite the sentences in the passive.

1 More than 162 million people use eBay.
eBay ____________.
2 The Channel Tunnel connects Britain and France.
Britain and France ____________.
3 Facebook bought WhatsApp for $22 billion.
WhatsApp ____________.
4 Steven Spielberg didn't direct *Jurassic World.*
Jurassic World ____________.
5 They make sushi with rice and raw fish.
Sushi ____________.
6 Did Tolstoy write *War and Peace*?
Was ____________.

3 Complete the text with the active or passive form of the verbs in brackets.

HIDDEN TREASURE

Treasure Detectives is a British TV show and it 1 ____ (watch) by more than 300,000 viewers. Each week, two different objects 2 ____ (examine) very carefully by experts to find out if they are valuable treasures or copies of original works.

Robert Darvell 3 ____ (contact) the programme and 4 ____ (ask) them to help him find out more about a painting he had. Robert's father 5 ____ (buy) a box of objects for £30 at an auction in 2003, which included a small painting. The painting 6 ____ (keep) in a drawer for many years and eventually it 7 ____ (give) to Robert.

After almost a year, Robert 8 ____ (tell) the truth about the painting on live TV. The experts 9 ____ (say) it was by the English artist, John Constable, and it was worth about £250,000! He was surprised, but very happy.

◀ Go back to page 80

10A Past perfect

We use the past perfect to describe an action that happened before another action in the past.

I arrived at the meeting late because I'd missed the train.
Justine hadn't studied for the exam so she failed it.
Had you met Sergio before you started the job?

We form the past perfect with *had* + the past participle of the main verb.

10.5	Past perfect
+	He'**d forgotten** his wallet so he couldn't buy anything.
–	We **hadn't tried** *ceviche* before we visited Peru.
?	**Had** you **trained** much before you ran the marathon?
Y/N	Yes, I **had**. / No, I **hadn't**.

Look! The contracted form of the past perfect is the same as the contracted form of *would*.
I'd seen him before. = I had seen him before.
I'd see him if I could. = I would see him if I could.

Narrative tenses

We usually use the past perfect with the past simple and the past continuous to show when actions happened.

When I got home, my husband made the dinner.

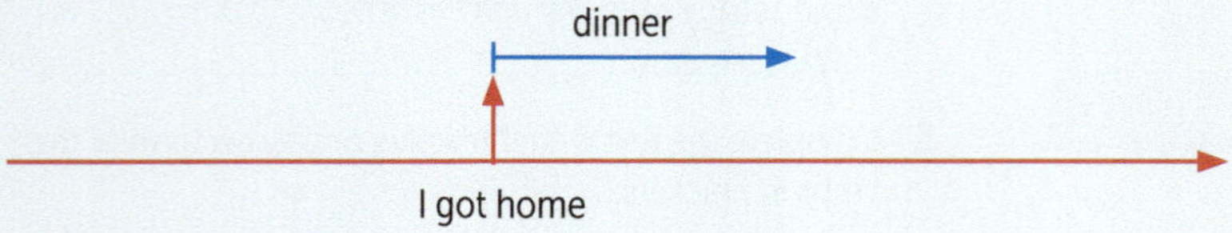
dinner
I got home

When I got home, my husband was making the dinner.

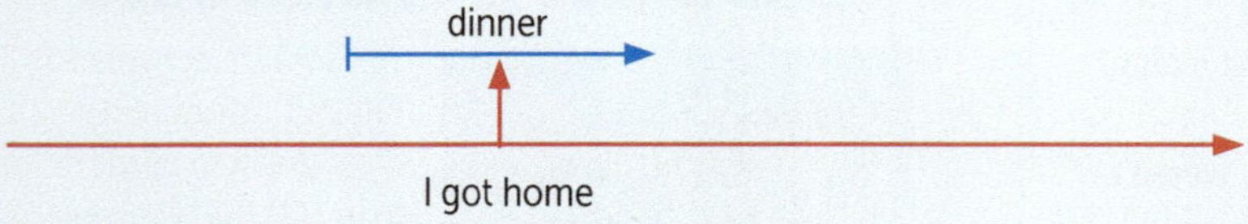
dinner
I got home

When I got home, my husband had made the dinner.

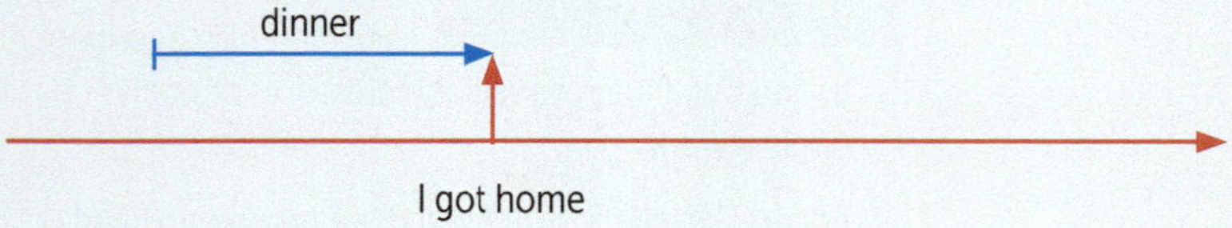
dinner
I got home

1 Match the halves to make sentences.

1 Sofia had seen the film before ______
2 Geoff felt very bad because ______
3 Susana hadn't had lunch, so ______
4 Paulo had grown a beard, so ______
5 When I got to the station, ______
6 Ali had finished the report when ______

a I got to work this morning.
b she felt very hungry.
c and she said it wasn't very good.
d the train had already left.
e I didn't recognize him.
f he'd forgotten his niece's birthday.

2 Complete the conversations with the past perfect form of the verbs in brackets.

1 **A** Why did they walk to university today?
B They __________ (have) a problem with the car.
2 **A** __________ you __________ (hear) about the problems at the airport before you left?
B No, I hadn't. Luckily, they __________ (not make) any changes to my flight.
3 **A** Rita bought me a book for my birthday, but I __________ (read) it before.
B It's my fault. She bought it because I __________ (recommend) it to her.
4 **A** Was Grandma pleased that the kids __________ (draw) a picture for her?
B Yes, she was. They __________ (not do) one for her before.
5 **A** __________ Ricky __________ (look) everywhere before he cancelled his credit card?
B No, he __________ (not look) in his sports bag. He found it there this morning.

3 Complete the text with the past simple, past continuous or past perfect form of the verbs in brackets.

On 21 April 1980, Rosie Ruiz 1__________ (cross) the finishing line of the Boston Marathon with a time of 2:31:56 – the fastest female time in Boston Marathon history. However, when she 2__________ (receive) the winner's medal, some judges 3__________ (become) suspicious because she 4__________ (not sweat) very much. Then, two students 5__________ (say) that they 6__________ (see) her join the race half a mile from the finishing line. Later, photographer Susan Morrow said she 7__________ (meet) Ruiz while she 8__________ (travel) on the subway in her running clothes at the time of the New York marathon, six months earlier. The judges 9__________(discover) that Ruiz 10__________ (do) the same thing to win the Boston Marathon.

◀ Go back to page 85

10C Reported speech

When someone speaks, we call what they say 'direct speech'. When we talk about what they said afterwards, we call it 'reported speech'.

'I don't like the website.' ⇨ *My boss said that he didn't like the website.*
'We reserved a room.' ⇨ *They told me that they had reserved a room.*

We use the verbs *say* and *tell* to report speech. We use *tell* with a noun or a pronoun when we want to say who the person was speaking to. We can add *that* to reported speech sentences.

'I'm sorry.' ⇨ *He said (that) he was sorry.*
⇨ *He told me (that) he was sorry.*

The tense of the verb usually changes when we report speech.

Direct speech		Reported speech
present simple	⇨	past simple
present continuous	⇨	past continuous
past simple	⇨	past perfect
present perfect	⇨	past perfect
past perfect	⇨	past perfect
am/is/are going to	⇨	*was/were going to*
will	⇨	*would*
can	⇨	*could*

Look! We also change pronouns and possessive adjectives in reported speech.
'I sold my car to Lenny.' ⇨ *He said that he'd sold his car to Lenny.*
'We'll send you the letter.' ⇨ *They said they'd send me the letter.*

10.12	Direct speech		Reported speech
present simple	'I drink too much coffee.'	⇨	She told me she drank too much coffee.
present continuous	'We're studying for the exam.'	⇨	They said they were studying for the exam.
past simple	'Karl didn't go to the shops.'	⇨	She said Karl hadn't gone to the shops.
present perfect	'I haven't been to Paris.'	⇨	He said he hadn't been to Paris.
past perfect	'We'd seen the film before.'	⇨	They said they'd seen the film before.
going to	'Michelle is going to drive home.'	⇨	He said Michelle was going to drive home.
will	'I'll open the letter.'	⇨	He told me he'd open the letter.
can	'Ruby can't swim.'	⇨	They told him Ruby couldn't swim.

1 Choose the correct words to complete the sentences.

1 My teacher *said / told* me that my English was improving.
2 The doctor *said / told* you had to stay in bed.
3 Viktor *said / told* he had made a big mistake.
4 Someone *said / told* us that you had started a blog.
5 They *said / told* everyone they would win the game.
6 The newsreader *said / told* that scientists had discovered a new planet.

2 Rewrite these sentences in reported speech.

1 'I'll see you on Tuesday.'
My mum told me ______________________.
2 'It's not going to rain this week.'
The weather forecaster said ______________________.
3 'I've never eaten a curry.'
Julieta said ______________________.
4 'We saw your brother at the airport.'
They told me ______________________.
5 'I hadn't heard the news.'
Bobby said ______________________.
6 'I can't come to your wedding.'
Ravi told me ______________________.
7 'I'm waiting for a phone call.'
My boss said ______________________.
8 'I don't do much exercise.'
Sandra said ______________________.

3 Write the direct speech for the reported sentences.

1 Sheila and Harold said that they wanted to tell me their news.
____
2 They told me that they'd been to Egypt on holiday.
____
3 They said they'd been excited because they'd never been there before.
____
4 Sheila said that she'd never ride a camel again.
____
5 Harold told me he was going to go back next year.
____

◀ Go back to page 89

11A -*ing*/infinitive verb patterns

We often use two verbs together. The form of the second verb changes depending on the first verb.

I want to learn a new language.
I enjoy learning new languages.

After some verbs, we use the infinitive with *to*.

11.2	infinitive with *to*
decide	She decided to travel the world.
arrange	We've arranged to meet at the airport.
expect	I expect to have the results next week.
forget	Marcus forgot to buy any paper for the printer.
hope	He hopes to be here soon.
agree	They haven't agreed to decrease the price.
can afford	He can't afford to go on holiday.
manage	The driver managed to stop the train.
learn	I'm learning to speak Arabic.
offer	They offered to pay for the meal.
plan	We're planning to open a new office.
try	Meenah's trying to finish the project on time.
want	My sister wants to find a new job.
would like	I'd like to have a rest now.
promise	Saul promised to help me with the work.

After other verbs, we use the -*ing* form.

11.3	-*ing* form
imagine	Can you imagine living until you're 150?
feel like	I feel like staying in bed all day.
enjoy	My son enjoys visiting his grandparents.
fancy	We fancy eating out tonight.
suggest	They've suggested installing some new software.
spend (time)	I spend a lot of time travelling to work.
miss	She misses seeing her friends.
finish	Tony's finished building the wall.
hate	I hate being late.
keep	Jorge keeps making mistakes.
like	He doesn't like cooking dinner.
love	I love playing golf.
can't stand	Ramon can't stand staying in a tent.
mind	They don't mind getting up early.
look forward to	I'm looking forward to seeing you at the party.

Look! After some verbs, we can use the infinitive with *to* or the -*ing* form, with no difference in meaning, e.g. *start* and *continue*.
It has started to rain. *It has started raining.*
He continued to study. *He continued studying.*

1 Choose the correct form of the verbs to complete the sentences.

1 Have you finished *to clean / cleaning* the kitchen?
2 Josh arranged *to meet / meeting* Natasha at the cinema.
3 She promised *to do / doing* her homework.
4 I don't mind *to wait / waiting* for you.
5 They agreed *to repair / repairing* my dishwasher.
6 You should learn *to use / using* the computer.
7 We didn't expect *to see / seeing* them again.
8 He spent the whole morning *to sunbathe / sunbathing*.
9 Our teacher keeps *to give / giving* us lots of homework.
10 She offered *to help / helping me* with my English.
11 David suggested *to cancel / cancelling* the meeting.
12 Don't forget *to bring / bringing* warm clothes.

2 Complete the conversation with the correct form of the verbs in brackets.

Julia Felipe and I have decided [1] ________ (move) back to Brazil.
Sophie Really? I thought you liked [2] ________ (live) in Britain.
Julia Yes, but we miss [3] ________ (see) our families and we'd like [4] ________ (have) our own house. We could never afford [5] ________ (buy) a place in London.
Sophie When are you planning [6] ________ (leave)?
Julia Well, we don't want [7] ________ (wait) too long, so we expect [8] ________ (go) some time in the next couple of months. I've already managed [9] ________ (find) a job, and Felipe is hoping [10] ________ (get) one soon.
Sophie It won't be the same here without you. Do you promise [11] ________ (keep) in touch?
Julia Yes, of course. And if you and Dan feel like [12] ________ (come) to Brazil for a holiday, you'd be very welcome.
Sophie That sounds great. Don't forget [13] ________ (give) me your email address before you go.
Julia Don't worry, I won't. We're trying [14] ________ (organize) a party before we go, so that we can say goodbye to everyone properly. Do you fancy [15] ________ (come)?
Sophie I hate [16] ________ (say) goodbye to people, but yes, I'd love to come!

◀ Go back to page 95

11C Articles

We use articles (*a*, *an* or *the*) before nouns. Sometimes we don't need to use an article.

11.14	articles
Indefinite article *a/an*	I have **a** pet dog and **a** pet cat.
Definite article *the*	**The** dog is much bigger than **the** cat.
No article	I love animals, especially dogs and cats.

We use the indefinite article *a/an*:

- to talk about a person or thing for the first time.
  I've got two children – a boy and a girl.
- to talk about a person's job.
  My sister's an engineer.
- in expressions of frequency or measurement.
  I see him once a week.
  The fish costs £10 a kilo.

We use the definite article *the*:

- if we have already mentioned the person or thing or we know which one is referred to.
  The boy is called Alex, and the girl is called Lucy.
- if there is only one of the thing.
  The sun is setting.
  I'll check on the internet.
- before some countries, especially if they have two words or are plural.
  I live in the UK, but my brother lives in the Philippines.
- for specific places in a town.
  I went to the bank / the cinema / the theatre.
- for musical instruments.
  She plays the guitar.
- for superlatives.
  He's the fastest runner in the world.

We don't use an article:

- to talk about things in general (plural and uncountable nouns).
  Dogs are my favourite animals.
  Pollution is a big problem today.
- for some places we visit regularly.
  I'm not going to work today.
  He's working at home.
  She had to go to hospital.
- for meals, days of the week, months and years.
  On Tuesday, I'm having lunch with Jack.
  August is the hottest month of the year.

1 Complete the sentences with *a/an*, *the* or – (no article).

1. We usually go to ____ cinema once or twice ____ month.
2. I bought ____ new car yesterday, but this morning ____ engine won't start.
3. He's one of five brothers. ____ youngest brother is ____ doctor.
4. She flew from ____ Venezuela to ____ USA.
5. Are you really scared of ____ spiders?
6. How long have you played ____ piano?
7. Neil Armstrong was ____ first man on ____ moon.
8. I hope you both find ____ happiness together.
9. What did you have for ____ breakfast this morning?
10. We have ____ dinner together three times ____ year.
11. She got ____ home from ____ work and went straight to ____ bed.
12. ____ Friday is ____ busiest day of ____ week for us.

2 Correct the mistakes or tick (✓) the sentences if they are already correct.

1. Is she student? ☐
2. I'm staying in bed this morning. ☐
3. Why don't you ask her out for lunch? ☐
4. Excuse me, where is museum? ☐
5. It's lovely day today. ☐
6. The life is hard sometimes. ☐
7. The driver of our taxi was from Mexico. ☐
8. I went to bank this morning. ☐
9. My wife has never liked tomatoes. ☐
10. It's best present I've ever had. ☐

3 Complete the text with *a/an*, *the* or – (no article).

sochi 201

Hexoskin is 1____ Canadian company founded in 2____ 2006. It wanted to create 3____ clothes that could record 4____ information about our bodies. That's why they developed 5____ smart shirt which contains lots of sensors. 6____ sensors collect data about the wearer's movements, heart rate and breathing and send it to 7____ computer. Ariane Lavigne is 8____ Olympic athlete who uses it, and she says 9____ technology gives her 10____ advantage over other snowboarders.

◀ Go back to page 99

12A Defining relative clauses

We use relative clauses to say which person, thing or place we are talking about.

He's the actor who was Sherlock Holmes on TV.
It's a machine which makes bread.
That's the restaurant where I used to work.

We use the relative pronouns *who* or *that* to talk about people.

The man who sits next to me at work was ill today.
I saw the woman that works in the post office in the park.

We use the relative pronouns *which* or *that* to talk about things.

There are companies which organize weddings for people.
Luigi enjoys films that make him laugh.

We use *where* to talk about places.

I want to visit the stadium where Manchester United play football.
Jorge works in the hospital where I was born.

12.2	defining relative clauses
To describe people	He's the teacher **who** taught me English. Did you see the children **that** were singing?
To describe things	That's the dog **which** bit me on the leg. I don't want a car **that** has a big engine.
To describe places	I'll meet you in the square **where** we met last time.

Look! *Who*, *which*, *that* and *where* refer to a person, thing or place that's already been mentioned, so we don't need to use another word again.
Snakes are the animals which ~~they~~ kill most people each year.
I'd prefer to see the doctor who ~~she~~ saw me last time.
Ronald went to the cinema where we saw the Star Wars film ~~there~~.

1 A Complete the sentences with *who*, *which* or *where*.

1 Did you get the email ________ I sent you yesterday?
2 This is the nightclub ________ Nicola met her boyfriend.
3 There's a meeting at 2.00 p.m. for all employees ________ work in the Sales Department.
4 The office ________ she spends most of her time is in Kuala Lumpur.
5 The person ________ started this company is now a millionaire.
6 My father-in-law doesn't like films ________ are too violent.

B In which sentences could you also use *that*?

2 Add the correct words: *who*, *which*, or *where*. Then match the halves to make sentences.

1 An umbrella is something *which* *f*
2 A DJ is someone ________ ____
3 A hospital is a place ________ ____
4 A credit card is something ________ ____
5 An enemy is a person ________ ____
6 A passport is a document ________ ____
7 A department store is somewhere ________ ____
8 A selfie stick is something ________ ____
9 A single parent is someone ________ ____
10 A prison is a place ________ ____

a you go when you're ill.
b you use when you travel abroad.
c you use to take a photo of yourself.
d brings up a child without a partner.
e criminals are sent.
~~f you use when it rains.~~
g plays music in a club or on the radio.
h you can buy lots of different things.
i someone hates.
j you use instead of cash to buy things.

3 Combine the pairs of sentences using *who*, *which*, *that* or *where*. Remember not to use words that aren't necessary.

1 That's the restaurant. We're going there tonight.
That's the restaurant where we're going tonight.
2 I know the man. He lives in that house.
____
3 Did you enjoy the film? You watched it last night.
____
4 They're the neighbours. They have lots of parties.
____
5 We've booked a holiday in the hotel. We stayed there last summer.
____
6 My sister-in-law works for a company. It develops apps.
____

◀ Go back to page 103

12C Uses of the *-ing* form and the infinitive with *to*

We use the *-ing* form after prepositions. In the negative, *not* goes before the *-ing* form.

Thanks for inviting me to your wedding.
I'm bored of not going out.
He's worried about failing his exam.

We also use the *-ing* form as the subject or object of a sentence. The *-ing* form functions as a noun.

Keeping in touch is so easy these days.
Reading is a great way to improve your English.
Not drinking soft drinks has helped me to lose weight.
John doesn't enjoy reading.
I love dancing.

We use the infinitive with *to* after adjectives. In the negative, *not* goes before the *to*.

I'm amazed to hear that they're going out with each other.
She was disappointed to lose the match.
It's impossible not to laugh when you watch this film.

We also use the infinitive with *to* to say why we do something (to express the purpose).

I went shopping to buy a new pair of shoes.
She left the office to meet a friend.
They're saving all of their money to get married.

Look! We use *for* + *-ing* form to explain the function of things, but we use the infinitive with *to* to explain the purpose of actions.
Function: *This button is for turning up the volume.*
Purpose: *You press this button to turn up the volume.*

12.6	*-ing* form/infinitive with *to*
After prepositions	I'm interested **in buying** a new laptop.
As subject/object of a sentence	**Cycling** is a great way to keep fit. I love **cycling**.
After adjectives	It's **easy to forget** he's only eighteen.
To express a purpose	We have to leave soon **to get there on time**.

1 Choose the correct words to complete the sentences.

1 Before *to say* / *saying* anything, please just listen to me.
2 She wants a better job *to earn* / *for earning* more money.
3 He's afraid of *to disappoint* / *disappointing* his father.
4 *To share* / *Sharing* photos is easy with Instagram.
5 I'm really sorry for *to miss* / *missing* your party.
6 I'm delighted *to tell* / *telling* you that we're getting married.
7 *To speak* / *Speaking* another language is really useful in business.
8 She's pleased *not to work* / *not working* for that company.
9 He gave me the ring *to look after* / *looking after* for him.
10 We thought about *not to go* / *not going* to the wedding.

2 Write sentences in the present tense using the *-ing* form or infinitive with *to*.

1 Drink / too much coffee / not be / good for you
Drinking too much coffee isn't good for you.
2 She really / enjoy / go to the cinema
______
3 It / not be / expensive / eat / here
______
4 She / not be / afraid of / make mistakes
______
5 Cook / with friends / be / a nice way to relax
______
6 We / delighted / hear your news
______
7 He / not be / very good at / keep in touch
______
8 I / go / to the gym / keep fit
______

3 Complete the text with the correct form of the verbs in the box.

be work study get act

[1]____ happily married for over 50 years isn't easy, but that's what Paul Newman and Joanne Woodward were. In 1950, Paul was working for his family's business, but he was more interested in [2]____ , so at the age of 25 he went to Yale University [3]____ Drama. He was lucky [4]____ a job as an actor in a play called *Picnic*, where he first met Joanne. After [5]____ together in the film *The long hot summer* a few years later, they got married. And the rest, as they say, is history.

◀ Go back to page 107

1A Personality adjectives

1 1.1 Match sentences 1–8 with pictures a–h. Listen and check.

1 Rosa is very **shy**. She doesn't like talking to people she doesn't know. ____
2 Sven is very **funny**. He makes the children laugh. ____
3 Irene is very **patient**. She can wait for a long time and doesn't get angry. ____
4 Marco always buys me a coffee when we go out. He's really **generous**. ____
5 Stefano is very **kind**. He's always happy to help me when I have a problem. ____
6 Jana watches TV all day and she never cleans the house. I think she's **lazy**. ____
7 Arturo is very **polite**. He opens the door for us when we visit. ____
8 Jin-Wu always tells the truth about everything. She's very **honest**. ____

a

b

c

d

e

f

g

h

2 A 1.2 Match the adjectives in the box below with the definitions in the table. Listen and check.

hard-working sociable dishonest serious
rude selfish unkind impatient

This type of person ...	adjective	opposite
1 only thinks about himself/herself.		
2 says and does things that hurt other people's feelings.		
3 works very hard.		
4 likes going out and meeting new people.		
5 doesn't like waiting for things.		
6 doesn't laugh very often.		
7 isn't very helpful to others.		
8 doesn't tell the truth.		

B Write the adjectives from exercise 1 in the 'opposite' column.

Look! We say *What is he/she like?* when we ask about personality.
What is your teacher like? *She's shy, but she's very kind.*

3 Choose the correct adjectives to complete the sentences.

1 Children can be very *impatient* / *unkind* / *dishonest*. They can say very bad things and make each other cry.
2 Paul prefers to be with people he knows. He's very *rude* / *patient* / *shy*.
3 I think Leo's *dishonest* / *rude* / *lazy*. He plays computer games all day and he doesn't do any work.
4 Marco's very *selfish* / *impatient* / *lazy*. He drinks all the milk in the fridge and doesn't think about the rest of us.
5 Amanda hates waiting for the bus. She's so *impatient* / *unkind* / *selfish*.
6 Anton is really *patient* / *generous* / *sociable* with his time and his money. He always buys me lunch when we meet.
7 Artur doesn't smile or laugh very much and he thinks a lot about all his decisions. He's very *hard-working* / *polite* / *serious*.
8 Semih's really *sociable* / *funny* / *kind*. He always makes us laugh when he tells us his stories.
9 Stella is a *lazy* / *dishonest* / *serious* person. She lies to people so they think she's clever.
10 Those children are very *polite* / *generous* / *honest*. If they break something, they always tell the teacher.

◀ Go back to page 4

1B Hobbies and socializing

1 1.7 Match the halves in each group to make phrases. Listen and check.

Online activities

1 download ____
2 go on ____
3 blog ____
4 play ____
5 shop ____

a social media (e.g. Facebook)
b about your opinions
c music/films/apps
d online
e videogames

Socializing

11 spend ____
12 meet up ____
13 meet ____
14 join ____
15 go ____

k a club
l out at night
m time with family
n new people
o with friends

Sports and games

6 keep ____
7 play ____
8 go ____
9 do ____
10 go to ____

f football/chess
g exercise/Pilates
h fit
i the gym/the swimming pool
j running/swimming

Other hobbies

16 bake ____
17 learn ____
18 relax ____
19 go to ____
20 collect ____

p at home
q concerts/the cinema
r an instrument/a language
s coins/records/stamps
t bread/cakes

2 Complete the sentences with the correct forms of the verbs in the box.

meet keep relax spend go join shop go on meet up do

1 It's important to ________ time with your friends and family.
2 Why don't you ________ a tennis club?
3 Karen usually ________ online because she is very busy.
4 I went to English classes to ________ new people.
5 I think swimming is the best way to ________ fit.
6 Anatol doesn't have many hobbies. He just ________ at home.
7 I hardly ever ________ social media. I prefer meeting people face-to-face.
8 Saturday night is a good time to ________ with my friends.
9 You need to be very fit to ________ gymnastics.
10 Martin ________ running every morning at 6.00.

◀ Go back to page 6

1C Useful verbs

1 1.15 Complete the sentences with the correct forms of the verbs. Listen and check.

1 **wear** / **carry**
It's a beautiful day. Why are you _________ an umbrella and _________ a coat?

2 **bring** / **take**
Could you _________ me to the party, please? Brian says he can _________ me back home afterwards.

3 **look** / **look like**
A: She _________ beautiful in that dress, doesn't she?
B: Yes, she _________ her mother.

4 **look forward to** / **expect**
I'm _________ seeing my cousins again. We _________ their train to arrive very soon.

5 **say** / **tell**
Don't _________ her about the party. Charlotte _________ that she loves surprises!

6 **miss** / **lose**
Here are our cinema tickets – don't _________ them! I don't want to _________ the start of the film.

7 **hope** / **wait**
I'm _________ for you at the restaurant. I _________ you're not going to be late.

8 **win** / **earn**
He doesn't _________ very much money as a writer, although he _________ lots of competitions.

9 **remember** / **remind**
I must _________ to buy some eggs. If I forget, please can you _________ me?

10 **go back** / **come back**
My parents are _________ from Greece today. They had a fantastic time. They want to _________ next year!

2A Choose the correct verb to complete questions 1–8.

1 Who do you *look like* / *look* in your family?
2 Are you *going back* / *coming back* to college in the autumn?
3 What did you *take* / *bring* with you to class today?
4 How do you usually *wear* / *carry* your things to class?
5 Do you always *remember* / *remind* to do your homework?
6 Do you ever *lose* / *miss* your mobile phone?
7 Do you always *say* / *tell* your parents the truth?
8 Where do you *hope* / *wait* to be in 10 years' time?

B Match questions 1–8 with answers a–h.

____ **a** Yes. We start in October.
____ **b** Nothing! I forgot my bag.
____ **c** I use a small backpack.
____ **d** Sometimes, but I normally carry it in my pocket.
____ **e** Of course! I'm very honest.
____ **f** I want to have my own company.
____ **g** No I don't. Sometimes I forget.
____ **h** My mother. We have the same eyes.

◀ Go back to page 9

3B Holiday activities

1 3.5 Complete the table with the words in the box to make phrases. Listen and check.

a museum   on a guided tour   abroad   a seat on a train   a resort
local attractions   sightseeing   camping   a hotel   a flight   a double room

go	visit	stay in	book

2 3.6 Match the sentences. Listen and check.

1 We always **sunbathe** on the beach. ____
2 I usually **buy souvenirs** for my family. ____
3 You can **hire a car** for a week. ____
4 On holiday, we usually **eat out** every night. ____
5 Let's **have a barbecue** at the weekend. ____
6 I sometimes **pack my suitcase** a week before we go. ____

a It's expensive but we like trying the local food.
b The weather looks good and the garden is tidy.
c That way I don't forget anything.
d The local market is the best place to find presents.
e I like relaxing and listening to the sea.
f It's a good way to see the countryside.

◀ Go back to page 24

2A *-ed/-ing* adjectives

1 2.5 Look at the pictures and complete the sentences with the *-ed* or *-ing* adjectives. Listen and check.

1 **amazed / amazing**
The magic show was __________!
I was __________. The magician did some incredible tricks.

2 **relaxed / relaxing**
I had a really __________ weekend.
I felt so __________ I had a sleep on Saturday afternoon.

3 **tired / tiring**
What a long day! I'm so __________ now.
It's __________ being a mother.

4 **interested / interesting**
I'm __________ in Roman History.
Do you have any __________ books on the subject?

ROMAN
HISTORY

5 **bored / boring**
The lesson was very __________ this morning.
I was so __________, I fell asleep!

6 **embarrassed / embarrassing**
I felt __________ when the computer stopped working.
I couldn't give my presentation.
It was very __________.

Error
try again

7 **annoyed / annoying**
I was __________ because Joe was playing loud music.
It's very __________ when people make lots of noise.

8 **disappointed / disappointing**
I failed my driving test last week.
I was really __________.
It's __________, but I can take the test again.

9 **excited / exciting**
I got my ticket for the music festival. I'm so __________!
It's always __________ to go to a live concert.

10 **frightened / frightening**
I don't like this. I'm __________ of heights!
I didn't think cleaning windows would be so __________.

11 **confused / confusing**
These instructions are very __________.
I'm completely __________.
I don't know what this means.

12 **surprised / surprising**
Ana received a __________ email this morning.
Ana was really __________ when she read the email.

2 Choose the correct adjectives to complete the sentences.

1 The lesson was really *interested / interesting* and all the students enjoyed it.
2 We were all *surprised / surprising* when we heard Katya's news.
3 The photos from the concert were really *disappointed / disappointing*.
4 Are you *excited / exciting* about moving abroad next year?
5 Horror films are *frightened / frightening*. I never watch them.
6 The exam questions were very *confused / confusing*. I didn't understand them at all.
7 I lost my phone, so I couldn't take any photos. It was very *annoyed / annoying*.
8 I was so *embarrassed / embarrassing* when I arrived late.

◀ Go back to page 13

2C Life stages

1 2.6 Match the phrases in the box with the pictures on the timeline. Listen and check.

~~be born~~ ~~die~~ get engaged go to university get your driving licence go to primary school get divorced fall in love retire get married grow up have children leave school go to secondary school start a career

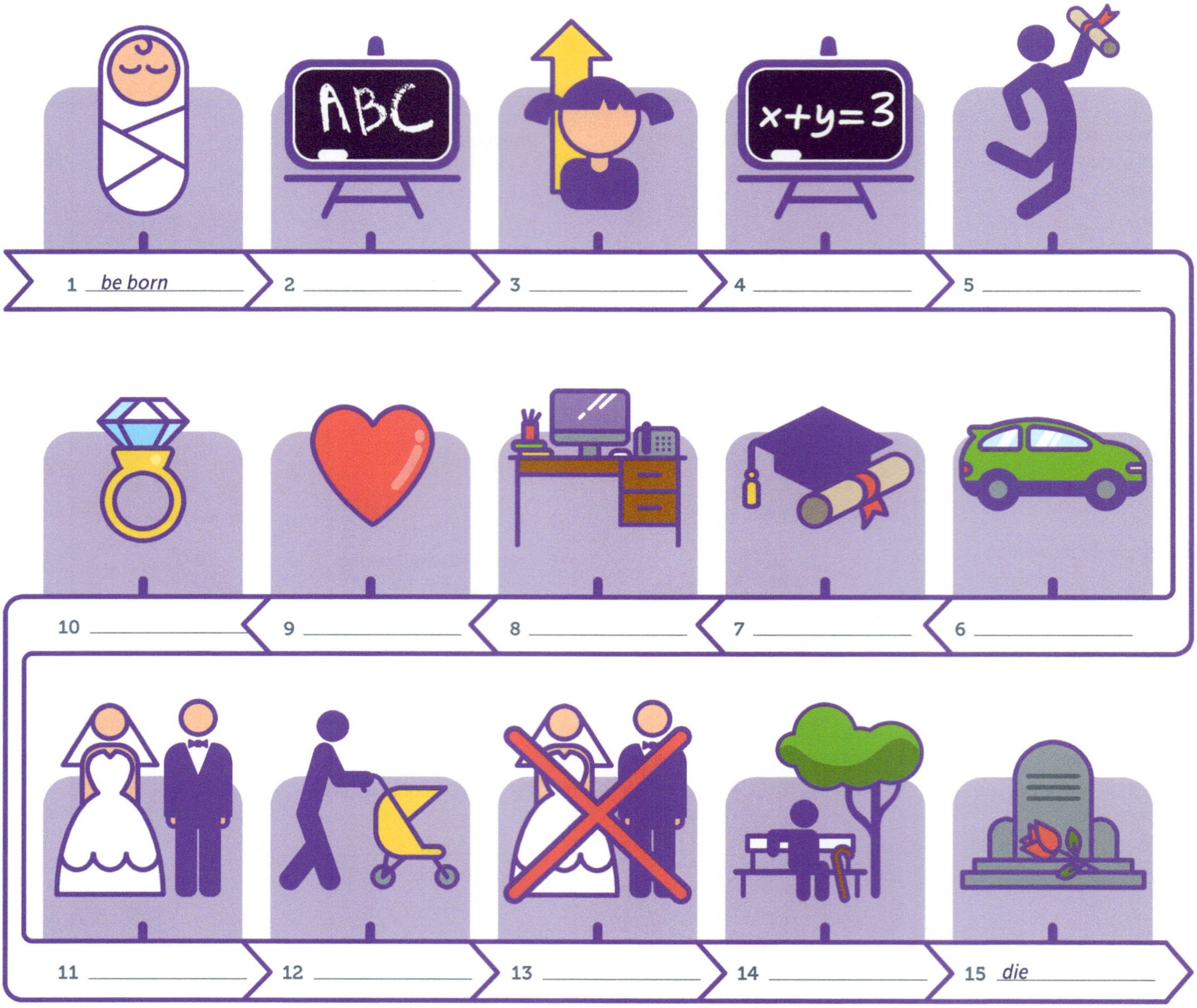

ABC
x+y=3
1 *be born*
2 ______
3 ______
4 ______
5 ______
6 ______
7 ______
8 ______
9 ______
10 ______
11 ______
12 ______
13 ______
14 ______
15 *die*

2 Match the halves to make sentences.

1 My grandmother was born ___
2 She grew up ___
3 She went to primary school ___
4 She left school when ___
5 She went to university ___
6 She started her career ___
7 There, she met ___
8 They got married ___
9 They had two children – ___
10 My grandmother retired ___

a my grandfather, also a doctor.
b at the age of 65.
c she was 18, in 1961.
d my mother and my uncle.
e on 14 April 1943.
f in 1966, after getting engaged.
g when she was five.
h on a farm near Liverpool.
i as a hospital doctor in London.
j to study Medicine.

3 Complete the text with the correct form of the life stages verbs.

1 My parents worked in lots of different countries, so I __________ with my grandparents in Madrid.
2 Luca __________ to his girlfriend last week. The wedding is in May, next year.
3 I want to __________ in the summer. Then I can drive to university every day.
4 Sandra's parents __________ ten years ago, but they are still friends and they often see each other.
5 Raoul works in that hospital. He says almost 30 babies __________ there every day.

◀ Go back to page 16

3A Useful adjectives

1 3.1 Match the adjectives in the box with the pictures 1–12. Listen and check.

ancient modern crowded famous busy lively messy polluted quiet ugly uncomfortable unusual

1 ____________

2 ____________

3 ____________

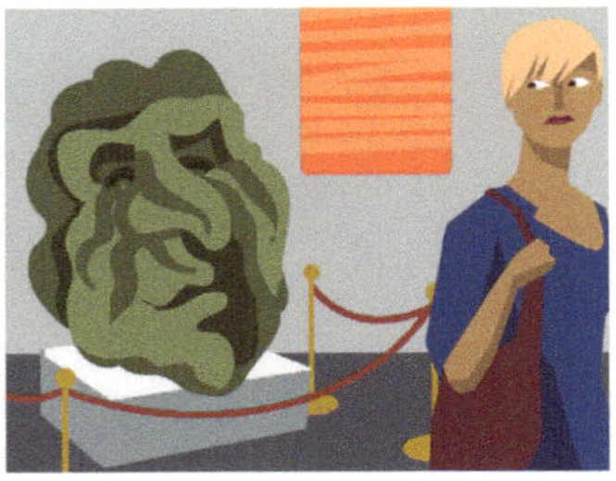

4 ____________

5 ____________

6 ____________

7 ____________

8 ____________

9 ____________

10 ____________

11 ____________

12 ____________

2 Choose the correct word to complete the sentences.

1 Our hotel room was really *uncomfortable* / *quiet*. We complained to the manager.
2 Petra is one of the most *lively* / *famous* archaeological sites in the Middle East.
3 You will love this restaurant – it's always very *lively* / *crowded*.
4 We went to the beach for our holiday but the water was really *polluted* / *messy*.
5 It's impossible to get on the buses at rush hour – they are so *lively* / *crowded*.
6 If you go to Egypt, don't miss the *ugly* / *ancient* temples in the south in Luxor and Aswan.
7 We loved Vietnam. The streets were so *busy* / *messy* with all kinds of vehicles and people.
8 He went all around the world and all he bought me was an *ugly* / *ancient* key-ring.
9 We went for a walk away from the city centre and found some *quiet* / *messy* streets.
10 We saw some very *unusual* / *uncomfortable* animals when we went to Australia.
11 There is a new building in the city centre – it's really *lively* / *modern*.
12 The children's rooms are always *unusual* / *messy* on holiday. It's hard work.

3 Complete the text with the correct adjectives.

My first trip to a foreign country was in 2015, when I visited Cambodia. My favourite place was Angkor Wat, which is one of the most [1] __________ archaeological sites in the world. There are hundreds of [2] __________ temples from the 12th century in an area of over 1 km^2! It's a very [3] __________ place but I'm very glad I went.

I went very early in the morning because it gets very [4] __________ later in the day and the buses get [5] __________. You can visit the site on your own, or hire a guide who can show you around and explain everything. Remember not to wear [6] __________ shoes, because you have to walk a lot!

◀ Go back to page 22

4A Jobs

1 4.1 Match the words in the box with the pictures 1–12. Listen and check.

lawyer accountant waiter/waitress receptionist surgeon firefighter scientist hairdresser journalist model salesperson farmer

1 ______________

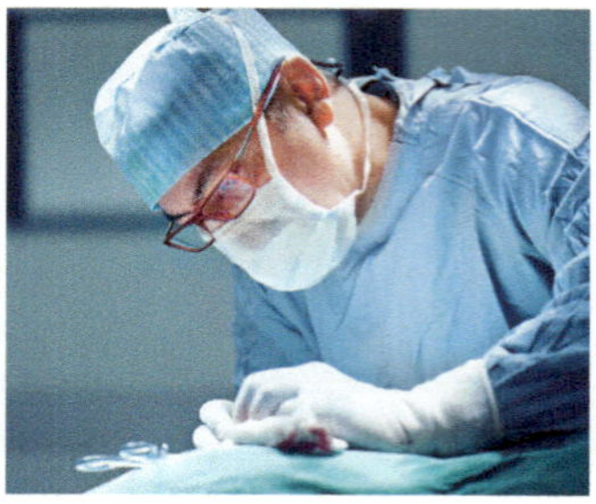

2 ______________

3 ______________

4 ______________

5 ______________

6 ______________

7 ______________

8 ______________

9 ______________

10 ______________

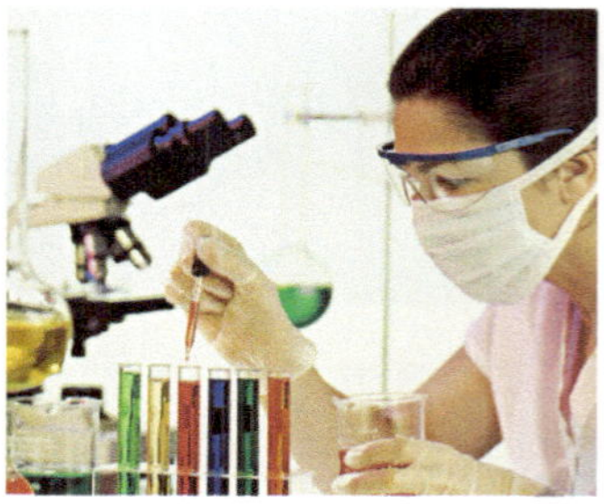

11 ______________

12 ______________

2 4.2 Match the words to make jobs. Listen and check.

1	fashion ____	a	guide
2	film ____	b	designer
3	football ____	c	officer
4	police ____	d	coach
5	security ____	e	reporter
6	shop ____	f	guard
7	tour ____	g	assistant
8	news ____	h	director
9	travel ____	i	attendant
10	flight ____	j	agent

3 Complete the sentences with the correct jobs from exercises 1 and 2.

1 Whenever I have my hair cut, I always tell the __________ all my problems.
2 I didn't know where to go on holiday, but the __________ suggested some good places.
3 I was worried about the operation, but the __________ said everything would be OK.
4 I went to buy a new shirt and the __________ was very helpful.
5 The __________ might lose his job. The team has lost ten games now!
6 Why don't you speak to a __________ before you sign this contract?
7 My mother is a __________ . She works for a company that develops new medicines.
8 Our plane was full, but the __________ was very helpful.
9 The concert was really crowded and a __________ said I couldn't go in.
10 I'm sure the company has financial problems. The __________ looks very worried!

◀ Go back to page 30

4C Phrases about work

1 4.11 Match the phrases with the pictures. Listen and check.

agree a salary	apply for a job	get a job offer
get a pay rise	get a promotion	have an interview
leave a job	see a job advert	start work	write a CV

COMPUTER PROGRAMMER
WANTED

1 __________

CV

2 __________

3 __________

HR DIRECTOR

4 __________

JOB OFFER

5 __________

6 __________

7 __________

8 __________

GENERAL MANAGER

9 __________

10 __________

2 Complete the sentences with the correct form of the verbs from exercise 1.

1 I would like to __________ for the job of assistant manager.
2 I'm so bored at work. I __________ my job in January.
3 My husband __________ a pay rise last week so we're going to buy a flat.
4 It looks like a fabulous new job. When do you __________ work?
5 I __________ a job advert in the paper last week. It looks really interesting!
6 My sister __________ a promotion to company director. We're all very pleased.
7 All the new jobs will be advertized next month. I need to __________ a CV.
8 I __________ three job offers in one week! I'm not sure what to do!
9 She can't go to the meeting on Tuesday. She __________ an interview for a new job.
10 The interview went well and I want the job, but we can't __________ a salary.

3 4.12 Match 1–8 with a–h to make expressions. Listen and check.

1 see	____	a interested in a career in ...
2 send	____	b a degree in ...
3 have	____	c on a training course
4 go	____	d an interview at any time
5 be	____	e for a salary between ...
6 look	____	f as an intern
7 attend	____	g a CV, an application form
8 work	____	h an advertisement, an advert

4 Complete the letter with the words in the box.

degree	interview	advertisement	salary	application	career

Dear Sir/Madam

I saw your 1 __________ for the job of Software Engineer and I'd like to apply. I am sending you my CV and an 2 __________ form.

I have a 3 __________ in Information Technology and am very interested in a 4 __________ in software development.

I am looking for a 5 __________ between £30,000 and £35,000 and I can attend an 6 __________ any time in the next two weeks.

I look forward to hearing from you.

Kind regards

Chloe Maxwell

◀ Go back to page 35

5A Health and medicine

1 5.1 Complete the problems 1–16 with the words in the box. Listen and check.

stomach ache	backache	broke	nosebleed	burned	cold	cough	cut
earache	flu	headache	hurts	sore throat	stressed	temperature	toothache

1 I ________ my hand.

TISSUES

2 I have a ________ .

3 I ________ my finger.

4 I ________ my leg.

5 I have a ________ .

6 I have a ________ .

7 I have a ________ .

8 I have a ________ .

9 I have ________ .

10 I have ________ .

11 I have a ________ .

12 I have a ________ .

13 I'm feeling ________ .

14 My knee ________ .

15 I have the ________ .

16 I have ________ .

2 Match problems 1–9 with possible solutions in the box. There may be more than one answer.

1 I don't feel well. I have a stomach ache. ________
2 Those boxes were heavy. I have backache now! ________
3 Ooh! I have a sore throat. ________
4 I'm worried about my nosebleeds. ________
5 I have a terrible headache. ________
6 I feel awful. I think I have the flu. ________
7 I'm stressed about work. ________
8 I burned my hand yesterday. It still hurts. ________
9 My foot hurts. I fell getting out of the car! ________

go to the doctor	call a friend
take some tablets	put some ice / cold water on it
rest in bed	have some hot lemon and honey
go and lie down	talk to your boss
have some chicken soup	put some cream on it
go to bed early every night	eat healthy food

◀ Go back to page 40

5B Collocations with *do, make, have* and *take*

1 ▶ 5.5 Complete the diagrams with *do*, *make*, *have* or *take*. Listen and check.

1 ________ : a break, a chance, your time, a deep breath

3 ________ : a rest, a chat, a good time, an argument, some tea/coffee

2 ________ : a list, a decision, an excuse, a mistake, an effort

4 ________ : something, exercise, your best, your homework

2 Complete the sentences with the correct form of the verbs *do*, *make*, *have* or *take*.

1 I ________ a bad argument with my parents last night.
2 Ahmet always finishes his work late and ________ an excuse.
3 If you want to make good sushi, you have to ________ your time.
4 Don't ________ any mistakes or you will need to start again.
5 She's a dancer so she ________ a lot of exercise.
6 We ________ a great time when we went to California.
7 Li Xiao ________ her best, but she failed the exam.
8 I don't have a reservation, but I'm going to ________ a chance and go.

◀ Go back to page 42

6A Phrasal verbs

1 ▶ 6.1 Match sentences 1–8 with the pictures a–h . Listen and check.

1 Can I **turn on** the air conditioning? ____
2 I'm going to **find out** who did this. ____
3 Oh no! We've **run out of** milk! ____
4 Why did the car **break down** here? ____
5 Please **throw away** bottles in this bin. ____
6 Can you **fill up** the car with petrol, please? ____
7 You should **tidy up** your bedroom. ____
8 I'm going to **look up** the word in a dictionary. ____

PLASTIC
GLASS
a

b

c

d

e

f

g

SCHOOL
h

2 ▶ 6.2 Match the phrasal verbs in **bold** with their meanings a–h. Listen and check.

1 I don't want to **carry on** with the course. It's boring.
2 If you want to get fit you should **take up** running.
3 I'm going to **look after** my sister's children tonight.
4 You need to **fill in** this form to get a passport.
5 Can you **give back** the money you owe me?
6 You should **give up** smoking. It's bad for you.
7 If you **hold on** for five minutes, I'll come too.
8 The snow will soon **turn into** water.

a wait
b continue
c stop
d start
e return
f care for
g complete
h become

3 Complete the sentences with the correct form of the phrasal verbs.

1 My car is awful. It ________ every month!
2 Yesterday, I ________ that I'm going to get a pay rise.
3 I'm going to ________ this pen. It's broken.
4 It rained at first, but then it ________ a beautiful day.
5 Two years ago, Colin ________ milk for health reasons.
6 The shop ________ size 8 jeans yesterday.
7 Can you ________ my cat while I'm on holiday.
8 Can we stop for lunch now? I can't ________ any longer.

◀ Go back to page 48

5C Emotions and feelings

1 5.10 Look at the pictures. Match sentences 1–12 with people a–l. Listen and check.

INTERVIEW
a
b
c
d

1 Roberto feels very **confident**. He thinks he'll get the job. ____
2 Mr Wallace doesn't like his job. He looks **miserable**. ____
3 Karen isn't worried about the interview. She's very **calm** today. ____
4 Peter hates interviews. He gets very **nervous**. ____

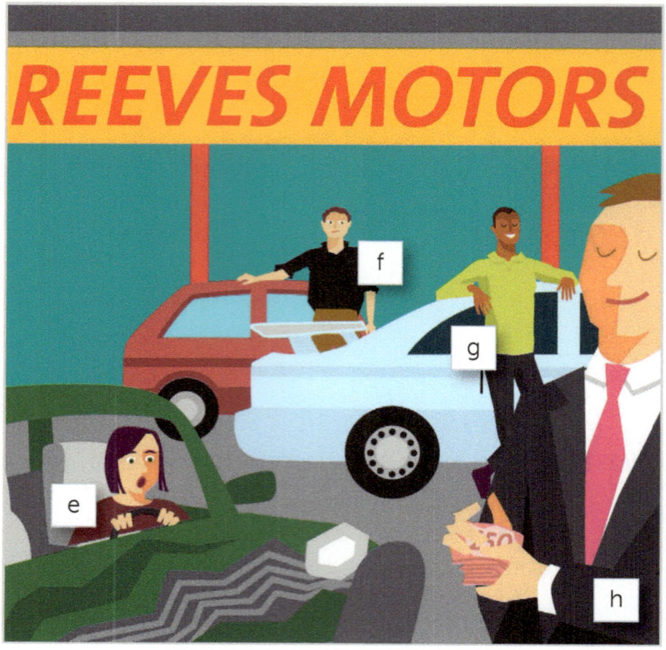
REEVES MOTORS
e
f
g
h

5 Kevin's very **proud** of his expensive new car. ____
6 Joe's **envious** of Kevin's car. He can't afford a new one. ____
7 Mr Reeves has made a lot of money. He's **delighted**. ____
8 Sally's very **upset** because she crashed her car. ____

i
j
k
l

9 Vikram loves his job. He's very **cheerful** today. ____
10 Lucia forgot Jess's birthday and is one hour late. She feels **guilty**. ____
11 Jess is celebrating her birthday on her own. She feels very **lonely**. ____
12 Mr Lee's **jealous**. He doesn't like his wife talking to Vikram. ____

2 Choose the correct words to complete the sentences.

1 I worked really hard for this exam. I'm *proud / confident / delighted* I will pass.
2 Claire's really *calm / guilty / upset* because her boss invited everyone to a party except her.
3 Pavel borrowed his neighbour's coffee machine and broke it. He feels really *guilty / envious / miserable*.
4 I was *cheerful / delighted / confident* when I got a pay rise and a promotion at work.
5 I moved to the city last year. I see lots of people but I still feel *envious / confident / lonely* sometimes.
6 My son won a writing competition. I'm so *proud / confident / delighted* of him.
7 My neighbour finishes work at 2.00 p.m. every day. I sometimes feel quite *upset / envious / guilty* of her!
8 When she listens to classical music she always feels very *cheerful / confident / calm*.
9 Jo doesn't like public speaking, but she's going to give a presentation this afternoon. She's really *lonely / nervous / upset*.
10 I feel *miserable / jealous / guilty*. My train was late, I lost my phone and now it's starting to rain!
11 Malika's son is only 3 years old. He gets *guilty / lonely / jealous* when she plays with her friends' children.
12 My boss was very *cheerful / delighted / proud* today. She was singing a song when she came into the office.

◀ Go back to page 44

6C The natural world

1A Match the landscapes in the box with pictures 1–3.

mountains rainforest coast

B 6.7 Match the words with the natural features a–r. Listen and check.

river ____
stream ____
rocks ____
branch ____
roots ____
wildlife ____

1 ______________
d
e
c
f
b
a

cliff ____
ocean ____
waves ____
shore ____
lightning ____
thunderstorm ____

2 ______________
i
j
g
k
h
l

cave ____
peak ____
valley ____
waterfall ____
lake ____
sunrise/sunset ____

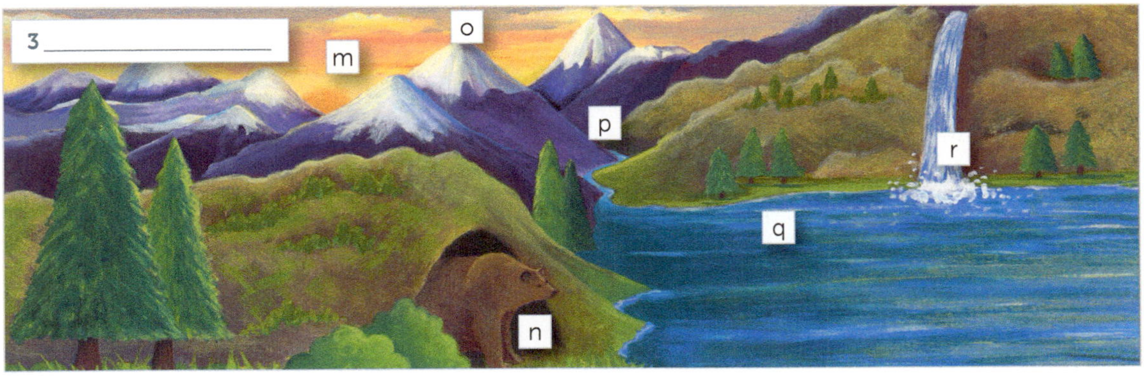
3 ______________
o
m
p
r
q
n

2 ~~Cross out~~ the word that is incorrect in each sentence.

1 It's difficult to take a photo of the *sunset* / *lightning* / *a wave* because you only see it for a second.
2 We saw a snake sitting on a *branch* / *rock* / *stream*.
3 You can drink the water from the *ocean* / *river* / *stream*.
4 You can hear the *cave* / *thunder* / *waterfall* from a long way away.
5 He believes that there are bears living in the *root* / *cave* / *valley*.
6 My feet got wet while I was walking along the *lake* / *shore* / *wildlife*.
7 She wants to climb up this *cliff* / *peak* / *wave*, but it's very difficult.
8 We didn't expect to see a *thunderstorm* / *the ocean* / *wildlife* on our beach holiday.

3 Complete the sentences with words a–h.

1 One of the driest places in the world is Death ____.
2 In Acapulco, people dive into the sea from tall ____.
3 Cairo is on the banks of the ____ Nile.
4 Niagara is an amazing ____ in the USA .
5 Every year, we drive along the Atlantic ____.
6 Surfers love going to Hawaii for its giant ____.
7 In 1963, a plane crashed when ____ hit it.
8 They say the Loch Ness Monster lives in a ____ in Scotland.

a River
b coast
c lake
d lightning
e cliffs
f Valley
g waves
h waterfall

◀ Go back to page 52

7A City features

1 7.1 Match the words in the box with the pictures 1–14. Listen and check.

apartment block pedestrian crossing street light signpost pavement bike lane fountain tunnel crossroads bridge bench litter bin statue traffic lights

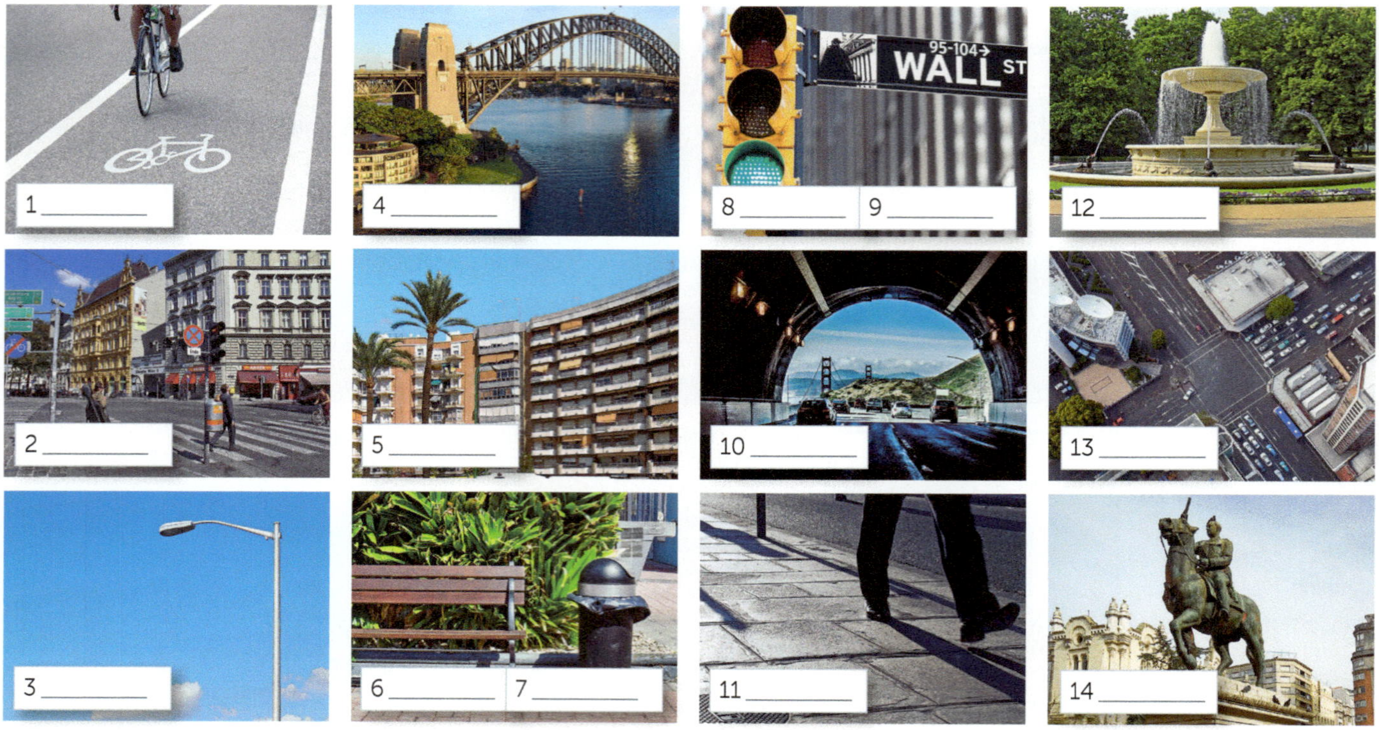
1 ________
4 ________
95-104→
WALL ST
8 ________
9 ________
12 ________
2 ________
5 ________
10 ________
13 ________
3 ________
6 ________
7 ________
11 ________
14 ________

2 Choose the correct options to complete the sentences.

1 The quickest way to the city centre is to go through the *bridge / tunnel*.
2 He stopped because the *street lights / traffic lights* were red.
3 Use the *pedestrian crossing / crossroads* – this road is dangerous.
4 This area is really dirty. I think it's because there aren't any *benches / litter bins*.
5 There's a big *statue / fountain* of a horse in the main square.
6 Follow the *signposts / pavement* for the national museum.
7 I don't like cycling here, there are no *apartment blocks / bike lanes*.
8 Go along this street, and turn right at the *crossroads / litter bin*.

◀ Go back to page 58

7B Transport

1 7.6 Match the words in the box with the definitions. Listen and check.

car park commuter delayed on time parking space passenger platform public transport rush hour traffic jam

1 The trains and buses people use to travel. ________
2 The area in a station where you get on and off a train. ________
3 A person travelling, but not driving. ________
4 Someone who travels to work each day. ________
5 An area or building where people leave their cars. ________
6 The time of day when most people are travelling. ________
7 A place where you can leave a single car. ________
8 Slow or late. ________
9 A long line of cars that move very slowly. ________
10 Not early or late. ________

2 7.7 Match the sentences. Listen and check.

1 The trains never **arrive on time**. ____
2 It **takes me** nearly two hours to get to work. ____
3 Shall I **give you a lift** to the shops? ____
4 I work at a local school, so I usually **go on foot**. ____
5 I prefer to **ride my bike** into town. ____
6 You need to **set off earlier**. ____
7 It's much quicker to **go by taxi**. ____
8 I have to **take a bus** and **a train** to work. ____

a I'm going into town anyway.
b That's why I always have my breakfast on the way.
c You will find one outside the station.
d I usually miss one of them!
e Last week I waited nearly 50 minutes on the platform.
f I always speak to people on the way.
g You're always late for work!
h It's faster than walking and there are good bike lanes.

◀ Go back to page 60

8A Food and drink

1 8.1 Match the words in the box with the pictures 1–20. Listen and check.

tomato sauce beef prawns cereal cucumber salmon lettuce peppers fruit juice pineapple strawberry lamb tuna cabbage coconut turkey flour peach aubergine apple pie

1 ______

2 ______

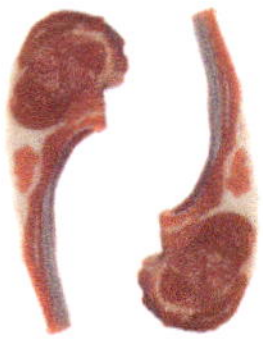
3 ______

4 ______

5 ______

6 ______

7 ______

8 ______

9 ______

10 ______

11 ______

12 ______

13 ______

14 ______

15 ______

16 ______

17 ______

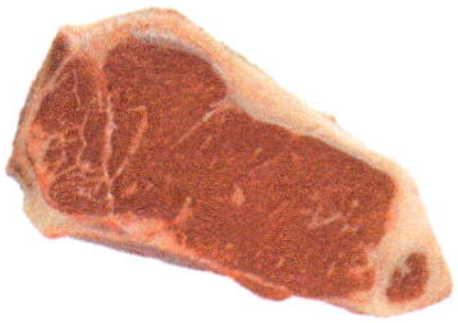
18 ______

19 ______

20 ______

2 Complete the sentences with the words in the box.

strawberries tuna cucumber coconut prawns fruit juice beef lettuce apple pie tomato sauce flour cereal

1 For breakfast, I usually have a bowl of ______ and a glass of ______ .
2 It's easy to make bread. You just need ______ , water and salt.
3 I'm allergic to seafood, I can't eat ______ .
4 The simplest pizza only has ______ and cheese on the top.
5 It's difficult to open the shell of a ______ , but the milk inside is delicious.
6 My grandmother is going to make an ______ for dessert tonight.
7 I'm going to make sushi tonight, so I need some rice and ______ .
8 She always has a salad with tomatoes, ______ and ______ for lunch.
9 In the summer, I love eating ______ and cream!
10 I ate some amazing ______ steaks in Argentina.

◀ Go back to page 66

8C Adjectives to describe food

1 8.8 Complete the descriptions 1–8 with the words in the box. Listen and check.

spicy unhealthy tasty raw fresh crunchy salty delicious sour disgusting healthy vegetarian bitter burnt creamy sweet

1 You can't eat that __________ toast. It will taste __________ !

2 Sashimi is made with __________ fish. There's not much fat or salt, so it's very __________ .

3 I don't eat meat so I ordered a __________ curry, but it was so __________ I had to drink lots of water!

4 I know chips are __________ , but mmm! They're very __________ !

5 I don't like black coffee – it's too __________ . I prefer a __________ hot chocolate.

6 In Morocco, they make tea with __________ mint and lots of sugar, so it's very __________ .

7 You can't eat these snacks quietly – they're so __________ . They're __________ too, but perfect with a cold drink.

8 Oh no! I can't use this milk, it tastes a bit __________ . My cake has to be __________ to win the competition.

2 Choose the correct words to complete the sentences.

1 **A** Do you remember those *tacos* we ate in Mexico that were full of chilli peppers?
B I'll never forget that. They were so *burnt / spicy / crunchy* that I started crying!

2 **A** How often do you go to the supermarket?
B Hardly ever. I think the market is the best place to buy *fresh / raw / spicy* ingredients.

3 **A** Is something wrong with your cake?
B Yes, I used too much sugar and now it's too *salty / tasty / sweet*.

4 **A** What's *lassi*?
B Oh, you'll love it! It's a *disgusting / bitter / creamy* drink from India made with yoghurt.

5 **A** I have some lettuce, cucumbers and red peppers in the fridge.
B Great! Then we can make a nice *crunchy / creamy / salty* salad for lunch.

6 **A** Do you like lemon juice?
B No, I don't. It's too *spicy / sour / raw* for me.

◀ Go back to page 70

9A Money verbs

1 9.3 Complete the sentences with the words in the box. Listen and check.

owe borrow can afford charge cost earn get paid be worth own pay back save spend waste lend

1 Excuse me, how much does this necklace __________?
2 In my opinion, football clubs __________ too much for tickets.
3 Waiters can __________ a lot of money from tips.
4 Can you __________ me $50 until I get paid next week?
5 He has a rare 1950s Rolex watch. It must __________ a fortune!
6 As well as their flat in London, they __________ a house in France.
7 They __________ most of their money on clothes.
8 How much money do you __________ to the bank each month?
9 The car isn't ours yet. We still __________ £5,000 to the bank.
10 I've left all my money at home. Can I __________ £20, please?
11 Don't __________ your money on lottery tickets – you'll never win!
12 He's trying to __________ for an expensive holiday next summer.
13 She's so rich that she __________ to buy anything she wants.
14 We normally __________ on the last day of the month.

2 Choose the correct words to complete the sentences.

1 Oh no, I've forgotten my wallet. Can you *borrow / lend / owe* me some money?
2 I can't go out tonight. I don't *earn / afford / get paid* until next week.
3 Excuse me, how much does this jacket *cost / worth / charge*?
4 I *spend / waste / save* almost half of my money on rent every month.
5 If you give me $200, I'll *borrow / owe / pay back* the money next week.
6 I bought the guitar for $500, but it's now *worth / cost / earn* almost double that.
7 My car is very old, but I can't *spend / afford / own* to buy a new one at the moment.
8 When I finish university, I will *owe / lend / charge* more than $10,000 to the bank.
9 I shouldn't go out this month. I need to *charge / earn / save* for a new computer.
10 Why did you pay *back / waste / earn* all your money on these comics?

◀ Go back to page 77

9B Shopping

1 9.5 Choose the correct verbs to complete the sentences. Listen and check.

1 Can I *pay by / pay with* credit card, or do I have to *pay by / pay with* cash?

2 I'd like to *exchange / return* this jacket – it's too big. Can I *exchange / return* it for a smaller one, please?

3 Can I *try on / fit* these shoes, please? I need to know if they *try on / fit* me.

4 You can *deliver / order* furniture online. Then the company will *deliver / order* it to your house.

2 9.6 Match the words in the box with the definitions 1–12. Listen and check.

changing room bargain receipt discount the sales cash refund till window shopping department store queue shopping centre

1 A product which a shop sells at a very good price. __________
2 A piece of paper that shows you have bought something. __________
3 A time when a shop sells things for a lower price than usual. __________
4 The place in a shop where you can try on clothes. __________
5 A line of people that are waiting for something. __________
6 The place where you pay for things in a shop. __________
7 The money that is returned when a product isn't suitable. __________
8 An amount or percentage off the usual price. __________
9 Money in the form of notes and coins. __________
10 Looking at products in shops without buying anything. __________
11 A large shop with areas selling different types of products. __________
12 A covered area with different shops. __________

3 Match the halves to make sentences.

1 I'm going to try on these jeans ____
2 I'm sorry, I can't give you a refund ____
3 Please join the queue for this till, ____
4 This morning I went window shopping ____
5 I bought this handbag for £15 in the sales – ____
6 I bought it at the department store because ____
7 If I pay with cash, ____
8 I ordered these online last week, ____

a can you offer me a discount?
b in the changing room.
c but you can only pay by credit card.
d it was a real bargain!
e if there's a problem, I can return it easily.
f but I'd like to exchange them for a different colour.
g if you don't have the receipt.
h in the shopping centre.

◀ Go back to page 78

10A Sports and competitions

1 10.2 Look at the football results. Complete the text with the verbs in the box in the correct form. Listen and check.

win beat score lose draw

On 28 May 2016, Real Madrid [1]_________ their rivals, Atlético, in the final of the UEFA Champions League. Ramos [2]_________ a goal first, but 65 minutes later, Carrasco managed to score again to [3]_________ 1–1. After extra time, Real Madrid were lucky to [4]_________ the game on penalties. Atlético were very disappointed to [5]_________ because in 2014, they had also lost to Real Madrid in the final.

UEFA
CHAMPIONS
LEAGUE
Real Madrid 1 - 1 Atlético
Ramos (15) Carrasco (79)
(5-3 on penalties)

> **Look!** We use *win* for a competition or award, and we use *beat* for another team or opponent.
> *Real Madrid won the Champions League.*
> *Real Madrid beat Atlético.*

2 10.3 Match the words in the box with the pictures 1–10. Listen and check.

athlete crowd player medal race referee spectator umpire trophy match

1 ____________

2 ____________

3 ____________

4 ____________

5 ____________

6 ____________

7 ____________

8 ____________

9 ____________

10 ____________

3 10.4 Read sentences. 1–4. Match the verbs in **bold** with definitions a–d. Listen and check.

1 Over 200 countries **take part** in the Olympic Games every four years. ____
2 It's difficult to **cheat** in sporting events, but some athletes still try. ____
3 Before you do any sport, you should always **warm up**. ____
4 I couldn't finish the marathon. I had to **give up** after 20 kilometres. ____

a break the rules to try to win a game or pass a test
b stop doing something because it's too difficult
c play in a game or competition
d do special exercises to prepare your body for sport

4 Choose the correct words to complete the sentences.

1 The *referee* / *umpire* showed three football players the red card.
2 I got injured because I didn't *give up* / *warm up* before the game.
3 My grandfather won a bronze *medal* / *race* in the Olympic Games.
4 The LA Lakers *beat* / *won* the Chicago Bulls by 123 to 118.
5 Serena Williams is a very successful *athlete* / *referee*.
6 Your team *cheated* / *scored*. This competition is for under 16s, but three of your players are 17 years old.
7 We *drew* / *lost* 0–0. It was a really boring game.
8 My sister was in the stadium, so when I watched the match on TV, I looked for her in the *crowd* / *spectator*.
9 The 100 metres *match* / *race* is my favourite part of the Olympics.
10 I'm terrible at tennis. I *beat* / *lost* my last match 0–6, 0–6, 0–6!

◀ Go back to page 84

10C Parts of the body

1 10.9 Match parts of the body a–x with the words 1–24. Listen and check.

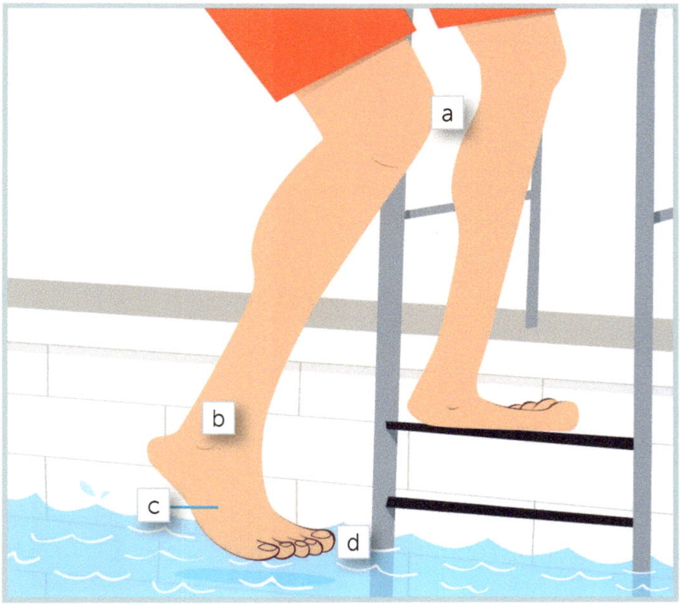
a
b
c
d

1 foot ____ **2** knee ____ **3** toes ____ **4** ankle ____

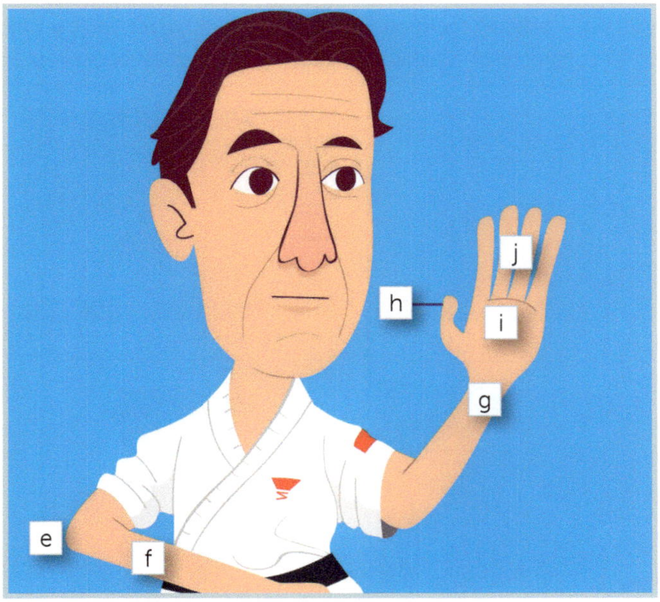
j
h
i
g
e
f

5 finger ____ **6** wrist ____ **7** elbow ____ **8** hand ____
9 arm ____ **10** thumb ____

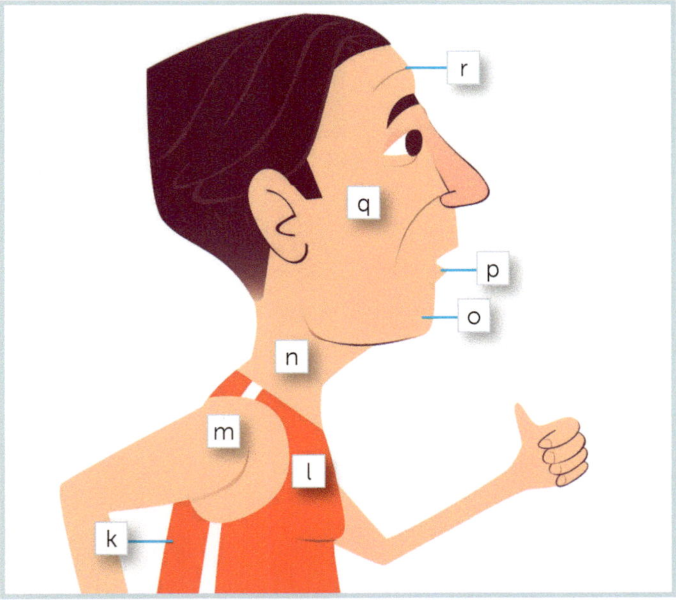
r
q
p
o
n
m
l
k

11 neck ____ **12** cheek ____ **13** chest ____ **14** lips ____
15 back ____ **16** chin ____ **17** forehead ____ **18** shoulder ____

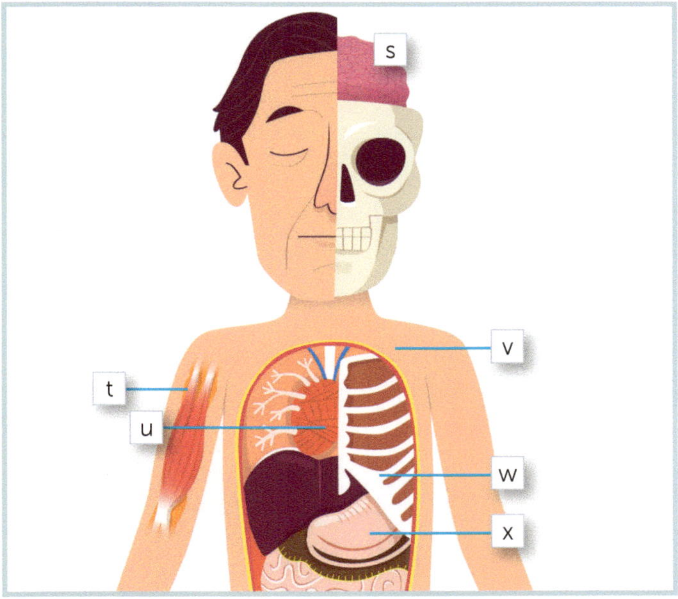
s
v
t
u
w
x

19 heart ____ **20** brain ____ **21** stomach ____
22 skin ____ **23** muscle ____ **24** bone ____

2 ~~Cross out~~ the word that is incorrect in each sentence.

1. I got injured in a rugby match and now I can't move my *cheeks* / *elbow* / *shoulder*.
2. She can't walk because she's hurt her *ankle* / *brain* / *toes*.
3. I can't write because something is wrong with my *fingers* / *lips* / *wrist*.
4. It was so cold, she was wearing a scarf around her *elbow* / *neck* / *shoulders*.
5. This shirt doesn't fit me because I have quite a big *chin* / *neck* / *chest*.
6. It's impossible for me to run a marathon because of my bad *ankle* / *fingers* / *knee*.
7. Put this cream on your *lips* / *muscles* / *bones* if they hurt.
8. You need to have a scan at the hospital to see your *bones* / *heart* / *forehead* properly.
9. In a warm-up, you need to stretch your *chin* / *arms* / *muscles*.

◀ Go back to page 88

11A Household objects

1 11.1 Match the words in the box with the pictures 1–20. Listen and check.

oven sink blanket cushion dishwasher bin duvet pillow fridge-freezer iron rug sheets wash basin tap air conditioning washing machine carpet chest of drawers central heating wardrobe

1 ____________

2 ____________

3 ____________

4 ____________

5 ____________

6 ____________

7 ____________

8 ____________

9 ____________

10 ____________

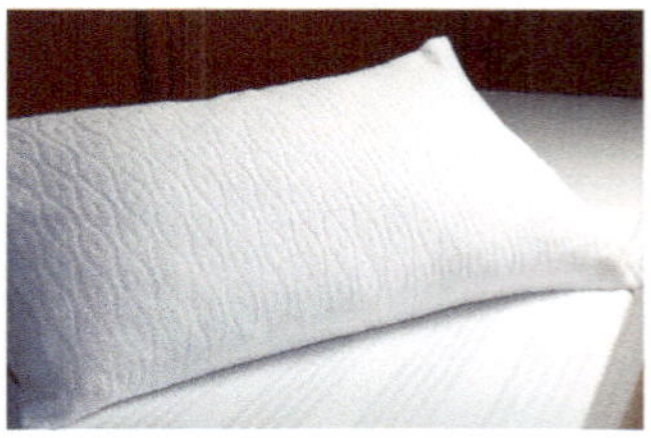
11 ____________

12 ____________

13 ____________

14 ____________

15 ____________

16 ____________

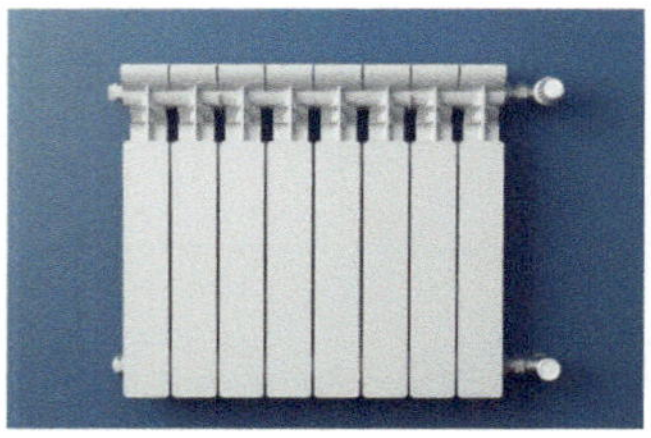
17 ____________

18 ____________

19 ____________

20 ____________

2 Choose the correct word to complete the sentences.

1 Can you put these glasses in the *wash basin / sink*, please? They're dirty.
2 We need new *pillows / cushions* for the sofa. What colour shall we have?
3 Let's move the *rug / carpet* to the middle of the room.
4 Could you turn on the *air-conditioning / central heating?* It's cold in here.
5 We have a new *dishwasher / washing machine*. My shirts are so clean these days!
6 Help me make the bed. Can you pass the *sheet / blanket* to put on top?

◀ Go back to page 94

11B Housework

1 11.6 Match the words in the box with the pictures 1–15. Listen and check.

mop the floor clear the table lay the table water the plants load the dishwasher do the ironing vacuum the carpet do the washing up sweep the floor take out the rubbish make the bed dust the furniture hang out the clothes do the washing put away the toys

1 ____________________

2 ____________________

3 ____________________

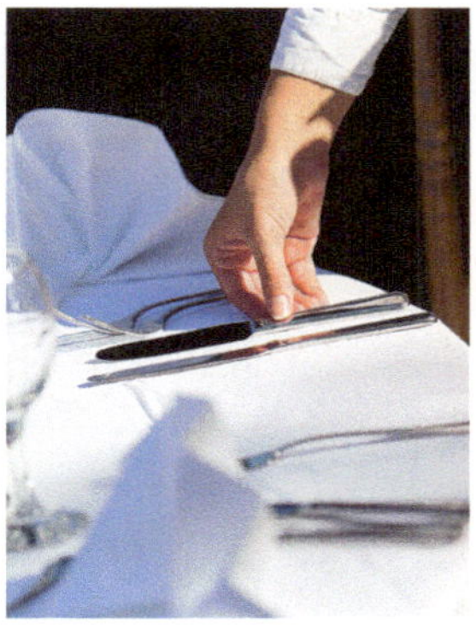

4 ____________________

5 ____________________

6 ____________________

7 ____________________

8 ____________________

9 ____________________

10 ____________________

11 ____________________

12 ____________________

13 ____________________

14 ____________________

15 ____________________

2 Choose the correct word to complete the sentences.

1 The first thing I do every morning is *lay* / *make* / *change* my bed.
2 You have to *do the washing up* / *do the washing* / *hang out the clothes*. The dishwasher is broken.
3 I have lots of allergies, so if I don't *clear* / *do* / *dust* the house every day, I start to sneeze and cough.
4 These plants will die if you don't *wash* / *water* / *clear* them more often.
5 Can you *hang out* / *take out* / *water* the clothes, please. They're very wet.
6 My dog leaves hairs on the rug, so I have to *vacuum* / *mop* / *clear* it every day.
7 What a wonderful meal! Can you help me *mop* / *clear* / *lay* the table?
8 My friends are coming to dinner in twenty minutes so I need to *clear* / *make* / *lay* the table.

◀ Go back to page 96

11C Words to describe materials and clothes

1 11.12 Complete the descriptions 1–10 with the words in the box. You will need to use some of the words more than once. Listen and check.

denim cotton plastic leather silk fur wood/wooden glass wool/woollen metal

1 A ________ shirt. It's made of ________ .

2 A ________ coat. It's made of ________ .

3 Some ________ boots. They're made of ________ .

4 A ________ tie. It's made of ________ .

5 Some ________ shoes. They're made of ________ .

6 A ________ jumper. It's made of ________ .

7 A ________ necklace. It's made of ________ .

8 Some ________ jeans. They're made of ________ .

9 A ________ ring. It's made of ________ .

10 Some ________ beads. They're made of ________ .

2 11.13 Match the adjectives with their opposites. Listen and check.

1 plain ____
2 smart ____
3 stylish ____
4 tight ____

a old-fashioned
b loose
c patterned
d casual

3 Look at the pictures. Are the sentences true (T) or false (F)? Correct the false sentences.

1 Helen is wearing a smart jacket. ____
2 She's wearing a silk scarf. ____
3 She's wearing tight trousers. ____

4 Joe is wearing casual clothes. ____
5 He's wearing a patterned jacket. ____
6 He's wearing a plain tie. ____

7 He has a wooden tennis racket. ____
8 He's wearing loose shorts. ____
9 He's wearing a plain T-shirt. ____

◀ Go back to page 98

12A Relationships

1 12.1 Put the words in the box in the correct columns. Listen and check.

cousin only child flatmate employer enemy stranger twin ex-husband stepsister bride colleague neighbour parents-in-law boss girlfriend groom single parent relative employee business partner classmate brother-in-law

family	couple	work/study	home	other

2 Complete the sentences with the words from exercise 1.

1 Daisy and I work in the same office. She's my ________ .
2 I'm an ________ . I don't have any brothers or sisters.
3 Harry and Luke share an apartment. They're ________ .
4 Carolina got divorced in 2013, but she still sees her ________ .
5 It was a lovely wedding. The ________ wore a long white dress, and the ________ wore a grey suit.
6 Our next-door ________ has just sold his house.
7 He's very friendly. He doesn't have an ________ in the world.
8 Her husband died, so she's a ________ to Emma, her daughter.
9 This is my ________ . We're not identical, but we look quite similar.
10 It's so friendly here. A ________ helped me when I was lost.

◄ Go back to page 102

12C Relationship verbs

1 12.5 Complete the sentences with the past simple form of the phrases in the box. Listen and check.

keep in touch go out (together) get back together ask (someone) out fall in love get on (well/badly) have (something) in common become friends get married introduce get to know go on a date break up

Couple get back together after 30 years

Hannah Mason from the UK and Gustavo Ramos from Argentina first met in 1985. They were both travelling in France after finishing university. A friend [1]________ Gustavo to Hannah, and they immediately [2]________ well. As they [3]________ each other better, they [4]________ good ________ . They discovered that they [5]________ a lot in ________ , including a love of travel.

Friendship turned to romance when Gustavo [6]________ Hannah ________ . They [7]________ to Gustavo's favourite restaurant in Paris, and before long they [8]________ in ________ . They [9]________ together for the rest of the summer, but they [10]________ when Hannah returned to the UK and Gustavo went home to Argentina.

They didn't [11]________ , and that could have been the end of the story. But, 30 years later, Gustavo moved to the UK and contacted Hannah. They realized they still cared for each other, so it wasn't long before they [12]________ . And their story ended happily when they [13]________ last year.

2 Choose the correct words to complete the sentences.

1 We don't *have / make / do* a lot in common – in fact, we're completely different!
2 I think I'm falling *on / in / for* love.
3 Are Charlie and Sarah really *leaving / going / getting* out together?
4 They're getting *marry / marriage / married* next year.
5 Do you get *on / in / out* well with your brother?
6 It was my boss who introduced me *with / for / to* my future wife.
7 The first date that we went *to / in / on* together was to a rock concert.
8 They had a big argument and decided to break *up / off / out*.
9 We were classmates, but we only *became / got / came* friends after we left school.
10 I first *became / arrived / got* to know her when we worked together in Istanbul.
11 Has Sam ever asked you *out / up / off* for dinner?
12 James and I are thinking of *going / getting / joining* back together.
13 You must *go / have / keep* in touch while you're away.

◄ Go back to page 106

1A Student A

1 Look at the activities and ask Student B questions with *How often … ?* Write down his/her answers.

1 go to the dentist ______
2 see a film at the cinema ______
3 buy clothes ______
4 check your phone ______
5 do exercise ______
6 eat in a restaurant ______

2 Answer Student B's questions using adverbs and expressions of frequency.

always usually sometimes often hardly ever never once/twice/three times a day/week/month every day/week/month

3 Tell the class what you found out about your partner.

1C Student A

1 Look at pictures 1–4. Ask Student B questions to guess what is happening.

A *Is the woman in picture 1 going for a walk?* B *No, she isn't.*

2 Answer Student B's questions about pictures 5–8.

2A Student A

1 Ask Student B *What did you do … ?* with the time expressions. Add the correct prepositions, if necessary.

A *What did you do in the summer?*
B *I studied for my exams, but I met up with friends, too.*

the summer yesterday 8.00 this morning last week 2015 two weeks ago

2 Answer Student B's questions.

2D Student A

1 Read sentences 1–5 to Student B and listen to his/her responses.

1 I fell over last week and broke my arm.
2 I got a new car for my birthday.
3 My brother found a wallet with $100 in it.
4 Yesterday was the best day ever!
5 I met someone famous yesterday.

2 Listen to Student B's sentences and respond to show you are interested.

B *I didn't get back from work until 10.00 p.m. last night.*
A *Poor you! What happened?*

2C Student A

1 Ask Student B questions about your mystery person and complete the table. Can you guess who she is?

When / born?		1935
Where / grow up?		Mississippi, USA
What / first job after leaving school?		Shop assistant
How many times / get married?		Once - to Priscilla
Have / children?		Yes – one, called Lisa Marie
How / become famous?		Made lots of records, including 'Jailhouse Rock' and 'Can't Help Falling in Love'
When / die?		1977

2 Answer your partner's questions about Elvis Presley. Remember, don't use his name! Can Student B guess who he is?

3A Student A

1 Complete the sentences with the superlative form of the adjectives in brackets and guess the answer. Student B will say if you are correct.

1 The __________ animals in the world are ... *(dangerous)*

crocodiles

sharks

snakes

2 The __________ sporting event was ... *(popular)*

FIFA WORLD CUP
Brazil World Cup, 2014

Beijing 2008
Beijing Olympics, 2008

Superbowl XLVI, 2012

3 The __________ car in the world is ... *(fast)*

Porsche 959

McLaren F1

Bugatti Veyron

4 The __________ place in the world is ... *(noisy)*

Times Square, New York

Champs Élysées, Paris

Exchange Square, Hong Kong

2 Listen to Student B's sentences. Look at the information and say if he/she is correct. Give more information using comparatives, superlatives, and *(not) as ... as*.

The Amazon isn't as long as the Nile, but it's longer than the Yangtze.

1 The Nile (6,853 km); The Amazon (6,437 km); The Yangtze (6,300 km)
2 *Nafea Faa Ipoipo*, Paul Gauguin ($300 million); *The Card Players*, Paul Cézanne ($274 million); *The Grand Canal*, Claude Monet ($35 million)
3 Manila, The Philippines (41,014 people/km^2); Cairo, Egypt (36,618 people/km^2); Buenos Aires, Argentina (13,680 people/km^2)
4 The Beatles (265 million albums); Michael Jackson (175 million albums); Madonna (166 million albums)

4D Student A

1 You phone a company to hire a car for one week. Call Student B and use the details below. Speak as quickly as possible!

Name: George Graddoll
Car: 5-door Subaru Impreza
Dates: Monday 1 March (12.00) – Sunday 7 March (18.00)
Credit card: Visa - 1225 5221 8426 3254

2 You work in a restaurant. Student B will call to book a table for tonight. Ask him/her questions and complete the form as accurately as possible.

Customer name: __________
Telephone number: __________
Number of people: __________
Time: __________
Special requirements: __________

3C Student A

1 Read the text about Harold Bride. Make questions for Student B. Use the answers to complete the story.

1 What / Harold Bride's job?
2 What / he / do / on 14 April at 11.40 p.m?
3 What / Captain Edward Smith / say?
4 What / water / force into the sea?
5 What / he / send from the radio room?

2 Answer Student B's questions to help him/her complete the story.

THE STORY OF A SURVIVOR

Harold Bride was working on the *Titanic* when the ship sank over 100 years ago. He was a [1] ________ who sent and received important information. He was on board when the ship began its journey from Southampton on 10 April 1912.

On 14 April at 11.40 p.m., Bride [2] ________ in his room when he heard a terrible noise. He woke up and went straight to the radio room to find out what was happening. Just after midnight, Captain Edward Smith came in and said that [3] ________ . He asked Bride to send an emergency signal to any other ships in the area. The nearest ship to respond was the *Carpathia*, but, unfortunately, it didn't arrive until after the *Titanic* sank.

While the *Titanic* was filling with water, Bride continued to send messages. However, the equipment eventually stopped working and Bride went to help release one of the last lifeboats, but the water forced the [4] ________ into the freezing sea.

Bride held onto the damaged lifeboat and, after hours in the water, some sailors rescued him and took him onto the *Carpathia*. He was badly hurt so he rested for a while, but later, he went to the radio room and began to send [5] ________ .

4A Student A

1 Ask Student B questions with *will*. Tick (✓) his/her answers in the table.

Do you think ...	likely	possible	unlikely	impossible
you will move house in the next five years?				
you will get a (new) job soon?				
you will become famous?				
you will live abroad in the future?				
you will learn to speak English fluently?				
you will do anything exciting this week?				

2 Answer Student B's questions using the phrases in the box. Give more information.

B *Do you think you will go on holiday next summer?*

A *Yes, I think I will. I'll probably visit my family in Miami.*

Yes, I think I will. Yes, I probably will.
Yes, I may. Yes, I might.
I don't think I will. I probably won't.
I definitely won't.

4C Student A

1 Student B has applied for a job at your company. You phone him/her to organize an interview. Look at your work diary and find a time to have the interview.

B *I'm free on Monday afternoon. Can we have the interview then?*

A *I'm sorry, I'm meeting with the marketing team. What about Monday morning?*

Monday	morning	
	afternoon	*meet with the Marketing team*
Tuesday	morning	
	afternoon	*visit the factory*
Wednesday	morning	
	afternoon	*meet with the Managing Director*
Thursday	morning	
	afternoon	
Friday	morning	*fly to Paris*
	afternoon	*have lunch with Pierre*

5A Student A

1 Tell Student B about your problems and write down the advice that he/she gives you.

Your problems	Advice
You can't sleep at night.	
You burned your hand while you were cooking.	
You have a bad headache.	
You have a nosebleed.	
You want to lose weight.	

2 Student B will tell you about a problem. Give him/her some advice using the ideas from the box and your own ideas.

do some exercise	drink so much coffee	eat junk food
eat more fruit	go to bed	go to the hospital
go to work today	lie down	lose some weight
put a bandage on it	work so hard	put some cream on it
rest	see a doctor	speak to a friend
stay at home	take the day off work	

You should ... *I think you should ...* *You shouldn't ...*
I don't think you should ...

5C Student A

1 Read the beginnings of sentences 1–6 to Student B. He/She will complete the sentences.

1 If I don't feel well tomorrow morning ...
2 If it snows this weekend ...
3 If I'm invited to a fancy dress party ...
4 If I don't have any homework tonight ...
5 If I have to cook dinner tonight ...
6 If I feel stressed at work ...

2 Listen to the beginnings of the sentences Student B reads to you. Choose the correct ending to complete the sentence and tell him/her.

... I might have a party to celebrate.
... I probably won't get a dog.
... I'll buy some new jeans.
... I'll take an aspirin.
... I might go to Cuba.
... I might get a promotion.

6A Student A

1 Complete the *Have you ever ...?* questions with the past participles of the verbs in brackets and ask Student B. He/She will always answer with *Yes, I have*. Ask him/her the past simple questions and decide if he/she is telling the truth.

2 Student B will ask you a *Have you ever ...?* question. You must always answer with *Yes, I have*. He/She will ask you more questions. If it is true, tell the truth. If it is not true, invent the details.

	Have you ever ...	Past simple
1	________ on TV? (be)	What programme were you on? What did you do? Did many people watch the programme?
2	________ something valuable by mistake? (throw away)	What was it? How much was it worth? Did you find it again?
3	________ karaoke? (sing)	When did you sing karaoke? Which song did you sing? Did you sing it well?
4	________ something and not given it back? (borrow)	What did you borrow? Who lent it to you? Were they angry about it?
5	________ a dangerous animal? (look after)	What kind of animal was it? Why did you have to look after it? Did you have any problems?

6C Student A

1 Complete the sentences with the correct form of the verbs in brackets. Decide if the sentence is true or false for you. Read your sentences to Student B.

1 If I ________ near the sea, I ________ swimming every day. (live / go)
2 I ________ a friend $50 if he/she ________ to borrow it. (not lend / ask)
3 If someone ________ to steal my bike, I ________ them. (try / stop)
4 I ________ scared if my friends ________ me to go mountain climbing. (feel / ask)
5 If I ________ outside in a thunderstorm, I ________ under a tree. (be / hide)

2 Listen to Student B's sentences. Decide if they are true or false. He/She will tell you if you are correct.

B *If I had more money, I'd buy a new car.*
A *False.*
B *Yes, you're right. If I had more money, I'd go on holiday.*

7A Student A

1 Student B has recently moved to an apartment in another country. Find out if he/she has done these things.

A *Have you unpacked your things yet?*
B *Yes I have. The apartment looks great.*

1 unpack your things
2 set up the Wi-Fi
3 meet your neighbours
4 explore the local area
5 register with a doctor
6 open a bank account

2 You are going to London on holiday tomorrow. Look at your 'to-do' list and answer Student B's questions.

Things to do

find my passport	✓ *(five minutes ago – in my desk)*
pack the suitcase	✗
book a hotel	✓ *(Astoria Hotel, Kensington)*
buy some sun cream	✓ *(went to shops an hour ago)*
ask friend to look after pet	✗
decide what to do in London	✓ *(city tour & shopping)*

7C Student A

1 Complete the sentences with the present perfect form of the verbs in the box and *for* or *since*. Guess the correct options and tell Student B. He/She will tell you if you are correct.

have collect be exist

HOLLYWOOD FACTS

1 The Oscars award ceremony ________ ________ ________ 1929. The winner of the Best Actor award that year was *an American / a German / a Russian* actor, Emil Jannings.

2 The actor Johnny Depp ________ ________ *Barbie dolls / teddy bears / toy cars* ________ his daughter was little.

3 Hollywood actress Christina Ricci ________ ________ afraid of *plants / spiders / flying* ________ most of her life.

4 The actress Angelina Jolie ________ ________ *Chinese lessons / a pilot's licence / a pet snake* ________ more than ten years.

2 Listen to Student B's sentences and tell him/her if they are correct.

1 There has been a big Hollywood sign in Los Angeles since 1923, but the first sign said 'Hollywoodland'.
2 *Spiderman* actor Tobey Maguire and Leonardo DiCaprio have known each other since they were children.
3 Actress Mila Kunis has played video games for many years.
4 Eva Marie Saint, who won an Oscar for *On the Waterfront* in 1954, has lived in Hollywood for over 60 years and still works as an actress.

8A Student A

1 You are going to cook a big lunch for a group of friends. Student B will tell you what ingredients he/she has. Look at the list of ingredients and use the phrases in the box to help you reply.

Great – that's enough. That's too much. That's too many.
That's not enough. We (only) need ...

INGREDIENTS
4 tins of tomatoes
1.5 kg of beef
2 red peppers
3 onions
1 pineapple
600g of strawberries
2 cartons of vanilla ice cream
2 litres of orange juice

2 You are going to cook a big lunch for a group of friends. Tell Student B what ingredients you have. He/She will tell you if you need more, less or if it is enough.

I have 500 grams of prawns.

MILK 1 LITRE
MILK 1 LITRE
PRAWNS 500 gm
FLOUR 1 KG
BUTTER 500gms
BUTTER 500g

8C Student A

1 You and Student B are starting work as cooks in a school canteen. Guess the missing words. Student B will tell you if you are correct.

SCHOOL KITCHEN GOLDEN RULES!

HYGIENE

1 You have to wear ________ at all times, but you don't have to wear gloves.
2 You mustn't wear ________ in the kitchen.
3 You must wash your hands before you start work.

COOKING

4 You must use ________ in all the dishes and you mustn't use too much salt or sugar.
5 You must wash all ________ , but you don't have to wash meat.
6 You have to throw away ________ in the black bins.

MENU

7 You have to prepare one vegetarian dish every day.
8 You don't have to serve ________ on Fridays.
9 On Thursdays, you have to make a curry, but you mustn't make the sauce ________ .
10 On Wednesdays, you have to make a Chinese dish, but you mustn't make ________ .

8D Student A

1 Invite Student B to one of the events below. If he/she refuses, try another one.

Die Meistersinger von Nürnberg Fri 6.00 p.m.
Over four hours of German opera at the National Theatre

Pencils through the ages Sat 11.00 a.m.
A talk about the history of pencils at the City Museum

Local chess competition Mon 1.00 p.m.
32 local players compete to win the tournament

Karaoke night Tue 7.00 p.m.
Sing your favourite songs all night

2 Student B is going to invite you to some events. Refuse as politely as possible every time.

9A Student A

1 Complete the quiz questions with *used to* and the verbs in brackets.

Before they were famous

1 The singer, Madonna, ________ (work) in a doughnut shop. **True** or False?
2 The actor, Brad Pitt, ________ (dress up) as a chicken to advertise a fast-food restaurant. **True** or False?
3 The founder of Microsoft, Bill Gates, ________ (sell) hot dogs at his local baseball stadium. True or **False**? (He used to work as a computer programmer.)
4 The actor, Johnny Depp, ________ (feed) the penguins at a zoo in Kentucky. True or **False?** (He used to sell pens.)
5 The actor and comedian, Jim Carrey, ________ (live) with his family in a VW camper van. **True** or False?
6 The hip hop artist, Kanye West, ________ (work) as a shop assistant in GAP. **True** or False?
7 The actor, Tom Cruise, ________ (work) as a chef in a Chinese restaurant. True or **False**? (He used to work in a hotel, carrying luggage for guests.)
8 The actress, Julia Roberts, and former US president, Barack Obama, ________ (sell) ice cream. **True** or False?

2 Take it in turns to read your quiz questions to your partner. The correct answers are in **bold**.

9C Student A

1 Complete sentences 1–6 with the passive form of the verbs in brackets.

1 Which famous item of clothing ________ by Dorothy in the film *The Wizard of Oz?* (wear)
a A pair of blue boots b A green hat c **A pair of red shoes**
2 When ________ the first *Superman* comic ________? (publish)
a In 1901 b **In 1938** c In 1959
3 In 2015, some drums that belonged to Ringo Starr from The Beatles were sold at auction. How much ________ they ________ for? (sell)
a **$1.75m** b $5.5m c $800,000
4 Who ________ the picture *Guernica* ________ by? (paint)
a Andy Warhol b Salvador Dalí c **Pablo Picasso**
5 Who ________ the film *Star Wars: The Force Awakens* ________ by? (direct)
a Steven Spielberg b **J.J. Abrams** c George Lucas
6 Who ________ the songs 'Umbrella' and 'Diamonds' ________ by? (sing)
a Beyoncé b **Rihanna** c Lady Gaga

2 **A** Read your questions and the three possible answers to Student B. He/She must try to answer. The correct answers are in **bold**.
B Try to answer Student B's questions.

10A Student A

1 A Guess the past perfect verbs to complete the sentences.

Kevin's flatmates were really angry with him because ...

1 he __________ all the food in the fridge.
2 he __________ to the supermarket.
3 he __________ the dirty dinner plates.
4 he __________ all the milk.
5 he __________ the kitchen.

B Read your sentences to Student B. He/She will tell you if you are correct.

2 Listen to Student B's sentences. Tell him/her if they are correct or not.

Last night, Miriam's friends organized a party for her. She was really surprised because ...

1 nobody had told her about it.
2 she hadn't seen some of her friends for years!
3 everyone had bought her a present.
4 she thought her friends had forgotten about her birthday.
5 all her friends had shouted "surprise!" when she came in.

10C Student A

1 You're a journalist. You interviewed Student B last week and made notes. Check the information with him/her and correct any mistakes.

A *Did you say that you were originally from South Africa?*
B *No, I told you that I was originally from Kenya.*

Student B
is originally from ~~South Africa~~ Kenya.
has lived in Argentina for ten years.
is married and has two children.
can't speak Spanish.
is going to the USA next week.
studied dance in the Netherlands.

2 Student B is a journalist who interviewed you last week. Correct what he/she says using the information.

B *Did you tell me that you were Irish?*
A *No, I said that I was Scottish.*

You're Scottish.
You moved to Kyoto in 2010.
You're learning to speak Japanese.
You've been to China twice.
You're going to take part in a marathon.
You won't go to the Olympics next year.

10D Student A

1 You are a passenger at an airport. Follow the diagram and use the phrases in the box to have a conversation with the information desk assistant.

Excuse me, I was hoping you could help me ... I'd also like to ask about ... Just one more thing. Can I double-check?
Could you give me some information about ... , please? Could I speak to someone about ... ?

Passenger (Student A)	Information desk assistant (Student B)
Ask if there's a delay on the 2.00 p.m. flight to Madrid. →	Apologize and explain that there is a 30-minute delay on this flight.
Ask which gate the flight is leaving from and how to get there. →	Say that the flight leaves from gate A22. Offer to print an airport map. Check the guest is satisfied.
Ask about a shop which sells newspapers and magazines. →	Explain that there are lots of shops, but suggest one on the third floor which has lots of foreign language newspapers.
Thank the assistant. →	Respond politely.

2 You are a receptionist in a hotel. Respond to Student B in a helpful way. Make offers and suggestions and check that he/she is satisfied.

Guest (Student B)	Receptionist (Student B)
Ask about the best way to get to the train station. →	Greet the guest and explain that the quickest way is to take a taxi. Offer to call a taxi for the guest.
Thank the receptionist. Say that you need to be at the station at 4.00 p.m. →	Check the guest is satisfied.
Ask the receptionist about a good place to have lunch. →	Recommend a restaurant on Queen Street. Give the guest a map and explain how to get there.
Thank the receptionist. →	

11C Student A

1 A Complete the questions with the correct article: *a*, *an*, *the* or – (no article).

1 Is ____ stress ____ big problem for you and your friends?
2 What's ____ best way to get ____ good job?
3 Have you ever been to ____ USA or ____ Canada?
4 What did you have for ____ dinner ____ last night?
5 Would you like to have ____ English lessons on ____ internet?
6 When was ____ last time you went to ____ cinema?

B Ask Student B the questions and listen to his/her answers.

12A Student A

1 Ask and answer questions with Student B to complete the crossword. Use the phrases in the box to make definitions with relative clauses.

B *What's 3 down?*
A *It's someone who is the leader of a country.*

> It's someone who/that ... It's a place where ...
> It's something which/that ...

1 E L B O 2 W
3 P
R 4 C A 5 M E R A
6 E 7 M
S 8 A I 9 R P O R T
I N U
10 D A 11 G 12 L O B E
E 13 G
N E 14 F I S H
15 T R

12C Student A

1 Answer Student B's questions. Use the table below. Tell him/her where you went and what you did.

B *What did you do yesterday?*
A *First, I went to the bank to take out some money.*
B *What did you do after that?*

Where	Why
the bank	take out some money
the shops	buy a new coat
the doctor	get the results of some tests
the market	get some fish
a café	meet some friends
the airport	pick up a friend from the USA

2 Ask Student B questions about what he/she did yesterday. Write down his/her answers in the table below.

A *What did you do yesterday?*
B *First, I went to the sports centre to have a swim.*
A *What did you do after that?*

Where	Why
the sports centre	*to have a swim*
the office	
the garage	
the hospital	
the hairdresser's	
the cinema	

12D Student A

1 Thank, congratulate or compliment Student B using phrases 1–5. Listen to his/her responses.

1 Wow, what a great presentation!
2 Your English is really good.
3 Thank you for dinner. It was delicious.
4 You found my wallet. Thanks a million!
5 Thanks so much for your help with the report.

2 Listen to Student B's thanks, congratulations or compliments. Respond using the phrases in the box.

> Thanks, it's just a second-hand one, though.
> It was a pleasure. They're lots of fun.
> Thanks. Yours is really nice too, actually!
> Oh, it's just something I did when I was at college.
> It wasn't just me. We're a team.

1A Student B

1 Answer Student A's questions using the frequency adverbs and expressions.

always usually sometimes often hardly ever never once/twice/three times a day/week/month every day/week/month

2 Tell the class what you found out about your partner.

3 Look at the activities and ask Student A questions with *How often … ?* Write down his/her answers.

1 download music ______________
2 send an email ______________
3 get angry ______________
4 cook dinner ______________
5 read a newspaper ______________
6 dance ______________

1C Student B

1 Answer Student A's questions about pictures 1–4.

A *Is the woman in picture 5 going for a walk?* B *No, she isn't.*

2 Look at pictures 5–8. Ask Student A questions to guess what is happening.

TAXIS
1
2
3
4

5
6
7
8

2A Student B

1 Answer Student A's questions.

2 Ask Student A *What did you do … ?* with the time expressions. Add the correct prepositions, if necessary.

31 December an hour ago the weekend February Friday night last month

B *What did you do on 31 December last year?*
A *I went to a street party with my friends and danced until midnight.*

2D Student B

1 Listen to Student A's sentences and respond to show you are interested.

A *I didn't get back from work until 10.00 p.m. last night.*
B *Poor you! What happened?*

2 Read sentences 1–5 to Student A and listen to his/her responses.

1 I have a new job.
2 My car didn't start this morning.
3 My sister wants to get married on a beach next year.
4 I had a terrible day yesterday.
5 I won a holiday to India in a competition.

2C Student B

1 Answer your partner's questions about Marilyn Monroe. Remember, don't use her name! Can Student A guess who she is?

When / born?		1926
Where / grow up?		California, USA
What / first job after leaving school?		Factory worker
How many times / get married?		Three times – to James Dougherty, Joe DiMaggio and Arthur Miller
Have / children?		No
How / become famous?		She made lots of films, including *Gentlemen Prefer Blondes* and *How to Marry a Millionaire*
When / die?		1962

2 Ask Student A questions about your mystery person and complete the table. Can you guess who he is?

3A Student B

1 Listen to Student A's sentences. Look at the information and say if he/she is correct. Give more information using comparatives, superlatives, and *(not) as … as*.

Crocodiles aren't as dangerous as snakes, but they're more dangerous than sharks.

1 snakes (50,000 deaths/year); crocodiles (10,000 deaths/year); sharks (20 deaths/year)
2 Brazil World Cup, 2014 (700 million viewers); Beijing Olympics, 2008 (600 million viewers); Superbowl XLVI, 2012 (110 million viewers)
3 Bugatti Veyron (415 km/h); McLaren F1 (408 km/h); Porsche 959 (317 km/h)
4 Times Square, New York (80 decibels); Champs Élysées, Paris (79 decibels); Exchange Square, Hong Kong (78 decibels)

2 Complete the sentences with the superlative form of the adjectives in brackets and guess the answer. Student A will say if you are correct.

1 The __________ river in the world is … *(long)*

The Amazon

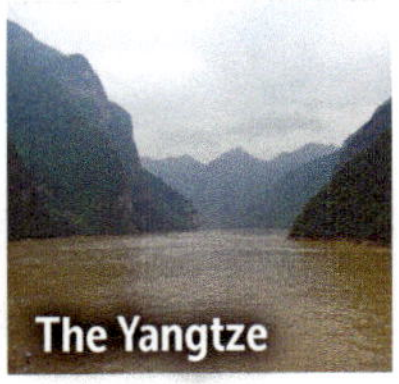
The Yangtze

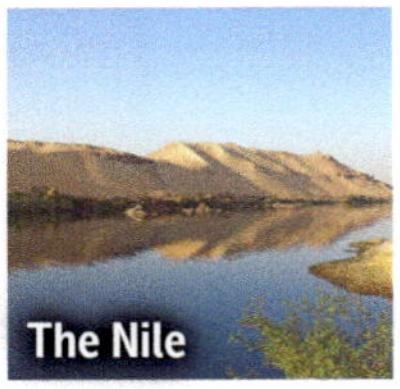
The Nile

2 The __________ painting ever sold is … *(expensive)*

The Grand Canal, Claude Monet

Nafea Faa Ipoipo, Paul Gauguin

The Card Players, Paul Cézanne

3 The __________ city in the world is … *(crowded)*

Buenos Aires, Argentina

Manila, The Philippines

Cairo, Egypt

4 The __________ musical artist is … *(successful)*

Madonna

Michael Jackson

The Beatles

4D Student B

1 You work for a hire car company. Student A will call to hire a car. Ask him/her questions and complete the form as accurately as possible.

Customer name: __________
Credit card: __________
Type of car: __________
Collection date and time: __________
Number of days: __________

2 You phone a restaurant to book a table for tonight. Call Student A and use the details below. Speak as quickly as possible!

Name: Lysandra Apostolakis
Phone number: 07700 9008831
Time: 7.00 (but may be late)
People: 8 adults, 4 children, 1 baby (need highchair for baby)

3C Student B

1 Read the text about Harold Bride. Answer Student A's questions to help him/her complete the story.

2 Make questions for Student A. Use the answers to complete the story.

1 When / the *Titanic* / begin / its journey?
2 Why / he / go / to the radio room?
3 What / name of the nearest ship?
4 What / happen / while / Bride / send / the messages?
5 What / Bride / hold onto / in the water?

THE STORY OF A SURVIVOR

Harold Bride was working on the *Titanic* when the ship sank over 100 years ago. He was a radio operator who sent and received important information. He was on board when the ship began its journey from Southampton on [1] ________ .

On 14 April at 11.40 p.m., Bride was sleeping in his room when he heard a terrible noise. He woke up and went straight to the radio room to [2] ________ . Just after midnight, Captain Edward Smith came in and said that the ship was sinking. He asked Bride to send an emergency signal to any other ships in the area. The nearest ship to respond was [3] ________ , but, unfortunately, it didn't arrive until after the *Titanic* sank. While the [4] ________ , Bride continued to send messages. However, the equipment eventually stopped working and Bride went to help release one of the last lifeboats, but the water forced the lifeboat and the men into the freezing sea.

Bride held onto the [5] ________ and, after hours in the water, some sailors rescued him and took him onto the *Carpathia*. He was badly hurt so he rested for a while, but later he went to the radio room and began to send personal messages from the survivors.

4A Student B

1 Answer Student A's questions using the phrases in the box. Give more information.

> Yes, I think I will. Yes, I probably will.
> Yes, I may. Yes, I might.
> I don't think I will. I probably won't.
> I definitely won't.

A *Do you think you will move house in the next five years?*
B *Yes, I might. My flat in the city centre is very small and I want to find a bigger one.*

2 Ask Student A questions with *will*. Tick (✓) his/her answers in the table.

Do you think ...	likely	possible	unlikely	impossible
you will go on holiday next summer?				
you will travel abroad this year?				
you will make any new friends this month?				
you will earn a lot of money in your next job?				
you will live to be 100 years old?				
you will eat in a restaurant next week?				

4C Student B

1 You applied for a job at Student A's company. He/She phones you to organize an interview. Look at your diary and find a time to have the interview.

A *I'm free on Monday morning. Can we have the interview then?*
B *I'm sorry, I'm visiting my aunt in hospital. What about Monday afternoon?*

Monday	morning	*visit Aunt Emma in hospital*
	afternoon	
Tuesday	morning	*go to dentist at 10.00*
	afternoon	
Wednesday	morning	
	afternoon	*go to Jenny's birthday lunch*
Thursday	morning	*have my piano lesson*
	afternoon	
Friday	morning	
	afternoon	*play piano at the jazz concert*

5A Student B

1 Student A will tell you about a problem. Give him/her some advice using the ideas from the box and your own ideas.

drink lots of water	drink so much coffee
eat so much chocolate	go on a diet
go to bed early	go to the pharmacy
go to the hospital	go to work today
hold it under cold water	hold your nose with a tissue
join a gym	move around too much
see a doctor	put some cream on it
take some tablets	sit down for a few minutes
smoke	take some medicine

You should ... *I think you should ...*
You shouldn't ... *I don't think you should ...*

2 Tell Student A about your problems and write down the advice that he/she gives you.

Your problems	Advice
You feel tired all the time.	
You cut your hand on a piece of glass.	
You have backache.	
I'm feeling stressed.	
You have a stomach ache.	

5C Student B

1 Listen to the beginnings of the sentences Student A reads to you. Choose the correct ending to complete the sentence and tell him/her.

... I won't make pasta.
... I might go as Superman.
... I'll probably watch a film.
... I'll speak to my boss.
... I'll stay in bed.
... I might go skiing.

2 Read the beginnings of sentences 1–6 to Student A. He/She will complete the sentences.

1 If I go on holiday this summer ...
2 If I decide to get a pet ...
3 If my boss thinks I'm doing a good job ...
4 If I pass my exams ...
5 If I have a headache ...
6 If I go shopping at the weekend ...

6A Student B

1 Student A will ask you a *Have you ever ...?* question. You must always answer with *Yes, I have*. He/She will ask you more questions. If it is true, tell the truth. If it is not true, invent the details.

2 Complete the *Have you ever ...?* questions with the past participles of the verbs in brackets and ask Student A. He/She will always answer with *Yes, I have*. Ask him/her the past simple questions and decide if he/she is telling the truth.

	Have you ever ...	Past simple
1	________ an email in English? (write)	When did you write it? Who did you send it to? Did you have any problems?
2	________ all night to see the sunrise? (stay up)	Why didn't you sleep? How did you feel? What was it like?
3	________ London? (visit)	When did you go there? Did you have a good time? What things did you see there?
4	________ money on holiday? (run out of)	Where did you go? Did you have any problems? How did you get more money?
5	________ your house keys? (lose)	How did you get into your house? Do you know where you lost the keys? Did you find them again?

6C Student B

1 Listen to Student A's sentences. Decide if they are true or false. He/She will tell you if you are correct.

A *If I had more money, I'd buy a new car.*
B *False.*
A *Yes, you're right. If I had more money, I'd go on holiday.*

2 Complete the sentences with the correct form of the verbs in brackets. Decide if the sentence is true or false for you. Read your sentences to Student A.

1 I ________ my friends if I ________ my driving test. (not tell / fail)
2 If I ________ a spider in the bathroom, I ________ and take it outside. (find / pick it up)
3 If I ________ a lot of money, I ________ it with my friends. (win / share)
4 I ________ an animal to eat if I ________ any other food. (kill / not have)
5 If I ________, I ________ all night and watch the sunrise. (not work / stay up)

7A Student B

1 You have recently moved to an apartment in another country. Look at your 'to-do' list and answer Student A's questions.

Things to do
meet your neighbours ✓ *(they're very nice)*
open a bank account ✗
explore the local area ✓ *(got back 15 minutes ago)*
unpack your things ✓ *(the apartment looks great!)*
set up the Wi-Fi ✗
register with a doctor ✓ *(went this morning)*

2 Student A is going to London on holiday tomorrow. Find out if he/she has done these things.

B *Have you bought some sun cream yet?*
A *Yes. I went to the shops an hour ago.*

1 buy some sun cream
2 decide what to do in London
3 book a hotel
4 find your passport
5 ask a friend to look after your pet
6 pack your suitcase

7C Student B

1 Listen to Student A's sentences and tell him/her if they are correct.

1 The Oscars award ceremony has existed since 1929. The winner of the Best Actor award that year was a German actor, Emil Jannings.
2 The actor Johnny Depp has collected Barbie dolls since his daughter was little.
3 Hollywood actress Christina Ricci has been afraid of plants for most of her life.
4 The actress Angelina Jolie has had a pilot's licence for more than ten years.

2 Complete the sentences with the present perfect form of the verbs in the box and *for* or *since*. Guess the correct options and tell Student A. He/She will tell you if you are correct.

know play be live

HOLLYWOOD FACTS

1 There ________ ________ a big Hollywood sign in Los Angeles ________ *1923 / 1953 / 1973*, but the first sign said 'Hollywoodland'.
2 *Spiderman* actor Tobey Maguire and *Leonardo DiCaprio / Kanye West / Joaquin Phoenix* ________ ________ each other ________ they were children.
3 Actress Mila Kunis ________ ________ *golf / video games / chess* ________ many years.
4 Eva Marie Saint, who won an Oscar for *On the Waterfront* in 1954, ________ ________ in Hollywood ________ over 60 years and still works as *a designer / an actress / a musician*.

8A Student B

1 You are going to cook a big lunch for a group of friends. Tell Student A what ingredients you have. He/She will tell you if you need more, less or if it is enough.

I have six tins of tomatoes.

ORANGE 1 LITRE
ORANGE 1 LITRE
BEEF 500gms
TOMATOES
TOMATOES
TOMATOES
VANILLA
VANILLA
VANILLA
STRAWBERRIES 300 gms

2 You are going to cook a big lunch for a group of friends. Student A will tell you what ingredients he/she has. Look at the list of ingredients and use the phrases in the box to help you reply.

Great – that's enough. That's too much.
That's too many. That's not enough.
We (only) need ...

INGREDIENTS
1 whole salmon
500g of prawns
1 lettuce
1 cucumber
250g butter
1 litre of milk
200g of flour
1 coconut

8C Student B

1 You and Student A are starting work as cooks in a school canteen. Guess the missing words. Student A will tell you if you are correct.

SCHOOL KITCHEN GOLDEN RULES!

HYGIENE

1 You have to wear a hat at all times, but you don't have to wear ________ .

2 You mustn't wear jewellery in the kitchen.

3 You must wash ________ before you start work.

COOKING

4 You must use fresh ingredients in all the dishes and you mustn't use ________ .

5 You must wash all raw fruit and vegetables, but you don't have to wash ________ .

6 You have to throw away all burnt food in the black bins.

MENU

7 You have to prepare ________ every day.

8 You don't have to serve salad on Fridays.

9 On Thursdays, you have to make a ________ , but you mustn't make the sauce too spicy.

10 On Wednesdays, you have to make ________ , but you mustn't make sweet-and-sour sauce.

8D Student B

1 Student A is going to invite you to some events. Refuse as politely as possible every time.

2 Invite Student A to one of these events. If he/she refuses, try another one.

Black-and-white night Thur 6.00 p.m.
Enjoy three films from the 1930s at Roxy Cinema

Crazy burger buffet Fri 7.00 p.m.
Eat as many hamburgers as you want for $12

Ballroom dancing lessons Sat 11.00 a.m.
Learn how to dance the waltz and cha-cha-cha

Benches of the world Sat 5.00 p.m.
An exhibition of Michael Lamb's photographs of benches

9A Student B

1 Complete the quiz questions with *used to* and the verbs in brackets.

Before they were famous

1 The singer, Beyoncé, ________ (sweep up) hair in her mum's hairdressing salon. **True** or False?

2 The actress, Jennifer Aniston, ________ (clean) salmon in a fish factory. True or **False**? (She used to clean toilets.)

3 The Australian actor, Hugh Jackman, ________ (teach) PE at a school in England. **True** or False?

4 The actor, Tom Hanks, ________ (sell) popcorn and peanuts at his local cinema. **True** or False?

5 The singer, Lady Gaga, ________ (work) in a library. True or **False**? (She used to work in a Greek restaurant.)

6 The actor, Sylvester Stallone, ________ (clean) the lions' cages at Central Park Zoo in New York. **True** or False?

7 The Rolling Stones singer, Mick Jagger, ________ (catch) rats at a London theatre. True or **False**? (He used to work in a hospital.)

8 The Russian billionaire, Roman Abramovich, ________ (sell) plastic ducks in a market. **True** or False?

2 Take it in turns to read your quiz questions to your partner. The correct answers are in **bold**.

9C Student B

1 Complete sentences 1–6 with the passive form of the verbs in brackets.

1 What famous items of clothing ________ by Harrison Ford in the *Indiana Jones* films? (wear)
a A hat and raincoat **b A hat and leather jacket** c A baseball jacket and cap

2 When ________ the first Sherlock Holmes story ________? (publish)
a In 1810 **b In 1887** c In 1935

3 In 2011, one of Marilyn Monroe's dresses was sold at auction. How much ________ it ________ for? (buy)
a $1.3m b $3.2m **c $4.6m**

4 Who ________ the sunflower pictures ________ by? (paint)
a Vincent Van Gogh b Henri Matisse c Salvador Dalí

5 What sort of car ________ by the mad scientist Doc Brown in the *Back to the Future* films? (drive)
a A Lamborghini b A Ferrari **c A DeLorean**

6 Who ________ the films *Titanic* and *Avatar* ________ by? (direct)
a James Cameron b Steven Spielberg c Ridley Scott

2 **A** Try to answer Student A's questions.

B Read your questions and the three possible answers to Student A. He/She must try to answer. The correct answers are in **bold**.

10A Student B

1 Listen to Student A's sentences. Tell him/her if they are correct or not.

Kevin's flatmates were really angry with him because ...

1 he had eaten all the food in the fridge.
2 he hadn't been to the supermarket.
3 he hadn't washed the dirty dinner plates.
4 he had drunk all the milk.
5 he hadn't cleaned the kitchen.

2 A Guess the past perfect verbs to complete the sentences.

Last night, Miriam's friends organized a party for her. She was really surprised because ...

1 nobody __________ her about it.
2 she __________ some of her friends for years!
3 everyone __________ her a present.
4 she thought her friends __________ about her birthday.
5 all her friends __________ "surprise!" when she came in.

B Read your sentences to Student A. He/She will tell you if you are correct.

10C Student B

1 Student A is a journalist who interviewed you last week. Correct what he/she says using the information.

A *Did you say that you were originally from South Africa?*
B *No, I told you that I was originally from Kenya.*

You're originally from Kenya.
You've lived in Argentina for eight years.
You're married and have one child.
You can speak Spanish fluently.
You're going to the USA next week.
You studied dance in Belgium.

2 You are a journalist. You interviewed Student A last week and made notes. Check the information with him/her and correct any mistakes.

B *Did you tell me that you were Irish?*
A *No, I said that I was Scottish.*

Student A
is ~~Irish~~ Scottish.
moved to Tokyo in 2010.
is learning to speak Japanese.
hasn't been to China before.
is going to take part in a 10 km race.
will go to the Olympics next year if it's possible.

10D Student B

1 You work on an information desk in an airport. Respond to Student A in a helpful way. Make offers and suggestions and check that he/she is satisfied.

Passenger (Student A)		Information desk assistant (Student B)
Ask if there's a delay on the 2.00 p.m. flight to Madrid.	→	Apologize and explain that there's a 30-minute delay on this flight.
Ask which gate the flight is leaving from and how to get there.	← →	Say that the flight leaves from gate A22. Offer to print an airport map. Check the guest is satisfied.
Ask about a shop which sells newspapers and magazines.	← →	Explain that there are lots of shops, but suggest one on the third floor which has lots of foreign language newspapers.
Thank the assistant.	← →	Respond politely.

2 You are a guest staying at a hotel. Follow the diagram and use the phrases in the box to have a conversation with the receptionist.

Excuse me, I was hoping you could help me ... I'd also like to ask about ... Just one more thing. Can I double-check?
Could you give me some information about ... , please? Could I speak to someone about ... ?

Guest (Student B)		Receptionist (Student A)
Ask about the best way to get to the train station.	→	Greet the guest and explain that the quickest way is to take a taxi. Offer to call a taxi for the guest.
Thank the receptionist. Say that you need to be at the station at 4.00 p.m.	← →	Check the guest is satisfied.
Ask the receptionist about a good place to have lunch.	← →	Recommend a restaurant on Queen Street. Give the guest a map and explain how to get there.
Thank the receptionist.	← →	Respond politely.

11C Student B

1 A Complete the questions with the correct article: *a*, *an*, *the* or – (no article).

1 Do you have ____ pet? What's ____ pet's name?
2 How many times ____ year do you go to ____ dentist?
3 Do you like ____ reading? Are you reading ____ book at the moment?
4 What time do you normally go to ____ bed at ____ night?
5 What's ____ worst food you've ever had in ____ restaurant?
6 Do you know anyone who is ____ architect or ____ designer?

B Ask Student A the questions and listen to his/her answers.

12A Student B

1 Ask and answer questions with Student A to complete the crossword. Use the phrases in the box to make definitions with relative clauses.

A *What's 3 across?*
B *It's a place where you can play football or go for a walk.*

> It's someone who/that ... It's a place where ...
> It's something which/that ...

PARK
WARDROBES
MAP
EXAM
DJ
EGG
LIFT
TOURIST

12C Student B

1 Ask Student A questions about what he/she did yesterday. Write down his/her answers in the table below.

B *What did you do yesterday?*
A *First, I went to the bank to take out some money.*
B *What did you do after that?*

Where	Why
the bank	*to take out some money*
the shops	
the doctor	
the market	
a café	
the airport	

2 Answer Student A's questions. Use the table below. Tell him/her where you went and what you did.

A *What did you do yesterday?*
B *First, I went to the sports centre to have a swim.*
A *What did you do after that?*

Where	Why
the sports centre	have a swim
the office	finish a report
the garage	get a light for my car
the hospital	visit my uncle
the hairdresser's	have my hair cut
the cinema	see the new *Batman* film

12D Student B

1 Listen to Student A's thanks, congratulations or compliments. Respond using the phrases in the box.

> No problem. I enjoyed working on it!
> It was no trouble at all. It was in my car.
> Do you think so? I didn't have much time to practise.
> Thanks, but I still need to improve.
> Well, thank you for coming to visit us!

2 Thank, congratulate or compliment Student A using phrases 1–5. Listen to his/her responses.

1 Did you paint this picture? It's fantastic.
2 I'm very grateful for your help at this difficult time.
3 I love your watch! It's cool.
4 Thanks for looking after the children.
5 Congratulations on your new car.

6D All students

1 You're going on a trip to a rainforest for one week. You can only take six of the items with you. Decide which are the most useful.

tent

mosquito net

torch

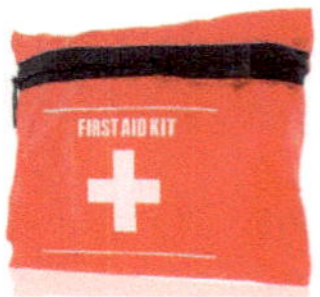
FIRST AID KIT
first aid kit

water-purifying kit

SUN
sun cream

knife

food

compass and maps

INSECT
insect repellent

cooking equipment

rope

2 In groups of four, discuss which six items you will take. Try to take turns politely.

11A Both students

1 In pairs, complete the sentences with the infinitive with *to* or the *–ing* form of the verbs in brackets.

Tell me about ...

1 something important you need __________ this week. (do)
2 a place you're planning __________ soon. (visit)
3 something you spend a lot of time __________. (do)
4 a person you'd like __________ more often. (see)
5 something you can't afford __________, but would love to have. (buy)
6 a household job you can't stand __________. (do)
7 a film you're looking forward to __________ at the cinema. (see)
8 a mistake you keep __________ in English. (make)
9 a food you would miss __________ if you lived in another country. (eat)
10 someone you expect __________ later today. (see)

2 In pairs, take turns asking and answering the questions.

A *Tell me about something important you need to do this week.*
B *I need to buy a birthday card for my mum. What about you?*
A *I need to take my car to the garage.*

3A Quiz results

For each answer A, score 0 points. For each answer B, score 1 point.

0–1 points = tourist. You're happiest sunbathing on a beach.

2–3 points = traveller. You like to do something more unusual on holiday.

4–5 points = adventurer. The best holiday for you is six months in the jungle!

5C Quiz results

For each answer A, score 0 points. For each answer B, score 1 point. For each answer C, score 2 points. For each answer D, score 3 points.

0–3 = Oh dear, you're quite miserable at the moment. Are you upset about something? If you talk to your friends or family, you'll feel better.

4–7 = You're not very happy at the moment. If you do something you enjoy, maybe you'll feel more cheerful.

8–11 = Great news, you're happy! If you're friendly and smile at everyone today, you'll make them feel happier, too!

12–15 = You're extremely happy! Are you delighted about something? What's the secret to feeling so happy?

6C Quiz results

How many answers did you get right?

0–1 = You probably wouldn't survive if you went on a weekend camping trip. It's safer for you to stay at home.

2–3 = If you were in a difficult situation, you'd probably survive, but don't take any risks. Always find out about the dangers of a place before you go.

4 = Wow! You'd know what to do if you were in the wild. If you could choose an exciting place for an adventure, where would you go?

6D Quiz results

How many times did you answer yes?

0–2 = You don't like taking risks. Be careful, if you always play it safe, you might miss out on opportunities in your life.

3–4 = You're happy to take a risk, but not too many. That's probably the best way to be.

5–6 = You're a real risk-taker! It can be exciting, but watch out, it can be dangerous, too!

Infinitive	Past simple	Past participle	Infinitive	Past simple	Past participle
be	was, were	been	make	made	made
become	became	become	meet	met	met
begin	began	begun	pay	paid	paid
bite	bit	bitten	put	put	put
break	broke	broken	read (/riːd/)	read (/red/)	read (/red/)
bring	brought	brought	ride	rode	ridden
build	built	built	ring	rang	rung
buy	bought	bought	rise	rose	risen
choose	chose	chosen	run	ran	run
come	came	come	say	said	said
cost	cost	cost	see	saw	seen
do	did	done	sell	sold	sold
dream	dreamt/dreamed	dreamt/dreamed	send	sent	sent
forbid	forbade	forbidden	sleep	slept	slept
forget	forgot	forgotten	speak	spoke	spoken
forgive	forgave	forgiven	spend	spent	spent
get	got	got	stand	stood	stood
give	gave	given	steal	stole	stolen
go	went	gone, been	stick	stuck	stuck
grow	grew	grown	swim	swam	swum
have	had	had	take	took	taken
hear	heard	heard	teach	taught	taught
hide	hid	hidden	tell	told	told
hold	held	held	think	thought	thought
keep	kept	kept	throw	threw	thrown
know	knew	known	understand	understood	understood
learn	learnt/learned	learnt/learned	wake	woke	woken
leave	left	left	wear	wore	worn
let	let	let	win	won	won
lose	lost	lost	write	wrote	written

Richmond
58 St Aldates
Oxford
OX1 1ST
United Kingdom

Printed in Brazil by Forma Certa
Lote. 800428
ISBN: 978-84-668-2095-0
CP: 641774
DL: M-10057-2017

Reprinted, 2024

Publishing Director: Deborah Tricker
Publisher: Simone Foster
Media Publisher: Sue Ashcroft
Content Developer: David Cole-Powney
Editors: Debra Emmett, Helen Ward, Ruth Cox, Emma Clarke, Fiona Hunt, Eleanor Clements
Proofreader: Peter Anderson
Design Manager: Lorna Heaslip
Cover Design: This Ain't Rock'n'Roll, London
Design & Layout: Lorna Heaslip, Oliver Hutton
Photo Researcher: Magdalena Mayo
***Learning Curve* video:** Mannic Media
Audio production: Tom, Dick and Debbie
App development: The Distance

We would also like to thank the following people for their valuable contribution to writing and developing the material:
Alastair Lane, Bob McLarty, Claire Thacker, Louis Rogers, Rachael Roberts, Pamela Vittorio (Video Script Writer), Belen Fernandez (App Project Manager), Rob Sved (App Content Creator)

Illustrators:
Simon Clare; Dermot Flynn c/o Dutch Uncle; Guillaume Gennet, Julien Kern and Liav Zabari c/o Lemonade; Joanna Kerr c/o New Division; Piers Sandford c/o Meiklejohn; The Boy FitzHammond and Beverley Young, c/o NB Illustration

Photos:
J. Jaime; J. Lucas; 123RF/ lightpoet; ALAMY/IanDagnall Laptop Computing, John Birdsall, Chuck Place, Granger Historical Picture Archve, All Canada Photos, Cofiant Images, ONOKY - Photononstop, Action Plus Sports Images, Arcaid Images, Jasminko Ibrakovic, Image Source Salsa, Radius Images, Pat Behnke, Ann Cutting, 360b, Heritage Image Partnership Ltd, Roger Bamber, Cultura Creative (RF), Blend Images, RosalreneBetancourt 10, Nick Gregory, BSIP SA, Trinity Mirror / Mirrorpix, Wavebreak Media ltd, Torontonian, Joy Sunny, SWNS, TP, IanDagnall Computing, PhotoEdit, Ammentorp Photography, Peter Barritt, Cliff Hide Stock, greenwales, caia image, eye35.pix, Carlos Guerra, Janine Wiedel Photolibrary, Peter Titmuss, Richard Heyes, Motoring Picture Library, Helen Hotson, Cephas Picture Library, ACORN 1, tommaso altamura, Steve Davey Photography, Image Source, Bill Cheyrou, Agencja Fotograficzna Caro, Kreative Photography, Imagedoc, Lou-Foto, Julie g Woodhouse, allesalltag, Stefano Carvoretto, MAX EAREY, wareham.nl (sport), Duncan Snow, Wilawan Khasawong, Brian Overcast, Design Pics Inc, Westend61 GmbH, Anton Stariskov, Elina Manninen, Aflo Co., Ltd., Alan Smith, Classic Image, Photos 12, D. Hurst, MBI, AF archive, PjrTravel, FineArt, moodboard, DonSmith, Jeramey Lende, epa european pressphoto agency b.v.; BNPS (BOURNEMOUTH NEWS & PICTURE SERVICE)/ Rijksmuseum/ BNPS; CATERS NEWS AGENCY/ Caters News Agency; GETTY IMAGES SALES SPAIN/Lumi Images/Dario Secen, Graham Monro/gm photographics, Jetta Productions, Thomas_EyeDesign, Photos.com Plus, David M. Benett, Astrid Stawiarz, Mark Metcalfe, CARL DE SOUZA, Alistair Berg, Toby Burrows, Sam Edwards, Dave Hogan, Barcroft, Maskot, Bloomberg, Bettmann, Don Arnold, Kari Lehr, PETER MACDIARMID, RENE SLAMA, Boston Globe, CHRISTOPHE ARCHAMBAULT, Caiaimage/Paul Bradbury, Image source, Paul Chesley, Thinkstock; HIGHRES PRESS STOCK/AbleStock.com; ISTOCKPHOTO/SeanShot, Pali Rao, oztasbc, jojoo64, SondraP, MollyNZ, Geber86, xijian, vgajic, sturti, olaser, miralex, mergez, alexsl, HASLOO, SolStock, DONOT6, Getty Images Sales Spain, Devasahayam Chandra Dhas, monkeybusinessimages, Osmany Torres Martín, alessandroguerriero, AleksandarGeorgiev, Tommaso Altamura, Nicolas McComber, warrengoldswain, travellinglight, stevecoleimages, Robyn Mackenzie, German-skydiver, digitalskillet, Wavebreakmedia, Petar Chernaev, Jaroslav Frank, wundervisuals, Squaredpixels, LuckyBusiness, Julia Nichols, Drazen Lovric, Dean Mitchell, elenaleonova, PeopleImages, Elenathewise, Dieter Meyrl, Daniel Ernst, Cathy Yeulet, ozgurdonmaz, mediaphotos, Yuri_Arcurs, Visiofutura, Jason Poole, David Sucsy, Bulent Ince, nataistock, bluehill75, calvindexter, MartialRed, Juanmonino, FangXiaNuo, Joel Carillet, FSTOPLIGHT, DeluXe-PiX, DeanDrobot, g-stockstudio, zhudifeng, pixdeluxe, milanfoto, dolgachov, cindygoff, SteveTram, OcusFocus, robertcicchetti, Maxiphoto, Kaan Ates, Huchen Lu, Anna Bryukhanova, Halfpoint, CactuSoup, yipengge, mihailomilovanovic, urbancow, rcaucino, pepifoto, lucky336, kyoshino, denphumi; MAYANG MURNI ADNIN; NASA/ NASA; REX SHUTTERSTOCK/Jonathan Player, ABC Inc/ Everett, Peter Brooker, Kippa Limited, Pixelformula, Newspix; SHUTTERSTOCK; SHUTTERSTOCK NETHERLANDS,B.V.; Project Jacquard/Levi's Strauss; Library of Congress/wikipedia; Carpigiani Gelato University; Niccolo Casas /EMBR labs; Optomen Television Ltd.; courtesy of Alex Deans; Pauline Van Dongen; Alastair Humphreys; freepic.com; Ringly Inc.; Jon Barlow; Dave Homcy; ARCHIVO SANTILLANA

Cover Photo: Jon Barlow

We would like to thank the following reviewers for their valuable feedback which has made Personal Best possible. We extend our thanks to the many teachers and students not mentioned here.
Brad Bawtinheimer, Manuel Hidalgo, Paulo Dantas, Diana Bermúdez, Laura Gutiérrez, Hardy Griffin, Angi Conti, Christopher Morabito, Hande Kokce, Jorge Lobato, Leonardo Mercato, Mercilinda Ortiz, Wendy López